Profiting from external knowledge

Profiting from external knowledge

How firms use different knowledge acquisition strategies to improve their innovation performance

Maarten Batterink

Innovation and sustainability series – Volume 3

Wageningen Academic
P u b l i s h e r s

ISBN: 978-90-8686-101-9
ISSN: 1875-0702

www.WageningenAcademic.com

First published, 2009

Wageningen Academic Publishers
The Netherlands, 2009

Table of contents

Preface and acknowledgements

When I reached the foot of the Alp d'Huez in the summer of 2007, it was perfectly clear to me what needed to be done to finish *La Marmotte*. By then I was completely exhausted after 160 km of cycling through the Haut Alpes in France. Still, I was really motivated to cycle the final 13.6 km to the top. It took a great deal out of me to reach the finish, and I was lucky that I made it, especially because it turned out to be even warmer than expected. Now, having completed this book, I see a clear parallel with the final year of conducting this research project. I knew that summer what needed to be done to complete the book, but I also realized that it was going to be a very difficult job. There is also a big difference. Whereas cycling to the top was something I did completely by myself (despite the support of friends along the roadside), finishing this research project would not have been possible without the help of so many. Here I would like to take the opportunity to thank them.

My special thanks go to my advisors, Onno Omta and Emiel Wubben. Onno, I thank you for the pragmatic guidance during the research and for constantly pushing me to improve my work and to get the best out of me. I also want to thank you for giving me the opportunity to continue working at the Business Administration group after my graduation. And Emiel, I thank you for always taking so much time to read and discuss my work in detail. Your enthusiasm and open-mindedness always made our meetings fruitful and pleasant. I also enjoyed our cooperation in the various research projects and conference visits, such as the Academy of Management Annual Conference in Philladelphia in 2007.

Furthermore, I greatly acknowledge the financial support from InnovatieNetwerk, and the Federatie Nederlandse Levensmiddelen Industrie (FNLI). I especially want to thank the members of my steering committee: Henk Huizing and Peter Oei from InnovatieNetwerk, Murk Boerstra from FNLI, August Sjauw-Koen Fa from Rabobank, Doeke Faber from VBN, Ad Juriaanse from NIZO, Roel Bol and Johan Gatsonides from LNV, and Olaf van Kooten from the Horticulture Production Chains group (WUR). Their research suggestions, and critical comments on and interpretations of the early research findings were essential to steer this research project in directions that promote meaningful results for society.

In addition, I would like to thank the members of my dissertation committee; i.e. Hans Dons, Cees Leeuwis, Olaf van Kooten, Hans Schenk and Wim Vanhaverbeke for evaluating this thesis and participating in the defence.

Chapter 4 is a result of the research project *Chain Innovation Benchmark*, a sub-project within the PROMSTAP project (INTERREG IIIC). I gratefully acknowledge the financial support from the EU, and the administrative support from the PromSTAP project. Many thanks go to the people from the innovation brokers who participated in the study, as well as to the related SMEs. In particular, I thank Rinus van der Waard from KnowHouse, Alfred Boeve from *my eyes*, Martin Hamer from GIQS and Emmanualle Gardère and Françoise Molegnana from

PEACRITT. I also thank Laurens Klerkx, who provided important ingredients to analyze the situation from a different angle and who became co-author of the paper underlying Chapter 4.

I greatly acknowledge the financial support from the Netherlands Organisation of Scientific Research (NWO, Dynamics of Innovation program, grant no.: 472-04-008). I also greatly acknowledge the anonymous companies that participated in the research project underlying Chapter 5. I especially want to thank the managers that were interviewed and who provided access to company documents relevant for the research.

Moreover, I acknowledge the friendliness and support from the staff of the Centre for Economic Micro data (Cerem) at Statistics Netherlands (CBS), where I executed the quantitative analyses of this research (see Chapters 2 and 3).

Many thanks go to the members of the Business Administration group of Wageningen University. It was a pleasure to work with them and I appreciate the friendship during coffee breaks, drinks and department trips. In particular I want to thank Ron Kemp for his assistance in the statistical analyses underlying a substantial part of this book and for the fruitful discussions we had on different aspects of my research. I also thank the MSc students Peter Schoch and Gerard Ensink, whose work were important contributions to this book. In addition, I want to thank the former PhD students who finished their research in the period 2005-2008, with whom I spent a lot of time – also after working hours. In particular I want to thank my former colleagues and paranymphs Wijnand van Plaggenhoef and Derk-Jan Haverkamp.

Finally, this book could not have been realized without the assistance and support of my family and friends. I want to thank my good friends Sietse en Gerda for always showing interest in my work, and especially in my personal life. Many, many thanks to my sister and brothers (in law): Moureen and Richard, Robbert, and Hans. You have always been essential for me to remain levelheaded.

De meeste dank ben ik verschuldigd aan mijn ouders. Pap en mam, jullie hebben mij altijd in alles onvoorwaardelijk gesteund, gedurende mijn studie, het promotieonderzoek, en alle andere dingen die ik in mijn leven heb ondernomen. Ik kan jullie niet genoeg bedanken daarvoor!

Last but not least, I want to thank Michelle – my fiancée. Michelle, thank you for being there for me all the time. There were so many times that I was pre-occupied with my work, but you always showed patience and understanding, and you encouraged me to stay focused. Thanks to you the last period of this project was so much nicer!

1. Introduction

This book discusses the important issue of how firms can profit from knowledge and capabilities from other organizations in order to improve their innovation performance. In recent years, innovation has become essential for the competitive advantage of firms in a growing number of industries (Christensen *et al.*, 1998; Hult *et al.*, 2004). Due to the fast development of technologies, changing customer demands, shortening of product life cycles, increased global competition and changing regulations, modern firms constantly have to look for new ways to prosper in this very dynamic business environment (Fagerberg, 2004; Porter, 1985; Teece *et al.*, 1997). Increasingly, innovation is regarded as the driver for economic change by national and international governments. Since in 2000 leaders of the European Union (EU) set out in Lisbon to build *the most competitive and dynamic knowledge-based economy in the world, capable of sustainable economic growth with more and better jobs and greater social cohesion*, innovation has become a prominent topic on EU and national policy agendas (European Commission, 2000, 2005; Kok, 2004). For example, in 2003, the Dutch government established the *InnovatiePlatform* with the aim of shaping better conditions, and making new connections in order to boost innovation and entrepreneurship (Innovatieplatform, 2008).

The importance of innovation has also been acknowledged by business. In the 2005 innovation survey initiated by the American Management Association (AMA) including 1,396 executives of large multinational firms in North America and Europe it was concluded that business regards innovation as crucial for the long-term survival of firms (Jamrog, 2006). However, innovation is associated with high failure rates as well (Booz-Allen & Hamilton, 1968; Hollander, 2002; Van Poppel, 1999), because many ideas for new products and processes do not enter the market or do not lead to commercial success once they enter the market. To put it more plainly, innovation is still a major challenge for firms. Therefore, an important management question is how a firm can renew its core technologies, products and processes as a basis for competitive vitality (Prahalad and Hamel, 1990; Sirmon *et al.*, 2007; Teece *et al.*, 1997).

It is perhaps therefore not surprising that modern firms treat the management of innovation as one of the basic business functions (Burgelman *et al.*, 2009; Janszen, 2000; Tidd *et al.*, 2005; Wheelwright and Clark, 1992). The management of innovation is concerned with monitoring the implementation of innovation projects from idea generation, development, and pilot testing all the way to industrial scale introduction. These innovation projects may entail improvements of existing products and processes, also referred to as incremental innovations, but also the development of radically new products and processes, that in turn may make existing ones obsolete (Christensen, 1997). Although it may be extremely difficult and take a lot of time to develop a radically new product, the rewards may be enormous, as it may lead to bring new competitive advantages and an upswing in turnover (Christensen *et al.*, 1998; Utterback, 1974; Utterback *et al.*, 1988).

Over the years innovation has received a lot of attention in a great number of academic disciplines, ranging from (business) management, economics, sociology and psychology, political sciences, to technical sciences (Gopalakrishnan and Damanpour, 1997). These disciplines offer different sets of research questions, use different units of analysis, and represent a wide range of meanings of the word 'innovation'. Even within the literature on innovation management, many different perspectives, different suppositions and approaches exist (Nieto, 2003). In the context of this book, innovation has been broadly defined as 'the exploitation of new ideas into new products, processes, services or business practice' (Pittaway et al., 2004).

It has become generally acknowledged in the innovation management literature that firms do not innovate in isolation (Chesbrough, 2003b; Gilsing, 2003; Lundvall, 1992; Powell et al., 1996; Teece, 1986; Von Hippel, 1988). Instead, firms increasingly look for ways to profit from knowledge in other organizations, like supply chain partners, universities and research institutes, and even competitors (Gemunden et al., 1996; Granstrand et al., 1992; Laursen and Salter, 2006; Omta, 2002). Firms may choose from several strategies for external knowledge acquisition (also referred to as governance modes), such as inter-organizational cooperation, venture capital investments, outsourcing of Research and Development (R&D), or licensing-in (Granstrand et al., 1992; Hagedoorn, 1990; Tidd and Trewhella, 1997). Chesbrough (2003) introduced the 'open innovation model', which emphasizes that the innovation process should be flexible and may cross organizational boundaries, so that it enables the transfer of knowledge and capabilities from and to other independent organizations (Chesbrough, 2003). According to the open innovation model, firms should not only consider internal, but also external knowledge, capabilities and paths to market.

In this book we concentrate on a number of knowledge acquisition strategies that can be regarded as types of open innovation, such as licensing-in of knowledge and technologies, and inter-organizational cooperation. Licensing-in is the purchasing of (product or process) technology, designs or marketing expertise, which are readily available in the market (Lowe and Taylor, 1998; Tidd and Trewhella, 1997). In inter-organizational cooperation different partners pool their resources and capabilities for the purpose of collaborative R&D (Hagedoorn, 2002; Nooteboom, 1999b; Sampson, 2007). In innovation networks, for instance, different organizations such as small firms and research organizations work together with the aim of developing a new product, process, or business practice. In addition to open innovation, firms can also merge with or acquire other firms in order to profit from external knowledge (Chakrabarti et al., 1994; Coff, 1999; Graebner, 2004; Granstrand et al., 1992; Hitt et al., 1996). Mergers and acquisitions (M&As) should be regarded as the situation where independent firms combine their operations into a consolidated firm. Whereas licensing-in and inter-organizational cooperation can be regarded as dedicated modes (i.e. the prime objective of such a mode is innovation or knowledge transfer), M&As involve other resources and business functions as well. In addition, the prime reason for M&As is often not to enhance the innovative potential, but to open new markets, or gain extra market share in existing markets (Bakker and Helmink, 2000; Chakrabarti *et al.*, 1994; Chakrabarti and Souder, 1987; Gerpott, 1995).

If firms try to acquire external knowledge, they will face several management challenges (Barney, 1999; Van de Vrande *et al.*, 2006). Several empirical studies have indicated that sourcing external knowledge can be time consuming, expensive and laborious (e.g. Katila and Ahuja, 2002; Laursen and Salter, 2006). Moreover, the management of inter-organizational cooperation is associated with complex issues such as appropriation concerns, motivational problems, leakage of sensitive information, and partner dependency (Gulati and Singh, 1998; Nooteboom, 1999b; Omta and Van Rossum, 1999). In the case of M&As, firms are faced with the additional complex process of integrating two different organizations, as they may face challenges of integrating different corporate cultures, resistance among personnel, and compromising ongoing work (Bakker and Helmink, 2000; Haspeslagh and Jemison, 1991; Schweiger, 2002).

Therefore, an important question for managers is whether external knowledge acquisition really contributes to innovation. Do the different knowledge acquisition strategies indeed lead to better innovation performance? And how is the process of acquiring external knowledge successfully managed? In this respect, the management of innovating firms should not only strategically consider which knowledge acquisition strategy is to be preferred if they want to profit from knowledge developed elsewhere, but they should also consider carefully how to manage their external knowledge acquisition processes. This book tries to address these management challenges. The main objective of this book is therefore as follows.

To analyze how firms can profit from external knowledge using different knowledge acquisition strategies.

In order to realize this objective, four empirical studies are carried out. The first two studies are presented in Part I of this book and are primarily concerned with the relevance of different strategies for acquiring external knowledge (such as licensing-in, outsourcing and cooperation), using a quantitative approach. Both studies use longitudinal data of industrial firms from Dutch Community Innovation Surveys (CIS, 1994-2004), which explore the innovation process inside firms. In Part II two qualitative studies are presented that concentrate on specific management challenges of two different knowledge acquisition strategies, namely inter-organizational cooperation and M&As. The first study provides in-depth information on innovation brokers orchestrating innovation networks of Small and Medium sized Enterprises (SMEs) in the agri-food sector, in different European countries. The second study provides in-depth information on the integration processes of the R&D function, following large (medium) high-tech M&As in life sciences sectors.

1.1 Part I: quantitative analyses

Part I of this book consists of two quantitative studies, which are concerned with the relevance of different knowledge acquisition strategies. The first study concentrates on the occurrence of different strategies to acquire external knowledge over time. In particular, the study concentrates on external knowledge acquisition strategies associated with open innovation. Next, the second study in Part I complements the first study by analyzing whether the different knowledge acquisition strategies are effective in improving the innovation performance.

1.1.1 Adoption of open innovation

Chapter 2 studies the extent to which firms use various strategies to acquire external knowledge. In particular, this study concentrates on the adoption of knowledge acquisition strategies that are associated with open innovation. As said, Chesbrough (2003) coined the term open innovation to introduce a model for managing innovation in large R&D-intensive firms. This model builds on the premise that if a firm wants to innovate successfully in the current highly dynamic business environment, the innovation process should get a more flexible structure, enabling the transfer and combination of external knowledge and capabilities. According to the open innovation model external innovative ideas and paths to the market are as important as internal ones, whereas in the 'closed innovation model' firms mainly generate their own ideas, carry out all innovation activities in-house, and develop and market all new products themselves (Chesbrough, 2003b). Several knowledge acquisition strategies have been associated with the open innovation model, such as licensing-in, outsourcing, venture capital investments, and cooperation (Chesbrough, 2003b; Chesbrough *et al.*, 2006; Van de Vrande, 2007). These knowledge acquisition strategies can imply relationships with different types of organizations, such as cooperation with suppliers, customers, competitors, and research organizations.

Yet, despite the recent emphasis on open innovation by innovation management scholars, the empirical evidence of its relevance to innovating firms has so far been limited to a small range of firms (Chesbrough, 2006). Most of the empirical evidence on the relevance of open innovation (e.g. Christensen *et al.*, 2005; Dittrich and Duysters, 2007; Fetterhoff and Voelkel, 2006) comes from high-tech industries, such as pharmaceutical, information technology and computers. Only anecdotal evidence suggests that open innovation can be beneficial for low-tech industries as well (e.g. Chesbrough and Crowther, 2006). Still, *it remains an open question whether the concepts of open innovation also apply to lower-tech or more mature industries* (Chesbrough, 2006: 4). In addition, whereas the relevance of open innovation is shown for a number of large firms, it remains unclear to what extent open innovation is also relevant for SMEs. Finally, much of the empirical evidence on open innovation, like the pivotal work by Chesbrough, is taken from US-based firms. *The relevance of open innovation to companies outside the US remains to be demonstrated* (Chesbrough, 2006: 5).

Given that a number of studies (e.g. Chesbrough, 2003b; Chesbrough and Crowther, 2006; Chesbrough *et al.*, 2006; Dittrich and Duysters, 2007) pointed at the importance of the open innovation model, there is a clear need for assessing its external validity. Therefore, in Chapter 2 we try to answer the question as to what extent innovating firms have adopted an open innovation strategy, by analyzing over an 11-year time period (1994-2004) the occurrence of different knowledge acquisition strategies, such as licensing-in, outsourcing, and cooperation among different types of firms.

Research Question 1 (RQ1): To what extent do different types (size and technology classes) of innovating firms pursue an open innovation strategy?

1.1.2 The impact of knowledge acquisition strategies on innovation performance

In addition to getting insight into the extent to which innovating firms pursue open innovation strategies, it is also important to know whether firms really profit from it. The management of innovating firms can choose between a variety of knowledge acquisition strategies, but which strategies are in fact effective? Is open innovation, as suggested by many scholars, really a successful strategy for firms? Or can firms just as easily rely on in-house innovation? Moreover, are knowledge acquisition strategies favorable for incremental improvements of existing products (incremental innovations) as well as completely novel innovations that are new to the market (radical innovations)? In addition to open innovation, M&As can also be regarded as a way of acquiring external knowledge in order to improve the innovation performance (e.g. Barney, 1999; Granstrand *et al.*, 1992; Van de Vrande *et al.*, 2006). However, are M&As really beneficial for innovation? These issues are central in Chapter 3. More specifically, the question is addressed as to how different knowledge acquisition strategies contribute to the performance of incremental and radical innovations. And what is the time frame within which performance effects can be expected?

So far, numerous empirical studies have investigated the impact of a single strategy for external knowledge acquisition on innovation performance, especially of inter-organizational cooperation (e.g. Miotti and Sachwald, 2003; Negassi, 2004; Sampson, 2007; Stuart, 2000), or to a lesser extent M&As (e.g. Ahuja and Katila, 2001; Cloodt *et al.*, 2006; Hagedoorn and Duysters, 2002a). Whereas studies on the relationship between cooperation and innovation tend to find a consistent positive relationship, studies on the relationship between M&As and innovation show mixed results (De Man and Duysters, 2005). Apparently, negative side-effects of M&As may dominate this relationship, e.g. job uncertainty, resistance to change, and clashing business cultures, all harming ongoing innovation trajectories. Some authors found a positive relationship between M&As and innovation performance in specific situations, for instance in the case of technology motivated M&As in high-tech industries (Ahuja and Katila, 2001; Cloodt *et al.*, 2006). The relationship between more market-based acquisition strategies for external knowledge acquisition, most notably licensing-in, and innovation performance has received much less attention. An exception is Tsai and Wang (2007), who found a positive relationship between licensing-in and innovation performance for firms that possess sufficient R&D to absorb the acquired knowledge.

Only a few studies have investigated the impact of different external knowledge acquisition strategies on innovation performance in an integrated way (Fey, 2005; Keil *et al.*, 2008; Rothaermel and Hess, 2007; Van de Vrande, 2007). However, these studies, like most of the studies within the inter-organizational context on innovation, focused exclusively on high-tech industries. As innovation is also important to other industries, it would be interesting to analyze the impact of different external knowledge acquisition strategies in industries other than high-tech as well. Therefore, Chapter 3 presents a statistical analysis of cross-sectional Dutch Community Innovation Survey (CIS) data that is concerned with the impact of different strategies for acquiring external knowledge on innovation performance. More specifically, we analyze the relationship between different strategies for external knowledge acquisition on the short- and long-term performance of incremental and radical innovations in innovative firms. Consequently, Chapter 3 focuses on the following research question.

Research Question 2 (RQ2): What is the impact of different external knowledge acquisition strategies on the short-term and long-term innovation performance of innovative firms?

1.2 Part II: qualitative analyses

Whereas in Part I a large dataset of Dutch industrial firms is analyzed to identify trends with respect to how firms profit from external knowledge, in Part II the objective is to analyze this phenomenon more in-depth. The first study in Part II concentrates on inter-organizational cooperation in SME innovation networks. Innovating in a network can be particularly challenging for SMEs, which often lack cooperation experience and have a limited absorptive capacity. More specifically, the study is concerned with the question how innovation brokers orchestrate SME innovation networks. In the second study the attention turns to how corporations in life-science industries profit from external knowledge acquired by means of M&As. M&As can be considered as the most far-reaching knowledge acquisition strategy in terms of organizational integration, and the integration of large firms with substantial R&D functions can be particularly difficult, especially in large firms with different business cultures and organizational systems. In addition, it is often stated that large firms lack the agility of SMEs and are as a consequence less well equipped to conduct (radical) innovation (Kemp *et al.*, 2003). While a merger or acquisition increases size, both arguments led us to make an in-depth study of the impact of different integration processes on the innovation potential in large-scale M&As. Therefore, the study concentrates on how innovation synergies are realized in terms of integration mechanisms and resource re-allocations in the case of the integration of two large firms following a merger or acquisition.

1.2.1 Orchestrating SME innovation networks

Chapter 4 deals with the management challenges that come with inter-organizational cooperation in innovation networks. Once a firm decides it will cooperate with other organizations to innovate, managers will face important questions, such as how to establish an innovation network of complementary actors? How to manage the cooperation between organizations with divergent interests and different cultures? How to ensure a fair balance in costs and benefits with the other partners in the network? And how to prevent leakage of sensitive information through the network?

Furthermore, SMEs in particular face several obstacles when they want to profit from external knowledge, such as limited absorptive capacity, and lack of joint research experience (Hoffmann and Schlosser, 2001; Kaufmann and Tödtling, 2002; Van Gils and Zwart, 2004). Nevertheless, SMEs often lack the essential resources and capabilities to successfully innovate in-house (Narula, 2004; Nooteboom, 1994), making inter-organizational relationships essential to them.

Intermediary organizations, also referred to as innovation brokers or network orchestrators, have emerged to assist SMEs to innovate in networks (Dhanaraj and Parkhe, 2006; Howells, 2006; Nooteboom, 1999b; Smits and Kuhman, 2004; Winch and Courtney, 2007). For instance, innovation brokers may support SMEs by identifying their innovation needs, articulating their knowledge demands, setting up partnerships and managing the inter-organizational cooperation processes (Howells, 2006). Within the literature on open innovation, innovation brokers are mentioned as important actors as well (Chesbrough, 2006: 10; Sousa, 2008). However, empirical knowledge on *how* innovation brokers operate successfully, and under which conditions, remains scarce (Boon *et al.*, 2008; Sapsed *et al.*, 2007; Winch and Courtney, 2007). In addition, it can be expected that innovation brokers are a rich source of information on how to successfully manage an open innovation network. Therefore, in Chapter 4 we want to answer the question as to how innovation brokers orchestrate SME innovation networks in the agri-food sector.

Research Question 3 (RQ3): How do innovation brokers orchestrate SME innovation networks in the agri-food sector?

In tackling this question, we apply an in-depth case study approach to analyze the network orchestration processes of four innovation brokers in the agri-food industry, in different European countries. The agri-food industry is an interesting setting in which to study network orchestration, because it has a high share of SMEs, and agri-food firms face substantial constraints when it comes to innovation. Studies concluded that economic considerations and insufficient innovation competencies are important barriers to innovation in the agri-food sector (Batterink *et al.*, 2006; Garcia Martinez and Briz, 2000). Moreover, Costa and Jongen (2006) pointed at some general barriers to agri-food innovation, such as a lack of concrete knowledge on how to organize the innovation process, especially in an inter-organizational setting. Innovation brokers can therefore potentially play a crucial role in SME innovation networks in the agri-food sector (Dons and Bino, 2008; Klerkx and Leeuwis, 2008b; Vanhaverbeke *et al.*, 2007).

1.2.2 Realizing innovation synergies in large M&As

Chapter 5 deals with the challenges that arise when firms want to profit from external knowledge and capabilities through mergers and/or acquisitions (M&As). We have already stated that, next to open innovation, firms can choose to merge with or acquire another firm in order to obtain new knowledge and capabilities. Whereas the knowledge acquisition strategies associated with open innovation are flexible in nature and imply that the involved firms remain autonomous, M&As should be regarded as a way to get permanent access to and full hierarchical control over innovative products, technologies, capabilities and assets (Chakrabarti *et al.*, 1994; Coff, 1999; Graebner, 2004; Granstrand *et al.*, 1992; Hitt *et al.*, 1996). M&As typically involve integrating the processes and resources of two firms, including perhaps unwanted resources (Barney, 1999; Gerpott, 1995). Moreover, as mentioned, in the case of M&As, the involved firms are faced with (corporate) cultural distance, resistance among personnel, and compromising ongoing work. It may therefore be not surprising that in general M&As are associated with high failure rates (Cartwright and Schoenberg, 2006; King *et al.*, 2004; Mueller, 1985; Ravenscraft and Scherer, 1987; Schenk, 2006; Seth, 1990) and with high levels of uncertainty when it comes to realizing innovation synergies (Bannert and Tschirky, 2004; Chakrabarti and Souder, 1987; Chatterjee, 1986)

Many authors, especially those residing in the organizational behavior stream of research, point at the Post M&A Integration (PMAI) process when explaining why M&As succeed or not (e.g. Bakker and Helmink, 2000; Birkinshaw *et al.*, 2000; Epstein, 2004; Haspeslagh and Jemison, 1991; Schweiger, 2002). Thus, integration and innovation managers alike need to ask themselves the following questions: Which specific innovation synergies can be expected from M&As? What integration mechanisms and resource re-allocations are required to realize these innovation synergies? And which factors contribute to successful integration of the R&D function? Surprisingly, however, to date only a few studies have investigated the PMI process of the R&D function in depth (e.g. Bannert and Tschirky, 2004; Gerpott, 1995; Grimpe, 2007).

In addition, there are a substantial number of characteristics of M&As (M&A context characteristics) that may determine whether innovation synergies can be expected or not (Gerpott, 1995). For instance, the size of an M&A, and the relatedness between the involved firms in terms of technologies possessed may determine the potential for synergy realization (Ahuja and Katila, 2001; Cloodt *et al.*, 2006; Prabhu *et al.*, 2005). However, most studies concentrating on the M&A context characteristics in explaining post M&A innovation performance, e.g. on the role of technological relatedness, consider the process of synergy realization (i.e. through post M&A integration) as a black box (e.g. Ahuja and Katila, 2001; Cloodt *et al.*, 2006). With this study, we aim to open this black box by concentrating on the M&A context characteristics as well as the post M&A integration process. More specifically, in line with the study of Cassiman *et al.* (2005), we link technological relatedness to specific R&D integration mechanisms, and subsequently to innovation synergy realization. The study presented in Chapter 5 focuses on the following research question.

Research Question 4 (RQ4): What is the role of technological relatedness in realizing innovation synergies in M&As?

In Chapter 5 we try to conceptualize innovation synergy realization in the context of M&As by analyzing in-depth the PMI process of large, medium- and high-tech M&As in the life science industry. Especially in high-tech sectors, M&As are an important mechanism to acquire external knowledge (Cloodt, 2005). Moreover, large high-tech M&As involve substantial R&D functions. Thus, even if access to R&D knowledge is not the prime reason for such M&As, the integration of the firms is likely to affect the R&D functions (Gerpott, 1995). Therefore, in such a setting, it is a clear management challenge to profit from the knowledge and innovation capabilities residing in the other firm.

1.3 Outline of the book

The remainder of this book is organized as follows. Chapters 2, 3, 4 and 5 present four separate empirical studies, each addressing one of the research questions that are stated in this introduction chapter.

Part I of this book comprises Chapters 2 and 3, which present quantitative analyses of CIS-data from the Netherlands, focused on the relevance of different strategies for acquiring external knowledge. Chapter 2 will focus on the trends with respect to the adoption of open innovation in low-, medium-, and high-tech sectors, and among small, medium and large-sized enterprises in the Netherlands in 1994-2004. Chapter 3 presents a quantitative study of Dutch industrial firms that investigates the impact of different external knowledge acquisition strategies on the short-term and long-term performance regarding both incremental and radical innovation.

Part II comprises Chapters 4 and 5 and presents in-depth case studies. Chapter 4 focuses on the management of SME innovation networks in the agri-food industry. This study explores how innovation brokers manage SME innovation networks to assist the cooperating SMEs overcoming their innovation and cooperation obstacles. The study presented in Chapter 5 includes in-depth case studies of 10 large high-tech M&As in the life-science industry in order to understand how innovation synergies are realized in terms of integration mechanisms and resource re-allocations.

Finally, Chapter 6 draws conclusions from the studies presented in this book, and indicates the main contributions to literature. This chapter ends with a discussion on the managerial implications for innovating firms.

Part I
Quantitative analyses

2. The adoption of open innovation. A longitudinal study of large firms and SMEs, in high-, medium-, and low-tech industries in the Netherlands

2.1 Introduction

This chapter was set up to answer the first research question.

RQ1: To what extent do different types (size and technology classes) of innovating firms pursue an open innovation strategy?

As we stated in the introductory chapter, open innovation was introduced as a new model for managing innovation in large R&D-intensive firms. Although suggested by several scholars, it remains unclear whether open innovation is also relevant for lower-tech or more mature industries and for Small- and Medium-sized Enterprises (SMEs). Therefore, to answer RQ1, we come up with two sub-questions:

a. Is there a noticeable trend of innovating firms adopting open innovation strategies?
b. Do SMEs and firms in low and medium-tech industries pursue open innovation strategies, or is open innovation exclusively the domain of large corporations and firms in high-tech industries?

In answering these research questions, we aim to arrive at a state-of-the-art view with respect to the relevance of open innovation in the Netherlands. In the present study we use longitudinal Dutch Community Innovation Survey (CIS) data of industrial firms from five subsequent surveys, covering the period 1994-2004, to identify the most recent trends with respect to open and closed innovation. As such, this study answers calls for longitudinal, cross-sectional research into the developments with respect to open innovation (Chesbrough, 2006; Laursen and Salter, 2006; West *et al.*, 2006). As Laursen and Salter (2004) state, *until greater research is undertaken on the nature of (external) search strategies over time, the full implications of open innovation will not be understood.* Using Dutch data, this research can also contribute to the existing literature by studying whether some elements of the open innovation model, derived mainly from (qualitative) research from US firms, are also relevant for EU-based firms (West *et al.*, 2006: 292).

The remainder of Chapter 2 is organized as follows. Section 2.2 presents a theoretical background and elaborates on the innovation process, highlighting the open innovation model and different strategies for external knowledge acquisition. Then, in Section 2.3 the data and methodology of our study is outlined. This section describes the properties of the Dutch CIS's, how the innovating firms are selected from the 5 subsequent innovation surveys and how the resulting samples compare. It furthermore describes how the different knowledge acquisition strategies associated with open innovation were measured, and what statistical method was used to substantiate our claims. Section 2.4 reports the findings of the empirical analyses on the CIS data. Finally, Section 2.5 contains the conclusions and implications, as well as suggestions for further research.

2.2 Theoretical background

2.2.1 The innovation process

The pivotal role of the management of the innovation process is to monitor the implementation of innovation projects from pilot testing to industrial-scale introduction. However, when tracing the literature on the management of innovation it becomes apparent that the way innovation is managed has changed dramatically over the years. The traditional view of innovation, especially in large firms, places the primary locus of innovation in the (corporate) research and development (R&D) department. This view is in line with the vertically integrated perspective on innovation and the importance of economies of scale in R&D (Chandler, 1990; Teece, 1986). Over the years, however, firms have increasingly spread innovation throughout the whole organization, which implies that different business functions, such as marketing, purchasing, manufacturing, have to cooperate (Wheelwright and Clark, 1992). In addition, external organizations are also increasingly included in the innovation process, like customers (Baker and Sinkula, 2005; Gassmann *et al.*, 2006; Roussel *et al.*, 1991), suppliers (Kamath and Liker, 1990; Petersen *et al.*, 2003; Ragatz *et al.*, 1997), competitors (Hamel *et al.*, 1989) or research organizations like universities (Fontana *et al.*, 2006; Mora-Valentin *et al.*, 2004; Schartinger *et al.*, 2002; Snyder and Blevins, 1986). In fact, successful innovating firms draw simultaneously from different external sources to keep up with the rapid technological and market developments (Laursen and Salter, 2006). As a consequence, a crucial part of the innovation process nowadays involves building and managing linkages with other organizations, in order to acquire the knowledge and capabilities residing there (Chesbrough, 2003b; Powell *et al.*, 1996; Rogers, 1996).

Chesbrough (2003b) coined the term open innovation to introduce a new model for managing innovation. Open innovation builds on the assumptions that in the current business environment, firms are faced with the increasing speed of technological developments, the growing mobility of highly experienced and skilled people, and the growing presence of venture capital (Chesbrough, 2003b). These developments, which are also referred to as 'erosion factors of closed innovation' have led to a diffusion of knowledge among firms of all sizes in many industries (Chesbrough, 2003b), so that *even the most capable R&D organizations must identify, connect to, and leverage external knowledge sources as a core process in innovation* (Chesbrough, 2006: 2). Therefore, in the open innovation model (Chesbrough, 2003a, 2003b, 2004; Chesbrough *et al.*, 2006) it is argued that if a firm wants to innovate successfully in the current highly dynamic environment, the innovation process should get a more open and flexible structure, allowing for the integration of external knowledge and capabilities (Chesbrough, 2003b). In this way, innovative ideas and technologies may come from outside the firm and innovative ideas may also be further developed by other firms, if it fits their business model better. It was, however, already widely accepted that innovation should be regarded as an interactive, cross-disciplinary and inter-organizational process (Lundvall, 1992; Von Hippel, 1988), so that in essence the notion of open innovation does not signify an altogether new phenomenon (Christensen *et al.*, 2005). The added value of the open innovation model is that it offers a more comprehensive and systematic framework for the way in which large high-tech firms manage these more externally oriented innovation processes (Christensen *et al.*, 2005).

The innovation process in SMEs differs substantially from that of large firms (Hoffmann and Schlosser, 2001; Nooteboom, 1994; Rogers, 2004). In contrast to many large firms, SMEs often do not have a structured R&D process, nor people working on innovation on a permanent basis. Moreover, Nooteboom (1994), for instance, addressed a number of characteristics of SMEs that can be considered as special strengths for innovation, such as highly motivated personnel, effective internal communication, little bureaucracy and much internal flexibility, and a high capacity for customization (Nooteboom, 1994). However, SMEs are traditionally confronted with many obstacles to innovation, such as a limited absorptive capacity (Menrad, 2004), lack of innovation funding (Caputo *et al.*, 2002; Kaufmann and Tödtling, 2002), lack of functional expertise, diseconomies of scale and the short-term perspective of management (Bessant and Rush, 1995; Kaufmann and Tödtling, 2002; Nooteboom, 1994). To overcome such obstacles, SMEs typically establish relations with external actors. Thus, there are specific drivers for SMEs to move towards an open innovation strategy, that may be different from the drivers towards open innovation in large firms. We will further discuss these issues in Chapter 4 on innovation brokerage.

2.2.2 Strategies for external knowledge acquisition

As we stated in the introductory chapter, the innovation literature has put forward a diversity of strategies, also referred to as governance modes, for connecting and leveraging external knowledge sources, such as technology in-licensing, R&D outsourcing, (different forms of) inter-organizational cooperation, corporate venture capital investments, or mergers and acquisitions (Granstrand *et al.*, 1992; Hagedoorn, 1990; Pisano, 1990; Tidd and Trewhella, 1997; Van de Vrande *et al.*, 2006). In the present chapter, we are primarily interested in those knowledge acquisition strategies that can be regarded as elements of open innovation. As noted earlier, the open innovation model emphasizes the flexibility of the innovation process, acknowledging and exploiting semi-permeable organizational boundaries. Implicitly, this means that flexible knowledge acquisition strategies in which the focal organizations remain autonomous, such as licensing-in, or inter-organizational cooperation, are associated with open innovation, whereas mergers and acquisitions imply high levels of organizational integration and are associated with closed innovation. Taking this into account and considering the possibilities of the CIS data we concentrate on licensing-in, outsourcing and (inter-organizational) cooperation as elements of open innovation.

First, technology or knowledge in-licensing (hereafter referred to as licensing-in) can be defined as the purchasing of (product or process) technology, designs or marketing expertise (adapted from Lowe and Taylor, 1998). As such, licensing-in is a means for innovating firms to exploit the innovation capabilities or intellectual property of another organization, which is readily available in the market. Technology licensing primarily enables firms to rapidly establish positions in new technological areas (Tidd and Trewhella, 1997). Usually, the licensee pays a fee and/or a royalty based on sales or a reciprocal flow of knowledge rights over a specific period of time (Lowe and Taylor, 1998). Second, with outsourcing, a particular part of the innovation process is carried out by another organization, the sub-contractor - e.g. a research institute, or another firm. The sub-contractor delivers particular knowledge or a technology specifically developed for, and to be controlled by the focal firm (Granstrand *et al.*, 1992; Hagedoorn, 1990). We consider that outsourcing does not specifically imply that an innovation (e.g. the new product) is completely developed by a third party (the sub-contractor). Outsourcing may also entail the development of a single part of a new product, or part of an innovation project. Third, cooperation implies that different partners work together and pool their resources and capabilities for the purpose of collaborative R&D, crossing organizational boundaries, while remaining autonomous organizations (Sampson, 2007). Cooperation may help firms to reap economies of scale in R&D and shorten development time while spreading the costs and risks of such new developments (Hagedoorn, 2002; Nooteboom, 1999b; Sampson, 2007). Thus, with cooperation each party contributes significantly to the innovation process, which implies that it does not include relationships involving the purchase of components or simply the funding of research (Emden *et al.*, 2006). Potential partners for cooperation include supply chain partners such as customers or suppliers, competitors, knowledge institutions like universities, or firms from other industries (Omta, 2002; Ritter and Gemunden, 2003). The rationale for cooperation can differ amongst the different types of partners. Cooperation within the supply chain, for instance, is associated with firms that lack market and technological knowledge, whereas cooperation with competitors is associated with exploiting economies of scale and reducing individual costs of innovation (Arranz and Fdez. de Arroyabe, 2008; Miotti and Sachwald, 2003). Cooperation with universities or research institutes is associated with firms that want to be at the technological frontier, targeting radically new products (Miotti and Sachwald, 2003). In the current dynamic business environment, innovating firms may cooperate with different types of partners simultaneously.

Given the recent emphasis on open innovation and its inter-organizational context, we expect that innovative firms have increasingly pursued open innovation strategies in the period 1994-2004. Thus, we expect that more and more industrial firms have opened up their innovation process by increasing the emphasis on licensing-in knowledge, engaging in outsourcing, or jointly developing innovations with other organizations, such as supply chain partners, competitors, or research organizations. Concordantly, we expect that a decreasing share of innovating firms rely exclusively on in-house innovation.

2.3 Data and methods

For this study we use data from the structured samples of 5 subsequent Community of Innovation Surveys (CIS) in the Netherlands, covering the period 1994-2004, which we further restricted to industrial sectors and firms with more than 10 employees[1,2]. The surveys were implemented by Statistics Netherlands, which is the official statistical bureau for the Netherlands and which is responsible for collecting, processing and publishing statistics to be used in practice, by policymakers and for scientific research (see www.cbs.nl). In the 1990s, the CIS was launched by the European Commission to track firms' innovation activities and has been conducted in several EU countries ever since. It is formally based on the OECD's Oslo Manual (e.g. OECD, 1996), which posits definitions for innovation and R&D-related concepts. The CIS draws on a long tradition of research on innovation[3], and so far CIS data have been used in many academic papers. Initially, CIS questionnaires were rather country-specific, but since 1996 (starting with CIS-2) the core of the questionnaire has been harmonized over the different countries. Moreover, the core of the questionnaire and the survey approach have remained the same for the successive CIS. As a consequence, the CIS data has great potential for longitudinal analysis. However, access to CIS data is still organized typically through the respective national statistics organizations[4]. Dutch CIS data have the huge advantage over CIS data from other European countries that Statistics Netherlands conducts the CIS every two years, instead of the standard four years. The additional Dutch editions (referred to as CIS2.5 and CIS3.5) are to a large extent similar to the 4-yearly European-wide editions, although Statistics Netherlands has experimented with new topics. As a consequence, not every item in the 4-yearly European-wide CIS is covered by the additional Dutch editions. For this study, however, all relevant items are available for the 5 editions, i.e. CIS2, CIS2.5, CIS3, CIS3.5 and CIS4.

Dutch CIS data contain innovation data of firms from industry, service, and other sectors such as agriculture, utilities, and building and construction. As the study concentrates on industrial firms, we excluded services and other sectors from the initial CIS samples. An important advantage of CIS data is that the firms include both publicly-listed as well as private firms, which makes this research a welcome contribution to the innovation management literature that mainly draws from publicly listed firms.

---

[1] The empirical part of this research was executed at the Centre for Economic Micro data (Cerem) at Statistics Netherlands (CBS). The views expressed in this book, however, are those of the author only.

[2] The questions in the CIS relate to the preceding three years (e.g. the CIS-4 (2004) relates to innovation activities in the years 2002, 2003 and 2004).

[3] Moreover, the reliability, validity and interpretability of the survey were established by extensive piloting and pre-testing before implementation within different countries (Laursen and Salter, 2006).

[4] Recently there have been attempts to integrate CIS data for the purpose of comparing different countries, but analyses of multiple EU countries is still burdensome. As a researcher, one has to contact and contract each national statistical office separately and a combined analysis is often impossible, because firm-level data are not allowed to leave the secured area of the national statistics offices.

For our study, we followed the structured sampling used for CIS by Statistics Netherlands (CBS). CIS were postal and voluntary. From firms with 10-49 employees a random sample was drawn, whereas all firms with 50 or more employees received a questionnaire. CIS-4 (2002-2004) was implemented in a similar way, although now a random sample was also drawn from the category '50-249 employees'. CIS-2.5 and CIS-3 comprise also firms with 10 employees or less, but for the sake of standardized comparison these firms were excluded from the analyses. From each of the surveys, we selected the innovating firms only, i.e. firms that indicated having developed at least one new or significantly improved product or process, and/or who indicated having a positive innovation budget. Table A1.1 in Appendix 1 provides the number of innovating firms in each sample. The samples in the later time periods are substantially smaller than samples in the first periods. This is mainly caused by the decrease of the shares of innovating firms over the period 1998-2002. Still, all sample sizes are substantial enough to allow for longitudinal analyses.

2.3.1 Measures

In order to assess the adoption of open innovation in different types of firms, we classified firms according to technology and size classes. The firms in the CIS database are classified by sector according to the Eurostat NACE classification. For our research we classified the distinguished industries according to the technological level, following the four OECD categories high-tech, medium high-tech, medium low-tech, and low-tech (OECD, 2007). This classification of technology classes is provided in Appendix 1 (Table A1.1).

In line with the size classification by Dutch Statistics, we identified three size classes: small (10-49 employees), medium (50-249 employees) and large firms (250 or more employees). This classification of size classes is provided in Appendix 1 (Table A1.2).

Furthermore, we concentrated on the following knowledge acquisition strategies, which can be regarded as indicators of open innovation: licensing-in, outsourcing, and cooperation with several types of partners. First, in the CIS surveys firms were asked to indicate whether they licensed-in knowledge or technologies for their innovation process. Second, in the CIS surveys firms were asked to indicate whether they outsourced particular parts of their innovation activities to other firms. Third, in the CIS surveys firms were asked to indicate whether they had cooperated with other organizations, that is, apart from outsourcing. Inter-organizational cooperation was defined in the questionnaire as *active participation in joint R&D and other innovation projects with other organizations (either other enterprises or non-commercial institutions)*. The surveys explicitly mentioned that pure contracting-out of work, where there is no active collaboration, is not regarded as cooperation. Furthermore, CIS also provides information on the type of partners involved in the cooperation. That enabled us to distinguish between different types of partners, like customers, suppliers, competitors, and knowledge institutions. Fourth, to trace the adoption levels of open innovation in Dutch industrial firms we also calculated the average number of partner types for cooperating innovative firms in the

Dutch industry. Note that to do this calculation we selected the cooperating innovative firms from the total set of innovative firms (see Appendix 1, Table A1.3 for the number of companies in the sub samples). Finally, we calculated to what extent firms combine different knowledge acquisition strategies (licensing-in, outsourcing and cooperation) within one period of time (see Figure 2.2).

2.3.2 Validity and reliability

In general, the response rates of industrial firms in the CIS turned out to be relatively high (e.g. 71% in 1996, 65% in 1998, 54% in 2000, 59% in 2002 and 71% in 2004). This high response rate may be due to the good reputation of Statistics Netherlands in the Dutch industry. In addition, the response rates for different industries and size classes are considered largely consistent with the overall response patterns of the CIS (CBS, 1998, 2000, 2002, 2004, 2006)[5]. The response may, however, be biased towards innovating firms, because innovating firms may be more inclined to respond to a questionnaire specifically dedicated to innovation. Such a response bias could be a problem when comparing innovating firms with non-innovating firms. However, we only performed the analyses on innovating firms. Moreover, there is no reason to believe that firms that pursue an open innovation-strategy are more inclined to respond to the survey, i.e. the so-called self-selection bias, as elements of open innovation (e.g. concerning cooperation) were only a minority of the many subjects covered by the CIS. In sum, it is unlikely that the samples suffer from response bias that would seriously hinder our longitudinal analysis.

Since we are interested in longitudinal trends in the adoption of open innovation, it is important that the sequential samples are comparable at the level of individual industries and technology classes, and at the level of size classes. It should be noted that the constructed dataset of innovating firms is not a panel dataset, because creating a panel dataset from the five successive CIS would dramatically reduce the number of firms for analyses, and would lead to a strong bias towards large firms. Instead we selected all innovating firms from each CIS and performed 2-proportions Z and Chi^2 tests to check whether the individual samples differed significantly in terms of the representation of the individual industries, and in terms of the representation of the size classes.

First, with respect to the representation of the individual industries in the different technology classes (i.e. low-, medium low-, medium high-, and high-tech) we compared the sample of each time-period with the final sample (CIS-4) and concluded that the samples with 14 industries and 5 time-periods differ significantly only on 7 out of 56 items (see Appendix 1, Table A1.1). More specifically, the sample of the low-tech industry in CIS-2 (1994-1996) and CIS-2.5 (1996-1998) contain significantly larger shares of textiles firms than the sample of the low-

---

[5] For a more detailed description of the methodology applied by Statistics Netherlands we refer to the CBS publication series 'Kennis en Economie' (in Dutch), in which the total results of the CIS are presented.

tech industry in CIS-4 (2002-2004), whereas in the CIS-4 there are relatively more food firms in the low-tech sub-sample than in CIS-2 and CIS-2.5. One explanation may be that the textiles sector in the Netherlands has diminished substantially over the past 2 decades, as many firms have stopped trading, or moved abroad. Next, the share of pharmaceutical firms in the high-tech sub-sample in CIS-2 is significantly smaller than in CIS-4. Finally, the share of firms representing 'automobile and other transportation means' is smaller in the sample of CIS-2, compared with the sample of CIS-4. Nevertheless, analysis of the more specific variables on open innovation for those industries revealed that these differences in representation of technology classes did not affect the conclusions. Altogether, the distribution of industries that makes up the technology classes is very similar over the years, so there is no reason to believe that this distribution will affect the analysis of the adoption of open innovation.

The total samples in the CIS-2 up to CIS-3.5 are also comparable to the sample of CIS-4 to the extent that they consist of comparable proportions of low-, medium low-, medium high-, and high-tech firms. The CIS-3.5 sample, however, comprises a relatively lower proportion of low-tech firms compared with the sample of CIS-4, whereas the proportion of medium high-tech industry in CIS-3.5 is slightly larger than in CIS-4. As we are interested in the adoption of open innovation among different technology classes, we also perform the analysis at the level of the technology classes, in addition to analyses at the overall industry level. Moreover, the small deviation of the sample composition of CIS-3.5 would not alter the conclusions with respect to open innovation adoption trends for the full period 1994-2004.

Second, the distribution of firms across size classes is presented in Appendix 2 (Table A1.2). With respect to size classes, Chi^2 tests revealed that the distributions compare relatively well over the years. The samples of CIS-2, CIS-3 and CIS-4 in particular, are not significantly different in terms firm size-distribution. The sample of CIS-3.5 (2000-2002), however, contains significantly fewer small-sized firms (10-49 employees), and more medium-sized firms (50-249 employees) than the other four samples. Furthermore, the sample of CIS-2.5 (1996-1998) contains significantly more small-sized and fewer large firms than the sample of CIS-3 (1998-2000). As we may expect that in general large and medium-sized firms are more likely to form linkages with other firms than small-sized firms, it is important to analyze developments with respect to the adoption of open innovation for different size classes separately.

2.3.3 Methods and data analysis

In the present study we analyse trends in the shares of innovating industrial firms within different categories engaged in different governance modes for external knowledge acquisition. Taking the indicators for licensing-in, outsourcing, and cooperation (with various types of partners), we calculated the share of innovating firms engaged in the respective knowledge acquisition strategy. We present the share of innovating firms and distinguish between technology classes (low-, medium low-, medium high-, and high-tech) and firm size classes, ranging from small (10-49 employees), to medium-sized (50-249 employees), up to large firms (250 or more employees). We performed '2-proportions z-tests' to determine whether the proportion of the firms pursuing a particular knowledge acquisition strategy has significantly increased or decreased compared with the previous period. The 2-proportions z-test is a statistical test to determine whether there is a significant difference between proportions (also referred to as the share or percentage) of two different independent samples (Churchill, 1999). In addition, we performed the same test to determine whether the proportions of firms pursuing a particular knowledge acquisition strategy in 2002-2004 has significantly changed, compared with 1994-1996. Regarding the case of the number of different types of cooperation partners, we ran an analysis using sub-samples of cooperating firms only. With an indicator for cooperating with different types of partners within one period, we performed a t-test to determine significant changes over time. In doing so, we were able to statistically justify our conclusions with respect to the longitudinal trends. In discussing the results of the longitudinal analysis, we focus mainly on significant changes over time in the adoption of open innovation.

2.4 Results

2.4.1 Adoption of an open innovation strategy

In Section 2 we indicated that there is an increased emphasis on external sources of innovation in the innovation literature (Chesbrough *et al.*, 2006), so we expect that the importance that firms attach to open innovation has increased in the period 1994-2004. Indeed, Table 2.1 shows that for the total industry the share of innovating firms that pursued an open innovation strategy (i.e. either in the form of licensing-in, outsourcing, cooperation, or any combination) in order to obtain access to external knowledge and capabilities has increased significantly in the period 1994-2004. This trend is most pronounced for small- and medium-sized firms, whereas larger firms were already inclined to pursue an open innovation strategy in 1994-1996. We derive from this that small and medium-sized firms are catching up with the larger firms in adopting an open innovation strategy. Next, as expected in high-tech industries there are relatively more firms with external relationships, compared with low- and medium-tech industries. Interestingly however, the difference between high-tech and low-tech in the levels of adoption of open innovation is decreasing. Table 1 indicates that whereas the difference in adoption of open innovation between high-tech and low-tech becomes more significant in 1994-2000, this difference becomes insignificant in 2002-2004. From this we deduce that in the period 1996-2004 low-tech industries are catching up with high-tech industries in adopting open innovation. Nonetheless, even in the period 2002-2004 almost one third of all innovating firms rely exclusively on their internal innovation capabilities and develop innovations without the help of other organizations (see Table 2.1).

When we switch focus from the general patterns in the adoption of open innovation to the patterns in the usage of specific knowledge acquisition strategies, we see that all three knowledge acquisition strategies associated with open innovation have been on the rise since 2000 (see Figure 2.1). Moreover, Figure 2.1 illustrates that innovating firms are more inclined

Table 2.1. Share of innovating firms using external knowledge acquisition strategies (e.g. licensing-in, outsourcing, cooperation).

	Size class (employees)	1994-1996 [a]		1996-1998 [a]		1998-2000 [a]		2000-2002 [a]		2002-2004 [b]	
Total industry	10-49	39%		43%		37%	*	46%	**	57%	**
	50-249	57%		57%		53%	**	64%	**	71%	**
	>250	83%		79%		80%		86%		90%	*
	Total	54%		55%		52%	**	63%	**	69%	**
High-tech	10-49	40%		50%		47%		66%		63%	**
	50-249	66%		62%		58%		70%		82%	*
	>250	94%		94%		94%		87%		90%	
	Total	58%		61%		62%		73%		76%	**
Medium high-tech	10-49	41%		46%		40%	*	55%		52%	*
	50-249	57%		60%		57%	**	68%		74%	**
	>250	84%		81%		79%		89%		93%	
	Total	56%		58%		55%	**	67%		70%	**
Medium low-tech	10-49	43%		43%		42%		36%	**	56%	*
	50-249	61%		58%		51%	*	61%	*	71%	*
	>250	89%		86%		86%		88%		89%	
	Total	57%		56%		51%		57%	**	68%	**
Low-tech	10-49	32%		37%		28%		30%	**	58%	**
	50-249	51%		51%		47%	**	62%		65%	**
	>250	78%		70%		71%		84%		88%	
	Total	49%		49%		45%	**	60%	*	68%	**
c		*		**		**		**			

[a] Reports z-test whether the percentage changes significantly between the two periods.
[b] Reports z-test whether the percentage in 2002-2004 changes significantly from 1994-1996.
[c] Reports z-test whether the percentage of the high-tech sector differs significantly from low-tech.
* P-value <0.05, ** P-value <0.01.

to engage in outsourcing or cooperation than in licensing-in. Whereas outsourcing was for a long time the most common strategy for innovating firms, in 2004 cooperation became most prominent. In the following sub-sections we elaborate on these trends and consider whether they are visible in the different technology and size classes.

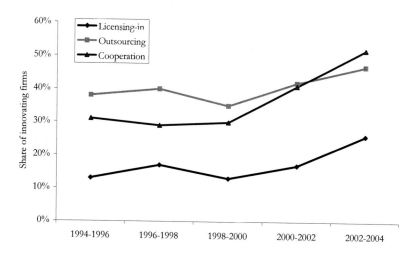

Figure 2.1. Share of firms using different knowledge acquisition strategies.

2.4.2 Licensing-in

The share of innovating firms licensing-in knowledge and technologies increased significantly in the period 1994-2004 (see Appendix 1, Table A1.4). More specifically, whereas the share of innovating firms that license-in knowledge or technologies fluctuated between 12% and 17% during 1996-2002, in 2002-2004 this share jumped to 27%. Taking a closer look at the different technology classes, we conclude that the increase in in-licensing firms is significant for all classes, except for high-tech. Over the years, the high-tech industries show the largest share of licensing firms, although the other technology classes are clearly catching up. It is also interesting to note that in the period 1998-2000 there was a small but significant decrease in the share of firms engaged in licensing-in, although this decrease turned out to be only temporary. When we focus on size classes, we see that in general large firms are more likely to engage in licensing-in than smaller firms. However, we find a dramatic increase in the share of smaller and medium-sized innovating firms that license-in (all highly significant, except for the medium-sized high-tech and small-sized medium high-tech firms), whereas for large firms the increase was much smaller (not significant). Apparently, in 1996-2004 the propensity of small and medium-sized firms to engage in licensing-in grew to a level almost comparable to the propensity of large firms to license-in.

2.4.3 Outsourcing

We also investigated whether the long dominant practice of outsourcing may indeed be associated with specific industries, especially those in supplier-dominated industries (Pavitt, 1984), such as the agricultural and textile industries, and major parts of the service sector. Firms in these industries often lack sufficient capabilities to innovate successfully. In such industries, technology suppliers are the main source of innovation, by providing the firms with custom-made and 'ready-to-use' technologies that improve the production processes, or improve the product quality.

In Dutch industry the share of innovating industrial firms engaged in outsourcing increased significantly for all size classes in the period 1994-2004 (see Appendix 1, Table A1.5). Whereas between 1996 and 2000 the share of innovating firms which outsourced at least a part of their innovation activities was about 35-40%, in the last two periods (2000-2002 and 2002-2004) this share increased significantly to 48%. Interestingly, from 1998 to 2000 there was even a significant decrease to 35%, but the subsequent periods showed a significant increase. However, despite the significant increase in outsourcing for the total industry, there are only a few significant increases in sub-classes. When considering the total period, only the medium and large firms in medium high-tech sectors, and the small- and medium-sized high-tech firms show a significant increase. In general, outsourcing is less prominent in low- and medium low-tech industries, compared with medium high-, and high-tech industries. Finally, in each time period the absolute shares of firms engaged in outsourcing are much higher for large firms compared with medium and smaller firms.

2.4.4 Cooperation

In several studies, Hagedoorn indicated that the absolute number of cooperative agreements increased significantly between the early 1980s and the late 1990s (e.g. 1990; 2002). Here we analyze developments with respect to inter-organizational cooperation in a more recent time period. We focus on inter-organizational cooperation in general and with different types of partners in particular.

Table 2.2 presents the share of innovating firms cooperating for innovation. These firms worked together with other organizations to jointly develop new products or processes. Taking the total industry, we see a highly significant increase in the share of cooperating firms from 31% in 2000 up to 53% in 2004, and the increase is present in all size-classes. Obviously, we can conclude that cooperation for innovation is becoming more and more common practice for innovating firms. Moreover, the share of cooperating firms initially remained more or less constant for the period 1994-2000, so we can deduce that the period 2000-2002 represent a turning point; there is a sudden and dramatic increase in the share of innovating firms that cooperate with other organizations. This trend is visible in all technology classes, although overall the absolute shares of firms cooperating for innovation is larger in high-tech industries, compared with the other technology industries. Interestingly, in medium low-tech and in high-tech the share of large innovating firms engaged in cooperation has not increased significantly. This can be explained by the fact that the share of large innovating firms cooperating for innovation was already at a high level (71%) in 1994-1996. In the period 2002-2004, 39% of the small, 53% of the medium-sized, and 80% of the large innovating firms cooperated for innovation. Similar proportions were found in the different technology and size classes. Altogether, this

Table 2.2. Share of innovating firms cooperating with other organizations for innovation.

	Size class (employees)	1994-1996 [a]	1996-1998 [a]	1998-2000 [a]	2000-2002 [a]	2002-2004 [b]
Total industry	10-49	19%	18%	18% **	26% **	39% **
	50-249	31%	30%	30% **	42% **	53% **
	>250	62%	54%	59% *	70% *	80% **
	Total	32%	29%	31% **	43% **	53% **
High-tech	10-49	22%	25%	23% **	50%	46% **
	50-249	40%	40%	39%	56%	70% **
	>250	71%	68%	75%	70%	83%
	Total	36%	37%	42% **	58%	63% **
Medium high-tech	10-49	17%	23%	21% *	32%	37% **
	50-249	30%	34%	30% **	45%	52% **
	>250	62%	55%	63%	69% *	87% **
	Total	31%	33%	33% **	45% *	52% **
Medium low-tech	10-49	26% *	16%	15%	19% **	39% *
	50-249	38%	30%	29% *	41% *	54% **
	>250	71%	60%	64%	73%	77%
	Total	37% **	28%	28% **	39% **	51% **
Low-tech	10-49	13%	14%	15%	13% **	37% **
	50-249	27%	21%	29%	35% *	47% **
	>250	57%	46%	47% **	70%	76% **
	Total	27%	23%	28% **	38% **	50% **

[a] Reports z-test whether the percentage changes significantly between the two periods.
[b] Reports z-test whether the percentage in 2002-2004 changes significantly from 1994-1996.
* P-value <0.05, ** P-value <0.01.

is a strong indication that there is a clear relationship between firm size and the propensity to cooperate with other organizations for innovation. Our findings with cooperation roughly confirm earlier findings (e.g. Arranz and Fdez. de Arroyabe, 2008; Fritsch and Lukas, 2001; Miotti and Sachwald, 2003; Negassi, 2004) that cooperation is positively associated with firm size and firms with relatively high levels of R&D (like in high-tech sectors). Interestingly, however, considering the low scores for small- and medium-sized firms in 1994-1996, we see that the longitudinal rise in the propensity to cooperate is most pronounced for small- and medium-sized firms.

Chapter 1

Cooperation with customers

Taking the total industry, we see that the share of innovating firms cooperating with customers increased from 18% in 1998-2000 to 33% in 2002-2004 (see Appendix 1, Table A1.6). Since the period 2000-2002 in particular more and more innovating firms work together with their customers on innovation. Firms do so to incorporate the user benefits when developing new products. In line with the general results, all technology sectors show parallel trends, with shares staying more or less steady in 1996-2000, but then increasing significantly in 2002 and even further in 2004. When we consider the different size classes, we see that only large firms in the medium-high-tech industries significantly increase cooperation with customers in 1994-2004. The explanation may be that in the period 1994-1996 already, especially in the other industries a substantial share of large innovating firms was already cooperating with customers (36% for large firms in total industry). In contrast, only 6% of the innovating small-sized low-tech firms worked together with customers in 1994-1996, whereas in 2004 this share was significantly larger (18%) but still below the 1994-1996 share (36%) for large low-tech firms. To conclude this section on cooperation with customers, we found that in Dutch industry firms have clearly opened up their innovation processes by cooperating with customers, but differences can be found between small, medium and large-sized firms.

Cooperation with suppliers

During 1994-2000 the share of innovating firms cooperating with suppliers remained steady at 17%, but this share increased dramatically to 31% in 2002, and to 42% in 2004 (see Appendix 1, Table A1.7). Obviously, these are not gradual increases, but represent a turning point in the period of 2000-2002. A closer look at the data reveals that there are similar trends in each of the technology and size classes. Only for large high-tech firms was the increase in cooperation with suppliers not significant. Moreover, by 2004 the proportion of large firms cooperating with suppliers was substantially larger in medium high-tech and low-tech industries than in high-tech industries. Similar to the trend concerning cooperation in general, the results show a clear relationship between firm size and the propensity to engage in cooperating for innovation with suppliers, with larger firms much more likely to engage in supplier cooperation than smaller firms. Finally, the results indicate that cooperating for innovation with suppliers has become more common than cooperating with customers.

Cooperation with competitors

Table A1.8 in Appendix 1 reports the developments with respect to cooperating on innovation with competitors. In absolute terms, cooperation with competitors is not as popular as cooperation within the supply chain. However, the trend we see in the total industry with regard to cooperation with competitors is similar to the trends we identified for cooperation within the supply chain (i.e. with customers and suppliers). From 1994 to 2000 the share of innovating firms cooperating with competitors remained steady at 9%, whereas in 2002 this share increased to 15%. However, instead of increasing even further in 2004, the share of innovating firms cooperating with competitors levelled off. Therefore, the increase in cooperation with competitors is not as clear as the increase in cooperation within the supply chain. Finally, when focusing on individual size classes within different technology classes we must conclude that the increase in cooperation with competitors is significant in just a few cases, i.e. all classes within medium to high-tech industries and only small-sized high tech firms.

Cooperation with knowledge institutions

In the total industry the share of innovating firms cooperating with knowledge institutions increased significantly in 1996-2004. Initially, the share of innovating firms cooperating with knowledge institutions remained constant at about 16% in 1994-2000, but increased significantly to 24% in 2000-2002 and to 31% in 2002-2004 (see Appendix 1, Table A1.9). Similar to the trend with respect to cooperation within the supply chain, but at lower levels, there is clearly a turning point in the period 2000-2002. Surprisingly, the increase in cooperation with knowledge institutions was significant for each of the four technology classes in the period 1994-2004. Nevertheless, this type of cooperation is more common in high-tech sectors than in low(er) tech industries. Interestingly, cooperation with knowledge institutions has become more popular in low-tech industries than in medium low-tech industries. Similar to cooperation with other types of partners, cooperation with knowledge institutions is more common for larger firms than small and medium-sized firms. Obviously, large innovating firms are more likely to have highly educated employees and technical experts who know how to link up, and who have the capacity to absorb the complex knowledge from universities and other research institutes. We deduce from this that large firms and firms in high-tech industries profit most from the basic and applied research conducted at knowledge institutions. This finding is in line with earlier findings of Laursen and Salter (2004) who concluded from their study of the CIS-3 data from the UK that large and more R&D-intensive firms are more inclined to use universities in their innovation activities than other types of firms.

Cooperation with different types of partners simultaneously

Having focussed in the previous four subsections on developments regarding individual types of cooperation partners, we now analyze the average number of cooperation partners per cooperating innovative firm. In modern business, innovative firms build linkages with a diversity of partners in order to acquire diverse knowledge to suit different parts of the innovation process (Chesbrough, 2003b). As such, firms working together with different types of partners are considered relatively 'open' with respect to innovation (Laursen and Salter, 2006).

For our subset of cooperating firms the results show that the average number of partner types increased from 2.1 in 1994-1996 to 2.6 in 2002-2004 (see Table 2.3). At first glance, this does not look very spectacular. However, it implies that there must be a substantial number of firms

Table 2.3. Average number of cooperation partners of cooperating innovative firms.

Size class (employees)		1994-1996 Mean	SD [a]	1996-1998 Mean	SD [a]	1998-2000 Mean	SD [a]	2000-2002 Mean	SD [a]	2002-2004 Mean	SD [b]
Total industry	10-49	1.8	(1.1)	2.0	(1.5)	2.1	(1.4)	1.9	(1.3) *	2.3	(1.4) **
	50-249	1.9	(1.2) **	2.3	(1.4) *	2.0	(1.4)	2.2	(1.3) **	2.6	(1.4) **
	>250	2.6	(1.5)	2.7	(1.5)	2.3	(1.7)	2.4	(1.4) **	3.1	(1.4) **
	Total	*2.1*	*(1.3)*	*2.2*	*(1.5)*	*2.1*	*(1.5)*	*2.2*	*(1.4) ***	*2.6*	*(1.4) ***
High-tech	10-49	1.8	(1.2)	2.4	(1.6)	2.0	(1)	2.2	(1.4)	2.7	(1.5) *
	50-249	1.9	(1.3)	2.1	(1.3)	1.9	(1.4)	2.1	(1.4)	2.6	(1.4) *
	>250	2.7	(1.4)	3.0	(1.6)	2.5	(1.8)	2.6	(1.6)	3.2	(1.4)
	Total	*2.1*	*(1.3)*	*2.5*	*(1.5)*	*2.2*	*(1.5)*	*2.3*	*(1.4) **	*2.8*	*(1.5) ***
Medium high-tech	10-49	1.8	(1.1)	1.8	(1.5)	2.3	(1.5)	1.8	(1.4)	2.3	(1.4)
	50-249	1.9	(1.1) **	2.5	(1.5) **	1.9	(1.2)	2.2	(1.4) **	2.8	(1.4) **
	>250	2.4	(1.5)	2.7	(1.3) *	2.1	(1.6)	2.3	(1.5) **	3.2	(1.3) **
	Total	*2.0*	*(1.2) **	*2.3*	*(1.5) **	*2.0*	*(1.4)*	*2.1*	*(1.4) ***	*2.8*	*(1.4) ***
Medium low-tech	10-49	1.7	(1.0) *	2.5	(1.7)	2.2	(1.4)	1.6	(1.4)	2.0	(1.4)
	50-249	2.0	(1.3)	2.3	(1.5)	2.2	(1.5)	2.2	(1.3)	2.3	(1.3)
	>250	2.4	(1.7)	2.4	(1.4)	2.7	(1.5)	2.6	(1.4)	2.8	(1.3)
	Total	*2.0*	*(1.3) **	*2.4*	*(1.5)*	*2.3*	*(1.5)*	*2.2*	*(1.3)*	*2.3*	*(1.3)*
Low-tech	10-49	1.8	(1.1)	1.6	(1.2)	1.8	(1.5)	2.0	(1.3)	2.1	(1.3)
	50-249	1.9	(1.2)	2.3	(1.2)	2.0	(1.5)	2.1	(1.3) *	2.6	(1.4) **
	>250	2.7	(1.5)	2.8	(1.4)	2.3	(1.9)	2.2	(1.4) **	3.1	(1.5)
	Total	*2.2*	*(1.4)*	*2.3*	*(1.4)*	*2.0*	*(1.6)*	*2.1*	*(1.3) ***	*2.6*	*(1.5) ***

[a] Reports t-test whether the means differ significantly between the two periods.
[b] Reports t-test whether the mean in 2002-2004 differs significantly from 1994-1996.
* P-value <0.05, ** P-value <0.01, SD stands for Standard Deviation.

Profiting from external knowledge

who incorporate at least 3 different types of innovation partners in their innovation processes. Despite the extra coordination costs of handling a large number of partners in the same time period, there seem to be many firms who know how to do this. Moreover, we considered only five different types of partners in total, which makes an increase from 2.1 to 2.6 rather substantial. For all the size classes there is a clear trend showing that cooperating firms include increasingly more types of partners in the innovation process. Overall large firms that cooperate for innovation do so with more different types of partners than smaller firms. Interestingly, the results show further that, when it comes to cooperation with different types of partners, there are relatively small differences between the technology classes. Only medium low-tech industries stay behind the industry averages. The longitudinal increase is most evident in the (medium) high-tech industries, but in the low-tech sectors cooperation with different types of partners is quite common as well. This finding suggests that when firms decide to cooperate with other organizations, they do this in innovation networks comprising different types of actors (see Chapter 4, where we analyze innovation networks).

2.4.5 Using multiple knowledge acquisition strategies simultaneously

Finally, we analysed to what extent firms combine different knowledge acquisition strategies (licensing-in, outsourcing and inter-organizational cooperation) within one period of time (see Figure 2.2). The results show that each combination of governance modes has increased in usage over the period 1994-2004[6], with the increase setting in from 2000. The most common combination of knowledge acquisition strategies is inter-organizational cooperation and R&D outsourcing (used by 35% of the innovating firms in the final period). Furthermore, we have calculated that there is a clear relationship between firm size and the extent to which innovating firms engage in different knowledge acquisition strategies within one period of time, similar to what we found for the individual knowledge acquisition strategies. Again, large firms have more resources and capabilities to engage in different knowledge acquisition strategies simultaneously and to absorb different sorts of knowledge from a wide variety of sources. Surprising as it may be, firms in high-tech industries are only a little more inclined than firms from the other technology classes to engage simultaneously in different knowledge acquisition strategies. However, the increase over time is apparent in all technology classes. This is another indication that even firms from low-tech industries are becoming more open.

---

[6] As with the individual knowledge acquisition strategies we analyzed the significant differences. The increases over the total period are significant for each of the technology and size classes. For some sub-classes (e.g. large companies in high-tech) the increase was not significant.

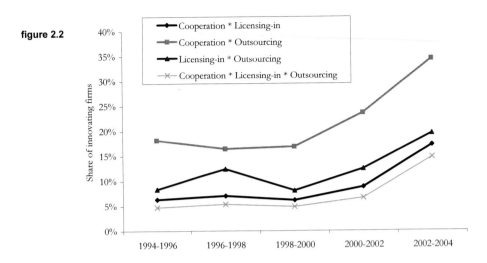

figure 2.2

Figure 2.2. Share of firms combining different knowledge acquisition strategies.

2.5 Discussion and conclusions

2.5.1 Conclusions

In this chapter we tried to answer the question as to what extent firms pursue an open innovation strategy. In doing so, we have investigated the adoption of open innovation in large firms and SMEs, in high-, medium-, and low-tech industries in the Netherlands. Various scholars in innovation management suggest that the innovation process of more and more firms is becoming increasingly open (e.g. Chesbrough *et al.*, 2006; Gassmann, 2006). These scholars emphasize the importance for innovating firms of building linkages to external organizations, so that they can profit from the knowledge and innovation capabilities residing there. Different knowledge acquisition strategies may facilitate the process of combining internal and external knowledge and capabilities. Our study, using longitudinal data of innovating firms in the Netherlands covering the period 1994-2004, provides support for the reasoning that an increasing share of innovating industrial firms pursue an open innovation strategy. In answering our two research sub-questions (see Section 2.1) we summarize the most important findings of this study.

First of all, the results of the study indicate that an increasing share of innovating firms in Dutch industry acquire external knowledge and capabilities through strategies associated with open innovation. As such, licensing-in, R&D outsourcing and inter-organizational cooperation have all become more common to innovating firms in the period 1994-2004. Whereas in the period 1994-1996 outsourcing was most popular to innovating firms, later inter-organizational cooperation became the primary governance mode for acquiring external knowledge and capabilities. Although the share of firms engaged in licensing-in increased as well, licensing-in remains less popular amongst innovating firms compared to R&D outsourcing and inter-organizational cooperation. More specifically, our results showed that suppliers have become the most popular partner for cooperation in the period 1994-2004, followed by customers and research organizations. Supply chain collaboration does seem to increase, considering the rise in cooperation for innovations. In contrast, the least popular cooperation partners, with less pregnant growth trends are competitors. Seemingly, competition negatively influences cooperation for innovation. We also identified a trend that Dutch innovating firms increasingly cooperate with different types of partners, within one time period. And yet, even in 2004, almost one third of the innovating firms rely exclusively on internal innovation capabilities. Such firms may miss out on ideas and opportunities that emerge outside the firm and are likely to lose competitive power. However, as Gassman (2006) proposes, *open innovation is not an imperative for every firm and every innovator*. Or, as Laursen and Salter (2006) conclude, there may be an optimum in the level of openness, as a focus on the external environment comes with certain costs. It would be interesting to know if, and, if so, to what extent firms that pursue an open innovation strategy perform better than firms with a closed innovation strategy. This issue could be an area for further research and will be tackled in Chapter 3.

Secondly, we analyzed whether the adoption of open innovation differs amongst different technology classes. As expected, firms in high-tech industries are more inclined to pursue open innovation strategies than firms in lower-tech industries, but this statement is challenged. Interestingly, the results indicate that firms in low- and medium-tech industries increasingly pursue an open innovation strategy. To date, empirical evidence for the relevancy of open innovation has mainly been derived from high-tech industries (e.g. Chesbrough, 2003b; Christensen *et al.*, 2005; Dittrich and Duysters, 2007). Only anecdotal evidence exists from low- and medium-tech industries (e.g. Chesbrough and Crowther, 2006). Our study clearly suggests that open innovation is also becoming a crucial aspect of managing innovation in low-tech industries. In a way, and surprisingly, low-tech firms are closing the gap with high-tech firms in adopting an open innovation strategy. Therefore, it suits the evidence to direct more research at the management of open innovation in lower-tech industries. In-depth case studies and observational research allows for a fuller description of how firms in low-tech industries manage open innovation, for instance how they cope with open innovation when intellectual property is difficult to protect through regular mechanisms such as patents.

Thirdly, in this study we investigated to what extent open innovation has been adopted by small-, medium- and large-sized firms. In line with our expectations, the results indicate that large firms are more open with respect to innovation than small- and medium-sized firms. Interestingly, however, the increase in adoption of open innovation is most apparent for small- and medium-sized firms. Whereas in 1994-1996 only a very small share of the small innovating firms used external knowledge acquisition strategies, this share has doubled for licensing-in and cooperation. Thus, we must conclude that small- and medium sized firms are catching up large firms in adopting elements of open innovation. We argue, therefore, that open innovation researchers should not overlook small- and medium-sized firms, as small- and medium-sized firms probably face particular challenges if they want to adopt an open innovation strategy and if they engage in different knowledge acquisition strategies.

Finally, our results indicate that there are clear 'pre- and post-adoption modes' (West *et al.*, 2006: 292) instead of gradual increases in open innovation adoption. More specifically, for inter-organizational cooperation, we identified the year 2000 as a turning point, as from that year on the share of firms engaged in cooperation increased dramatically. For technology licensing-in this turning point was in 2002. Only for R&D outsourcing did we identify a trend towards a more gradual increase in adoption. One would have to speculate for possible explanations for this turing point. One explanation could be that especiallty since around 2000 innovation policy instruments started promoting innovation in cooperation and networks. In that case, innovation policy in the Netherlands seems to be effective. Another explanation could be the economic downturn in the EU right after the turn of the century. Economic recessions are characterized by lower levels of investments, also in innovation, which would urge firms to take new routes and team up with other organizations in order to share costs.

2.5.2 Limitations and suggestions for further research

We are aware of the limitations of our study. First, large-scale firm level surveys miss certain subtleties, as questions may for instance not always fit within the context of all sectors involved. As a consequence, we used rather basic indicators of open innovation with limited sophistication. For instance, a limitation of the CIS data is that it was not possible to assess the importance of cooperation (e.g. with a particular type of partner) for the focal firm's innovation process, or to assess the importance of cooperation for specific innovative output (e.g. a successful new product). Moreover, CIS did not allow us to provide insights into the firm's motives for engaging in specific organizational forms for innovation. In order to acquire a more detailed understanding of the motives and relative importance of open innovation for firms, complementary research is needed that takes a more in-depth look at firms' innovation processes. Such research could take individual innovation projects as the unit of analysis. An obvious limitation is that secondary data is not fully under the control of the researcher. Despite the huge potential that came with 5 subsequent community innovation surveys, some variables were left out in later surveys (most notably the one on the acquisition of firms), something we would have liked to see happen differently. As a consequence, we were forced to abandon investigations on the developments with respect to M&A activity of innovating firms, as a means to acquiring knowledge. Finally, restricted by the possibilities of CIS, our study only focused on how external sources of innovation enter the firm. Future research may also focus on how internal sources of innovation leave the firm, as this is also an important aspect of the open innovation model (Chesbrough, 2003b). Perhaps future CIS can cover this topic.

2.5.3 Concluding remarks

Our findings provide sector-wide evidence of the relevance of open innovation. Open innovation, as coined by Chesbrough (2003), truly is a phenomenon that has infiltrated the mindset of innovation managers, not only of high-tech and large firms, but increasingly also of low- and medium-tech firms and SMEs. In fact, our results indicate that nowadays for most firms innovation management has an inter-organizational dimension. It therefore becomes crucial for firms to have the adequate capabilities to manage innovation in an inter-organizational context, as there are typical management challenges associated with, for instance, inter-organizational cooperation. The firms for whom open innovation is something new, most notably the small- and medium-sized firms, may in particular lack such capabilities. These firms could set up learning trajectories for teams to work in an inter-organizational context. Moreover, they should try and reap the rewards of the learning trajectories of other organizations (this is one of the issues dealt with in Chapter 4).

Since the Lisbon Agenda was laid down in 2000, European policy makers have really begun to emphasize that innovation is crucial for a modern economy and that different actors must interact and cooperate to foster innovation and entrepreneurship. This has resulted in several policy measures, including those to stimulate cooperation. The results of this study indicate that since the turn of the century innovating firms have become more open with respect to innovation and that many firms have started to cooperate for innovation. Apparently, at least part of the ambition stated in Lisbon has been fulfilled, although further policy instruments may be directed more specifically at small- and medium-sized firms.

To conclude, this study answers calls for up-to-date assessments of open innovation (Chesbrough, 2006; West *et al.*, 2006) by presenting the case of Dutch industrial sectors. Such an assessment was especially needed outside the US, because to date most empirical evidence of open innovation has been from the US (Chesbrough, 2006). The 5 longitudinal Community Innovation Surveys in the Netherlands, covering the period of 1994-2004, offered a good opportunity to do so. Clearly, it would be interesting to know whether similar trends to those found in this study arise in other countries. Finally, future CIS editions will show whether the trends identified in this chapter will continue, or not, or whether the adoption of open innovation has reached its peak.

3. The impact of different knowledge acquisition strategies on innovation performance. An empirical assessment of the Netherlands

3.1 Introduction

Chapter 3 aims to answer the second research question:

RQ2: What is the impact of different external knowledge acquisition strategies on the short-term and long-term innovation performance of innovative firms?

In the introduction we explained that innovation has become extremely important in determining the competitive advantage of firms in a growing number of industries (Christensen *et al.*, 1998; Hult *et al.*, 2004). Firms constantly look to improve existing products and processes, but they also develop radically new products, that in turn may make existing products obsolete (Christensen, 1997). Innovation scholars have come up with different taxonomies of novelty of innovation that span from incremental innovations, which involve the adaptation, refinement and enhancement of existing products, to radical innovations, which involve technological breakthroughs leading to entirely new products, processes and services (Freeman and Soete, 1997; Henderson and Clark, 1990; Tushman and Anderson, 1986). Although it may be extremely difficult to develop a radically new product, the rewards can be enormous, with a potential increased competitive advantage and an upturn in sales (Christensen *et al.*, 1998; Utterback, 1974; Utterback *et al.*, 1988).

In fact, modern innovating firms are often engaged in a diversity of innovation projects, ranging from incremental to radical innovation. These firms try to innovate rapidly to leave behind competitors, but they also engage in long-term projects to support strategic goals. To this respect, firms engage in exploration, which refers to innovation activities oriented at inventing new technologies, and/or in exploitation, which refers to innovation activities oriented at making refinements in existing technologies (March, 1991). To cover this broad range of innovation activities, firms may need different sorts of knowledge and capabilities. Therefore, innovating firms may engage in diverse external knowledge acquisition strategies simultaneously, each with different (dis)advantages and management challenges (Faems *et al.*, 2005; Van de Vrande *et al.*, 2006). As a consequence, the way the different knowledge acquisition strategies impact the performance of innovations can be different. It may be surprising to learn that to date there is little empirical research examining the performance and competitive implications of firms' knowledge acquisition strategies, or, as they are often called, firms' governance decisions (Leiblein *et al.*, 2002; Van de Vrande, 2007; Veugelers and Cassiman, 1999). Therefore, in our study we concentrate on the impact of knowledge acquisition strategies related to open innovation (licensing-in, outsourcing, and cooperation), as well as major firm acquisitions, on the innovation performance of innovating firms. Moreover, we are interested in the innovation performance of firms that choose not to profit from external knowledge and that carry out all their innovation activities exclusively within their own organization.

Our study builds on the work of Laursen and Salter (2006) who empirically assessed the impact of using multiple sources of knowledge in the innovation process on innovation performance. They concluded that searching information from external actors widely and deeply is curvilinearly (taking an inverted u-shape) related to innovation performance, which provides empirical evidence of the relevance of open innovation. The added value of our study over the one by Laursen and Salter (2006) is that we analyze *how* companies profit from external knowledge in terms of knowledge acquisition strategy. Moreover, in contrast to the study of Laursen and Salter (2006) our study considers both short- and long-term innovation performance effects.

The present study is based on a statistical analysis of two successive Dutch community innovation surveys (CIS), which explore the innovation process inside firms. We selected a large cross-section from Dutch industry (686 innovating firms) to analyze the impact of different knowledge acquisition strategies on a firm's innovation performance.

The remainder of this chapter is organized as follows: in the next section (Section 3.2) we provide a theoretical background and develop propositions on the relationship between different knowledge acquisition strategies and a firm's innovation performance. We make a distinction between licensing-in, outsourcing, and cooperation (all considered as open innovation strategies), mergers and acquisitions, and in-house innovation. Section 3.3 explains how we selected our sample from the Dutch CIS data. Furthermore, Section 3.3. describes the dependent, independent, as well as the control variables used in this study, and it details the methods for testing the propositions. Section 3.4 reports the results, and details to what extent our propositions have been confirmed. The final section (Section 3.5) contains the discussion and conclusions.

3.2 Theoretical background

We briefly indicated in the introductory chapter (Section 1.1) that in the (innovation) management literature the strategies for external knowledge acquisition are often referred to as 'governance modes' (e.g. Fey, 2005; Van de Vrande *et al.*, 2006). Governance modes for external knowledge acquisition can be placed on a continuum between market-based transactions and hierarchical modes of full integration (Gulati and Singh, 1998; Hagedoorn and Sadowski, 1999; Powell, 1990; Ring and Van de Ven, 1992; Williamson, 1985), with hybrid governance modes like inter-organizational cooperation in between (see Figure 3.1). In the case of market-based governance modes there is little organizational integration and little organizational control, whereas in the case of a hierarchy the focal firm possesses full control of the acquired knowledge and capabilities. In addition, with market-based governance modes the level of flexibility is high, which implies that it is a temporary transaction which is relatively easy and

Figure 3.1. Governance modes for external knowledge acquisition and the degree of organizational integration.

inexpensive to stop. With a hierarchical governance mode, such as an acquisition, the acquired firm is often integrated into the acquirer's organization which implies low flexibility, since it is difficult and expensive to stop or undo the acquisition once the acquired firm is integrated. As a consequence, in situations where the outcomes of the effort are highly uncertain, e.g. in the early stages of research an development (R&D), flexible governance modes may be the best alternative (Van de Vrande *et al.*, 2006). Moreover, when the focal firm's resources and capabilities concerning a specific technology are weak, licensing-in or outsourcing may be the preferred option (Tidd & Trewhella, 1997).

In the inter-organizational context it is important to divide knowledge into information and know-how (Dyer and Singh, 1998). Information is easily codifiable and transmittable knowledge, without loss of integrity, and is associated with facts, proposition and symbols (Kogut and Zander, 1992). Know-how, on the other hand, is tacit, sticky and residing in individuals (Dyer and Singh, 1998; Kogut and Zander, 1992). Technological know-how is often tacit which implies it is difficult to transfer from one firm to another (Larsson *et al.*, 1998) and requires the direct participation of specialists (Grant, 1996). When it is necessary to transfer or combine highly tacit or socially complex knowledge, governance modes of substantial organizational integration, such as the acquisition of a firm, may therefore be the best alternative (Bresman *et al.*, 1999).

In the present study we focus on four fundamentally different knowledge acquisition strategies, covering the total spectrum of governance modes for external knowledge acquisition (see Figure 3.1) and analyze the performance differences of choosing between the different strategies. The first is licensing-in, which is a typical example of a market-based governance mode. The second and third are outsourcing and inter-organizational cooperation, which can both be regarded as a hybrid governance mode. In Section 2.2.2 we explained that licensing-in, outsourcing and cooperation are typical open innovation strategies, as there is an emphasis on a flexible innovation process, which allows for the transfer of knowledge across organizational boundaries. The fourth is the acquisition of a firm, which can be regarded as a hierarchical governance mode. It should be noted that many sub-modes exist (Granstrand *et al.*, 1992), related to the modes we concentrate on, and that scholars use different labels for the same mode. In addition to the knowledge acquisition strategies, we include in-house innovation as another mode of innovation, because a firm can also decide not to engage in external knowledge acquisition and to innovate completely by itself.

3.2.1 Open innovation

Whereas in Chapter 2 we identified that innovating industrial firms are increasingly applying an open innovation strategy, especially in the form of cooperation and outsourcing, we are here concerned with the question as to whether open innovation actually contributes to the innovation performance of innovating firms. Given the emphasis of innovation management scholars on the importance of open innovation (Chesbrough, 2003b; Christensen *et al.*, 2005; Dittrich and Duysters, 2007; Gassmann, 2006; Vanhaverbeke *et al.*, 2007; West and Gallagher, 2006), we formulate the following proposition:

Proposition 1
P1: Open innovation; licensing-in (P1a), outsourcing (P1b), cooperation (P1c), is positively related to the innovation performance of innovative firms.

In the sections below, we detail the logic of this proposition by elaborating on the three knowledge acquisition strategies associated with open innovation: licensing-in, outsourcing, and cooperation.

Licensing-in

Licensing-in knowledge or technologies, also referred to as inward licensing (but hereafter called licensing-in), is placed on the left side of the continuum as it involves relatively little organizational integration. Licensing-in can be defined as the purchasing of (product or process) technology, designs or marketing expertise (adapted from Lowe and Taylor, 1998). As such, licensing-in is a means for innovating firms to exploit the innovation capabilities or intellectual property of another firm, which are readily available in the market. Foremost, licensing-in enables firms to rapidly establish positions in new technological areas (Hagedoorn, 1990; Tidd and Trewhella, 1997). Usually, the licensee pays a fee and/or a royalty based on sales or a reciprocal flow of knowledge rights over a specific period of time (Lowe and Taylor, 1998). The main advantage of technology licensing is that a firm does not need to make upfront capital investments for building or buying the assets in question (Teece, 1986). Moreover, the innovating firm can profit from subsequent improvements to the technology.

An important disadvantage of licensing-in can be that the technology is often not exclusively licensed to the buying firm (Grandstrand *et al.*, 1992), unless the buying firm obtains the exclusive rights. As a consequence, in many cases competitors may profit from the knowledge that is available on the market, so that licensing-in is not likely to lead to a sustainable competitive advantage. Another disadvantage is that the knowledge or technology involved in the agreement is not specifically developed for the licensee, which implies that it may still have to be adjusted to its specific requirements. Finally, licensing-in typically involves technologies of limited sophistication (Hagedoorn, 1990), or knowledge that is easily codifiable and seems less appropriate for tacit and socially complex knowledge.

Nevertheless, in the 1990s licensing-in had already been identified as an important way for firms to profit from external knowledge (Tidd and Trewhella, 1997). Moreover, in a study of 128 manufacturing firms in the UK, it was found that licensing-in could be associated with sectors in which the pace of technological change is high, i.e. with highly competitive and uncertain markets (Lowe and Taylor, 1998). However, studies on the direct impact of licensing-in on innovation performance at the firm level are still scarce. Only a recent longitudinal study of 341 Taiwanese electronics-manufacturing firms provided evidence for the positive effect of licensing-in on innovation performance, as long as the firm has sufficient internal R&D to absorb the knowledge at stake (Tsai and Wang, 2007). In line with the emphasis of open innovation scholars on the importance of licensing-in knowledge and technologies to complement internal R&D (e.g. Chesbrough, 2003a; Chesbrough, 2003b), we expect that licensing-in positively impacts innovation performance.

Outsourcing

The second governance mode for external knowledge acquisition on the continuum is outsourcing (see Figure 3.1). In the case of outsourcing, a particular part of the innovation process is carried out by another organization, the sub-contractor - e.g. a research organization, or another firm. The sub-contractor delivers particular knowledge or a technology specifically developed for, and to be controlled by the focal firm (Granstrand *et al.*, 1992; Hagedoorn, 1990). In contrast with licensing-in, outsourcing can involve clear-cut pieces of research and development and may as a result be better absorbed by the outsourcing firm. For instance, an innovating firm may pay a university to carry out fundamental research and develop a new technology, which the firm can utilize in future products and processes.

Outsourcing is primarily a strategy for firms who prefer to deploy their scarce resources to their core competences. Other organizations may just be better equipped for carrying out specific types of R&D (e.g. knowledge institutions). From a resource-based perspective, we could argue that a firm will outsource those activities in which it is not particularly specialized or that are 'non core', because the firm is less capable of performing those activities (Barney, 1999; Mol, 2005). However, outsourcing can be expensive, e.g. ex ante in terms of search and negotiation costs and ex post to execute and enforce the contract (Granstrand *et al.*, 1992; Mol, 2005; Veugelers and Cassiman, 1999). Finally, outsourcing may lead to the 'hollowing' of firms (Leiblein *et al.*, 2002), especially when they comprise business critical functions such as innovation.

The relationship between outsourcing and a firm's innovation performance has so far not received a lot of attention in the innovation management literature. Some empirical studies have shown that outsourcing is associated with firms that have sufficient internal R&D (Mol, 2005; Veugelers and Cassiman, 1999) and that R&D outsourcing is positively associated with a firm's R&D spending (Veugelers, 1997). Surprisingly, however, the amount of empirical testing of the direct impact of R&D outsourcing on a firm's innovation performance is scarce. A rare example is a study by Fey (2005), who found in a sample of 107 large R&D intensive firms that R&D outsourcing was negatively associated with R&D performance. However, it is well established in the innovation management literature that R&D outsourcing is an important strategy in supplier-dominated industries (Pavitt, 1984). In line with the principles of the open innovation model, we can argue that even the most innovative firms will need to outsource some parts of the innovation process to organizations that are better equipped for it. Therefore, we expect a positive relationship between R&D outsourcing and innovation performance.

Cooperation

Moving further along the continuum towards more integrated governance modes, we arrive at cooperative modes (in this chapter referred to as cooperation), such as research partnerships or joint development agreements (Granstrand *et al.*, 1992; Hagedoorn, 1990). Several sub-modes of cooperation exist with different levels of organizational integration, but most modes can be characterized either as contractual agreements or equity-based ventures (Hagedoorn *et al.*, 2000; Sampson, 2007). Moreover, the majority of cooperative activities in the context of innovation are based on contractual agreements, whereas to a lesser extent cooperative modes exist that include equity investments such as Joint Ventures (Hagedoorn *et al.*, 2000). Cooperation implies that different partners work together and pool their resources and capabilities for the purpose of collaborative R&D, crossing organizational boundaries, while remaining autonomous organizations (Sampson, 2007). In this way, firms can obtain access to and exploit resources and capabilities necessary for the creation of value that are not readily available in the market, or that require time to build up (Ahuja, 2000; Becker and Dietz, 2004; Das and Teng, 2000; Kogut, 1988; Miotti and Sachwald, 2003). Moreover, inter-organizational cooperation may help firms to reap economies of scale in R&D and shorten development time while spreading the costs of such new developments (Hagedoorn, 2002; Nooteboom, 1999b; Sampson, 2007).

Contrary to licensing-in or outsourcing, cooperation entails considerable levels of organizational integration and enables mobility and/or contact between R&D and (other) technical employees (Sampson, 2007). Such interactions are an important prerequisite for transferring and combining tacit and socially complex knowledge (Grant, 1996; Larsson *et al.*, 1998).

Although there are several potential benefits associated with inter-organizational cooperation, there are also some intrinsic problems (Gulati and Singh, 1998; Hamel, 1991; Larsson *et al.*, 1998; Nooteboom, 1999b; Sampson, 2007). For instance, inter-organizational cooperation involves some degree of competitiveness among partners which may lead to 'learning races' (Hamel, 1991; Larsson *et al.*, 1998). There are similar concerns about the risk of unwanted knowledge spill-over to the partner (Omta and Van Rossum, 1999; Sampson, 2007). Other typical problems with cooperation are appropriation concerns (Gulati and Singh, 1998) and cultural differences between the partners (Nooteboom, 1999b; Omta and Van Rossum, 1999).

Nevertheless, several empirical studies, that take into account various number of characteristics (e.g. sector, the type of firms or type of cooperation), identified in general a positive relationship between inter-organizational cooperation and innovation performance (Faems *et al.*, 2005; Miotti and Sachwald, 2003; Negassi, 2004; Rothaermel and Hess, 2007; Sampson, 2007; Van de Vrande, 2007). This positive relationship was also confirmed in a literature review on the relationship between alliances and innovation performance (De Man and Duysters, 2005).

3.2.2 Mergers and acquisitions

Mergers and acquisitions (M&As) are placed on the far right side of the continuum of governance modes for external knowledge acquisition (Figure 3.1), since they involve the highest levels of organizational integration. Firms increasingly acquire or merge[7] with other firms in order to get access to and full hierarchical control over innovative products, technologies and capabilities (Chakrabarti *et al.*, 1994; Coff, 1999; Graebner, 2004; Granstrand *et al.*, 1992; Hitt *et al.*, 1996).

In contrast to the other knowledge acquisition strategies discussed in this chapter, M&As typically involve the processes and resources of a complete firm, including perhaps 'unwanted resources' (Barney, 1999; Gerpott, 1995), which implies that more than just the innovative products, technologies and capabilities are part of the deal. Moreover, it should be noted that innovation is often not the main motive for a merger or acquisition, especially for major M&As. But even then, M&A can have a substantial (positive or negative) impact on the innovation processes of the firms that are combined (Cassiman *et al.*, 2005). For instance, M&As are associated with many types of integration problems affecting the innovation process negatively, such as cultural differences (e.g. Brock, 2005; Epstein, 2004), the loss of key inventors (e.g. Ernst and Vitt, 2000) and loss in productivity of R&D employees (e.g. Paruchuri *et al.*, 2006). As a consequence, the costs of acquiring and integrating a firm often exceed the benefits, which implies that many M&As should be considered as a failure (Cartwright and Schoenberg, 2006; Schenk, 2006). In addition, it may take substantial time, often years, before integration has completed and (innovation) synergies are realized (Haspeslagh and Jemison, 1991; Puranam *et al.*, 2006).

It is perhaps therefore not surprising that several empirical studies showed that, on average, firms engaging in mergers or acquisitions experience a neutral effect on or even a decline in innovativeness (De Man and Duysters, 2005). However, a recent study of pharmaceutical firms (Van de Vrande, 2007) found that acquisitions have a positive effect on innovation performance measured as patent counts, but a negative effect when patents referred to radical innovations or so-called pioneering technologies. Moreover, in high-tech sectors and in the case of moderate

---

[7] Scholars often do not distinguish between mergers and acquisitions, as in reality most mergers are in fact acquisitions with one firm controlling the other. Driven by the possibilities with the CIS data, the focus in this study is on large / major firm acquisitions: firm acquisitions that resulted in at least 10% growth in turnover (See also the operationalization, Section 3.3.3).

relatedness (with respect to the relevant technologies and knowledge) between the two firms, acquisitions do have a positive effect on innovation performance (Ahuja and Katila, 2001; Cloodt *et al.*, 2006). Apparently, there is greatest potential for learning and innovation when the knowledge bases of the firms to be integrated are diverse enough to encourage creativity and novel solutions, but also have sufficient overlap to be able to understand and assimilate each other's specific knowledge. Nevertheless, as said, most studies on the impact of M&A on innovation performance found a neutral or negative impact (De Man and Duysters, 2005). Especially when analyzing a cross section of the industry, and when including both technological and non-technological motivated M&As, it is even likely that M&As have a negative impact on innovation performance (Ahuja and Katila, 2001; Cloodt *et al.*, 2006). We formulate Proposition 2 accordingly.

Proposition 2
P2: M&As are negatively related to the innovation performance of innovative firms.

3.2.3 In-house innovation

Carrying out R&D and other innovation activities internally is regarded as crucial for innovating firms, so that they have sufficient 'absorptive capacity', which is the ability to recognize and adapt externally acquired knowledge (Cohen and Levinthal, 1990). Therefore, in itself, in-house innovation activities are important for firms that want to innovate in an open setting. In Section 2.4.1 we showed that many firms do not engage in licensing-in, outsourcing and/or cooperation, which suggests that these firms carry out all innovation related activities exclusively in-house (here labeled in-house innovation). In-house innovation can be contrasted with open innovation, as firm's that innovate in-house focus on control and assume that all required knowledge and capabilities are available within the organization. We argue, however, that firms that rely exclusively on their internal R&D and internally possessed knowledge perform less on innovation compared with firms that acquire external knowledge and capabilities, because those firms innovating in-house will miss opportunities and because they will be not able to catch up with the fast technological developments (Chesbrough, 2003b). Moreover, firms exclusively relying on in-house innovation may suffer from the Not Invented Here (NIH) syndrome (Katz and Allen, 1982), as employees from the firms may become suspicious about external ideas and prefer own ideas. Therefore, and in line with the earlier propositions, we expect that innovating in-house (which implies that the firm is not engaged in any of the external knowledge acquisition strategies discussed in this chapter) is negatively related to the innovation performance of innovating firms. Consequently, we formulate Proposition 3 as follows:

Proposition 3
P3: In-house innovation is negatively related to the innovation performance of innovative firms.

3.3 Data and methods

3.3.1 Data

For the present study we use data from two subsequent Community of Innovation Surveys (CIS) in the Netherlands[8,9]. The first of the two surveys (generally abbreviated as CIS-3) was implemented in 2001 and refers to innovation activities in the three-year period 1998-2000. Similarly, the second survey (CIS-4) was implemented in 2005 and refers to 2002-2004.

The questionnaires were postal and voluntary and firms were promised confidentiality. For the CIS-3, a random sample was taken from firms with 10-49 employees, whereas all firms with 50 or more employees received a questionnaire. CIS-4 was implemented in a similar way, although a random sample was also taken from the category '50-249 employees'. As a consequence, large firms are more likely to be included in two successive surveys. Unlike CIS-4, CIS-3 contained firms with 10 employees or less, but these firms were excluded from the sample. The CIS-3 was sent to 4,890 and CIS-4 to 4,146 industrial firms, with response rates of 54% and 71% respectively. The response rates for different sectors and size classes are largely consistent with the overall response pattern (CBS, 2002, 2006).

From the CIS-3 sample with industrial firms we selected all innovating firms: industrial firms that claimed they had innovated and/or who specified a positive innovation budget in the previous 3 years. We selected only innovating firms, because the focus in our study is exclusively on the questions on innovation activities (like the ones on external knowledge acquisition), which were not answered by firms without innovation activities and innovation output. Including these so called non-innovators in the sample would increase the probability of finding significant relationships in regression analysis, whereas for a sample of innovating firms the same relationships may be not evident, or in a worst case even have a different direction. By only selecting innovating firms, we were able to perform our analyses with a more representative sample than some previous studies using CIS (for instance, Laursen and Salter (2006) who analysed the total sample of firms in the UK-CIS), including non-innovating firms. We arrived at an initial sample of 1,654 innovating firms from Dutch industry in CIS-3.

To enable assessment of the impact of different knowledge acquisition strategies on innovation performance over a longer period, we restricted our sample further by selecting only the innovating firms in CIS-3 that were also present in the CIS-4 sample. As said in Section 3.2, it may take some time before acquired knowledge is integrated in the focal firm's innovation process and results in innovative output, especially for the knowledge acquisition strategies

---

[8] The empirical part of this research was executed at the Centre for Economic Micro data (Cerem) at Statistics Netherlands (CBS). The views expressed in this book, however, are those of the author only.

[9] General information on CIS data has been provided in Section 2.3. Here we will only discuss the characteristics of the data and other information that are relevant for the study presented in Chapter 3.

involving more organizational integration, especially the acquisition of a firm. After eliminating the cases with missing values, we came to a final sample of 686 firms for which we could track the innovation performance over a longer period of time. We checked to what extent the longitudinal sample of 686 firms is similar to the original selection of innovating firms in CIS-3 in terms of the variables used in this study. This check indicates that the longitudinal sample is similar to the original CIS-3 sample of innovating firms on the dependent, independent, and control variables, except for firm size (see Table A2.1 in Appendix 2). It turned out that the longitudinal selection contains larger firms than the original CIS-3 sample of innovating firms. We have already explained that large firms are more likely to be included in two subsequent surveys.

3.3.2 Dependent variables

Following a recent stream of innovation studies (e.g. Laursen and Salter, 2006; Miotti and Sachwald, 2003; Negassi, 2004; Raymond et al., 2006) the indicator for innovation performance in this study is the 'share of sales derived from new products developed in the last three years'. Patent counts are regarded a good proxy for innovation performance in high-tech sectors (Hagedoorn and Cloodt, 2005). However, patent counts do not necessarily capture the (commercial) success or effect of the innovation and are less applicable for firms from low-tech sectors. After all, not all innovations are patented. The variable 'share of sales from new products' not only measures whether a firm has been innovating, but also the impact of these innovation activities on its sales. More in particular, in line with Laursen and Salter (2006) we distinguish between the fraction of sales from new products new to the market (associated with radical innovation), and the fraction of sales from new products new to the firm only (associated with incremental and imitative innovation).

For firms engaged in a major acquisition in particular, the innovation performance may only improve a considerable time after the official deal, as it often takes years to integrate the two innovation functions (Ahuja and Katila, 2001; Cloodt et al., 2006; De Man and Duysters, 2005). Hence, we analyze the impact of different governance modes for external knowledge acquisition on both short- and long-term innovation performance. Therefore, we use variables for short-term innovation performance (measured in CIS-3) and long-term innovation performance (measured in CIS-4). Thus, the short-term innovation performance relates to the share of sales of 2000 from innovations introduced in the years 1998-2000, whereas the long-term innovation performance relates to the share of sales in 2004 from innovations introduced in 2002-2004.

3.3.3 Independent variables

The indicators for the different knowledge acquisition strategies were all taken from CIS-3. Firms had to indicate whether they had been involved in licensing-in (of knowledge or technologies), outsourcing, and cooperation for their innovation activities in the period

1998-2000. It was explicitly stated in the questionnaire that pure outsourcing of R&D was not regarded as inter-organizational cooperation. Furthermore, we included an indicator for M&As. A question in the CIS asked whether the firm undertook a major acquisition, i.e. an acquisition resulting in an increase in the total turnover by at least 10%. It should be noted that, unlike with the other knowledge acquisition strategies, this question was not specifically addressed in the innovation context. We constructed binary variables for each of the knowledge acquisition strategies. These variables have the value 1 when the firm had indicated that it used the strategy in question, and 0 if the firm did not. We also constructed a new variable based on a combination of other variables, indicating whether the firm does not make use of any of the strategies for external knowledge acquisition. This variable has the value 1 when the firm is not involved in either licensing-in, R&D outsourcing, inter-organizational cooperation, or firm acquisitions. In this way, our new variable is used as an indicator for 'in-house innovation'.

3.3.4 Control variables

In line with existing empirical studies analyzing determinants of innovation, and driven by the possibilities of the CIS, we included a number of control variables. First, we included firm size, measured as the natural logarithm of the number of employees. In general, larger firms are more likely to introduce innovations, although the relative effect of such innovations on turnover is expected to be lower, compared to smaller firms (Batterink *et al.*, 2006; Mohnen and Dagenais, 2002). Second, we included a measure of innovation intensity, measured as the firm's total innovation expenditures divided by its turnover. Innovation intensity is a slightly broader concept than R&D intensity, as it captures both pure R&D expenditures and other innovation expenditures, such as costs for introducing or implementing an innovation. Innovation intensity is, therefore, a good indicator for the relative extent to which the focal firm is engaged in innovation. Third, we check whether a firm is part of a group, as firms belonging to a group (or conglomerate) may be able to benefit from innovation activities from elsewhere within the group. The variable has the value 1 if the firm is part of a group, and 0 if not. Fourth, we check the level of 'openness' of the focal firm towards external sources of information required for innovation activities. Firms can be classified according to their 'openness' towards external knowledge, and may have several search strategies for relevant information (Laursen and Salter, 2004; Laursen and Salter, 2006). It is expected that the more open a firm is, the more different types of knowledge acquisition strategies are required to facilitate external knowledge acquisition. Therefore, we constructed a variable, in line with Laursen and Salter (2006), that captures the extent to which the focal firm searches for innovative ideas and relevant information from different external sources (labeled search breadth). The CIS contains a question about the importance of drawing from a number of different information sources, such as suppliers, customers, competitors, universities and other (public or private) research institutes, or other types of sources (like fairs, magazines, existing patents). The firms were asked to indicate the degree of use for each source (0= not used, 1 = limited importance, 2 = important, 3 = very important). We coded each of the sources with 1 when the firm in question reported that the information source was 'important' or 'very important'. Consequently, the search variable gets the value 0 if the firm indicated there was no important external information source and 6 if the firm considered each of the 6 identified external information sources important or very important. Finally, we included 15 sector dummies to check for a difference in sector propensities to innovate. Moreover, checking for sector differences is important because the share of sales from new products is largely influenced by the Product Generation Life Cycle (PGLC) of the firm's sector. The PGLC concept refers to the sum of the product life cycles of all related products belonging to one product generation (Maidique and Zirger, 1985), something which may vary among sectors (Fortuin, 2006). It is therefore necessary to check for the sector when using the indicator 'share of sales from new products' as dependent variable. The furniture sector, which consisted of the most firms in the sample, was used as the reference category. A further description of the variables is provided in Table 3.2.

3.3.5 Methods

The dependent variable in the analysis is the percentage of innovative sales, which ranges between 0 and 100. Since this variable is (double) censored, a Tobit regression analysis is applied (Green, 2003). The assumption of normality of residuals in the standard Tobit models is not satisfied in our case, because the variables reflecting innovation performance are somewhat skewed. Other studies facing similar problems with respect to skewness and departure from normality, have proposed a log-transformation of the Tobit model (Kemp *et al.*, 2003; Klomp and Van Leeuwen, 1999; Laursen and Salter, 2006; Raymond *et al.*, 2006). We apply this approach and make the following transformation of the dependent variables: innovative sales transformed = ln(1+ innovation sales).

3.4 Results

3.4.1 Descriptive results

In Table 3.1 we present the key variables across industrial sectors. Overall, we find that the shares of sales from new products from incremental innovations of both 2000 and 2004 are substantially larger than the shares of sales from new products from radical innovations. Obviously, it is much more demanding for firms to invest in radical innovation, i.e. products that are truly innovative and new to the market. Surprisingly, however by 2004 the shares of sales from incremental innovations have dropped substantially till 12% compared with 21% in 2000. The decrease in the share of sales from incremental innovation may be explained by the economic downturn in the EU right after the turn of the century. With respect to the variables for knowledge acquisition strategies, we see that in 2000 outsourcing was used by the largest percentage of innovating firms (40%), followed by cooperation (33%), licensing-in (13%), and the acquisition of a firm (5%). This low percentage of firms making acquisitions is not surprising as this governance mode is the most far-reaching with respect to organizational integration and often the most expensive one. We conclude from this that innovating firms

Table 3.1. Key variables by sector.

Sector	N[c]	Share of sales from: Incremental innovation 2000[a]	Radical innovation 2000[a]	Share of sales from: Incremental innovation 2004[a]	Radical innovation 2004[a]	Licensing 2000[b]	Outsourcing 2000[b]	Cooperation 2000[b]	Acquisition 2000[b]	In-house 2000[b]
Food and drink	88	17.1	4.5	10.0	4.7	0.0	37.5	25.0	8.0	51.1
Textiles	21	22.8	5.3	7.1	11.0	14.0	57.1	38.0	10.0	28.6
Paper	40	17.0	5.2	13.9	3.3	10.0	32.5	38.0	5.0	47.5
Printing and publishing	35	16.9	1.3	5.6	3.0	11.0	14.3	23.0	3.0	60.0
Furniture	94	18.6	4.2	8.7	4.0	19.0	40.4	34.0	2.0	42.6
Petrol	6	19.5	18.5	4.2	0.8	0.0	33.3	50.0	17.0	16.7
Chemical basic products	29	14.8	2.5	8.6	3.3	21.0	48.3	59.0	3.0	20.7
Pharmaceuticals	20	30.2	3.3	9.0	6.4	31.0	60.0	51.0	22.0	20.0
Chemical end products	36	25.5	6.6	13.3	6.5	6.0	25.0	36.0	14.0	52.8
Plastics	39	23.4	4.2	13.7	6.2	13.0	35.9	23.0	5.0	48.7
Basic metals	24	17.0	3.4	8.4	4.0	17.0	41.7	42.0	4.0	33.3
Fabric. metal products	87	19.4	3.1	10.9	6.0	16.0	36.8	37.0	3.0	47.1
Machinery	91	23.9	10.1	16.3	8.7	15.0	42.9	23.0	5.0	42.9
Electrical	48	28.8	11.3	20.8	11.6	31.0	60.4	54.0	4.0	20.8
Automobile and transport	28	29.1	9.4	16.6	7.8	4.0	46.4	29.0	4.0	35.7
Total industry	686	21.1	5.6	12.2	5.9	13.0	40.1	33.0	5.0	42.0

[a] Mean share of sales from incremental or radical innovation of sector.
[b] Share of firms in sector engaged in this governance mode for external knowledge acquisition.
[c] Number of firms in the sample.

are more likely to engage in flexible governance modes for acquiring external knowledge than governance modes with a more permanent character. Moreover, sectors traditionally associated with high levels of innovation (e.g. pharmaceutical, electrical) have a relatively high share of firms engaged in licensing-in and cooperation. Interestingly, in the food and drink and the petrol sector there was no licensing activity at all in 2000. Finally, 42% of the firms in the sample are not involved in any knowledge acquisition strategy, as they innovate completely in-house.

Descriptive information on the variables used in the regression models is provided in Table 3.2. It presents the means of the dependent (after the transformation) and independent variables (that we discussed before). The mean firm size is 323 employees (which corresponds to 4.94, after a natural log transformation). The average innovation intensity of the innovating firms in our sample is 2.7. It is somewhat surprising that 80% of the firms in the sample belong to a holding or other legal grouping of firms. Such firms may be able to capitalize on innovation activities carried out elsewhere in the organization. Dutch innovating firms indicated that on average they search for about two different types of external information sources that are important for their innovation activities. A closer look at the data reveals that customers and suppliers are the most important sources of information, followed by competitors and lastly knowledge institutions.

Finally, Table 3.3 shows that there is relatively little correlation between the main independent variables, which indicates there are no problems with multicolinearity (Hair *et al.*, 1998). However, as explained in Section 3.3.3, the indicator for in-house was constructed from the indicators of the different knowledge acquisition strategies. Consequently, there is a relatively high correlation between the indicator for in-house innovation and the indicators for the knowledge acquisition strategies. To avoid problems with multicolinearity, we should run separate analyses including the in-house innovation indicator and excluding the indicators for the different knowledge acquisition strategies (see the next section).

3.4.2 Results of the statistical analyses

We ran separate Tobit regression analyses to assess the impact of different knowledge acquisition strategies on short-term innovation performance (Models 1 and 2) and long-term innovation performance (Models 3 and 4), and distinguished between incremental innovation (Models 1 and 3) and radical innovation (Models 2 and 4)[10]. Table 3.4 presents the results of the Tobit regression analysis. The table provides the coefficients, standard

---

[10] In addition to the models presented in Table 3.4, we analyzed similar models including additional variables to test for interaction effects between the knowledge acquisition strategies. For Models 1-4 (with the same dependent, independent and control variables) we constructed three variants, with one interaction variable per comparable model. As none of the interaction terms turned out to have a significant impact on innovation performance, and they do they influence the relationships in the Models 1-4, we do not present the models with interaction terms here.

Table 3.2. Descriptives and explanations of the variables (N=686).

Variable	Description	Value (range)	Mean	SD
Dependent variables (innovative sales)				
Incremental 2001	The share of sales derived from new or significantly improved products that were new to the firm (LN transformation)	metric	0.18	0.16
Radical 2001	The share of sales derived from new or significantly improved products that were new to the market (LN transformation)	metric	0.05	0.09
Incremental 2005	The share of sales derived from new or significantly improved products that were new to the firm (LN transformation)	metric	0.10	0.15
Radical 2005	The share of sales derived from new or significantly improved products that were new to the market (LN transformation)	metric	0.05	0.10
Control variables				
Size (LN employees)	Total number of employees in 2000 (LN)	metric	4.94	1.18
Innovation intensity	Total innovation expenditures in 2000 divided by the total turnover in 2000	metric	0.027	0.24
Firm part of group	Is the firm part of a group? (1=yes, 0 = no)	ordinal	0.80	0.40
Search breadth	Number of different types of external information sources used for innovation that were important (possible sources are 1 customers, 2 suppliers, 3 competitors, 4 universities, 5 research organizations). Value range: 0-6	ordinal	2.08	1.52
Independent variables				
Licensing-in	Firm active in technology/knowledge licensing in the period 1998-2000 (1=yes, 0 = no)	ordinal	0.13	0.34
Outsourcing	Firm active in R&D outsourcing in the period 1998-2000 (1=yes, 0=no)	ordinal	0.40	0.49
Cooperation	Firm active in inter-organizational cooperation aimed at innovation in the period 1998-2000 (1=yes, 0 = no)	ordinal	0.33	0.47
Acquisition	Firm acquired (at least) one firm in 1998-2000, which resulted in at least 10% turnover growth (1=yes, 0 = no)	ordinal	0.05	0.22
In-house (no external linkages)	This variable has the value 1 in the case the firm is not active in both licensing-in, outsourcing, cooperation, and acquisition	ordinal	0.42	0.49

Table 3.3. Correlations among the independent and control variables (N=686).

	1	2	3	4	5	6	7	8	9
1 Firm Size	1								
2 Innovation intensity	0.06	1							
3 Firm part of group	0.11 *	0.03	1						
4 Search breadth	0.13 *	0.03	0.01	1					
5 Licensing-in	0.07	0.02	0.08 *	0.16 *	1				
6 Outsourcing	0.21 *	0.08 *	0.10 *	0.24 *	0.20 *				
7 Cooperation	0.28 *	0.01	0.10 *	0.24 *	0.18 *	0.32 *	1		
8 Acquisition	-0.04	-0.01	-0.01	0.03	0.04	-0.02	0.03	1	
9 In-house	-0.20 *	-0.06	-0.13 *	-0.27 *	-0.33 *	-0.70 *	-0.60 *	-0.2 *	1

* P-value <0.05.

errors and significance levels of the control and independent variables for each model. The most important model parameters are provided as well. For instance, Model 1 was based on 686 observations, from which 130 were left-censored (that is, 0 percent share of sales from incremental innovations), and 3 were right-censored (share of sales from incremental innovations of 100%). The Likelihood Ratio (LR) Chi^2-statistics provide the best indication of the predictive power of a model, as it indicates the improvement over the 'constant only' model. Table 3.4 shows that the four models provide better predictive power than the 'constant only' models, because the Chi^2 statistics are highly significant. Furthermore, Table 3.4 provides a Pseudo R^2 which also gives an indication of the predictive power of the models. In addition, Models 5-8 are comparable with Models 1-4, but they contain the composite variable 'in-house' instead of the knowledge acquisition strategies variables (see Table 3.5). As we explained, this variable is composed of the other independent variables, so in-house innovation could not be included in the original models including the different knowledge acquisition strategies. Hence, the additional Models 5-8. Note that the Models 1-4 with specific indicators of knowledge acquisition strategies show better predictive power (see LR Chi^2 statistics) than the comparable Models 5-8 with one independent variable (in-house innovation) that is composed of the knowledge acquisition strategies variables.

The independent variables are relevant for the proposition testing. We find strong support for Proposition 1a, stating that licensing-in is positively related to the short-term innovation performance. Models 1 and 2 in Table 3.4 show there is a positive, significant relationship between licensing-in and the short-term performance of both incremental and radical innovation. Interestingly, especially the relationship with radical innovation is highly significant ($P<0.01$). In contrast, Models 3 and 4 show that there is no significant relationship between licensing-in and long-term innovation performance. A market-based governance mode like licensing-in appears to be a beneficial way to acquire external knowledge that is readily available in the market and that can be promptly integrated into existing innovation activities. Moreover, the competitive advantage of licensing-in seems to be temporary, probably because the standardized knowledge or technology at stake is available on the market, and thus also available to competitors.

Proposition 1b stated that outsourcing is positively related to a firm's innovation performance. Models 1 and 2 show that outsourcing is significantly, positively related to the short-term performance of incremental innovations in 2000, but not of radical innovations (see Table 3.4). In contrast, when we look at the innovation performance in 2004 we see a highly significant relationship between outsourcing and the performance of radical innovations (see Model 4), whereas the positive relationship with the performance of incremental innovations is significant at the 10%-level (see Model 3). Apparently, for radical innovation it takes some time before the outcomes of outsourced R&D become visible in terms of innovative sales, whereas for incremental innovations companies also benefit in the short term from outsourcing. In sum, we find partial support for Proposition 1b.

We find strong support for Proposition 1c, asserting that there is a positive relationship between cooperation and innovation performance. There is a significant and positive relationship with the performance of both incremental and radical innovation performance in 2000 (Models 1 and 2) and 2004 (Models 3 and 4, see Table 3.4). Cooperating with other organizations for innovation activities seems to be a successful way for developing both incremental and radical new products, as the innovations of cooperating firms contribute substantially to the sales of the firm. Interestingly, this holds for both short-term and long-term innovative sales.

The combined results with respect to licensing-in, outsourcing, and cooperation, provide substantial evidence that open innovation is positively related to the innovation performance of innovating firms, thereby providing support for Proposition 1.

We found no support for Proposition 2, which predicted a negative relationship between the acquisition of a firm and innovation performance. Whereas, Models 1 and 2 show there is no significant relationship between acquisitions and short-term innovation performance (indicating a neutral relationship), acquiring a firm has a significant positive impact on long-term innovation performance (Models 3 and 4, see Table 3.5). Thus contrary to our expectations, there is no negative relationship between a firm acquisition and innovation performance, rather in the long term there is even a significant positive relationship. This result would be in line with the literature on M&A (e.g. Ahuja and Katila, 2001; Puranam *et al.*, 2006), which suggests that it takes quite a while before the post-acquisition integration process has been completed and innovation synergies are realized. Moreover, the coefficients in Models 3 and 4 indicate that, compared with the other two knowledge acquisition strategies, in the long run, acquiring a firm has the largest positive impact on innovation performance. To conclude, Proposition 2 is partly rejected.

Table 3.4. Tobit regressions with knowledge acquisition strategies explaining innovation performance.

Model	Model 1			Model 2			Model 3			Model 4		
Year	2000			2000			2004			2004		
Dependent variable	Incremental innovation			Radical innovation			Incremental innovation			Radical innovation		
	Coefficient	S.E.[a]	b	Coefficient	S.E.[a]	b	Coefficient	S.E.[a]	b	Coefficient	S.E.[a]	b
Control variables												
Constant	0.136	(0.040)	***	-0.150	(0.036)	***	-0.209	(0.057)	***	-0.225	(0.051)	***
Size (LN employees)	-0.006	(0.006)		0.015	(0.006)	***	0.012	(0.009)		0.006	(0.008)	
Innovation intensity	0.062	(0.029)	**	0.034	(0.023)		-0.022	(0.050)		-0.006	(0.040)	
Firm part of group	-0.017	(0.018)		0.005	(0.016)		0.048	(0.026)	*	0.061	(0.023)	***
Search breadth	0.014	(0.005)	***	0.004	(0.004)		0.024	(0.007)	***	0.011	(0.006)	*
Food and drink	-0.017	(0.028)		0.007	(0.025)		0.038	(0.039)		0.028	(0.034)	
Textiles	0.013	(0.045)		0.014	(0.039)		0.055	(0.061)		0.064	(0.052)	
Paper	-0.039	(0.035)		0.021	(0.031)		0.050	(0.049)		-0.048	(0.047)	
Printing and publishing	-0.016	(0.037)		-0.043	(0.035)		-0.047	(0.055)		-0.016	(0.048)	
Petrol	0.043	(0.076)		0.153	(0.063)	**	-0.051	(0.110)		-0.125	(0.115)	
Chemical basic products	-0.040	(0.039)		-0.041	(0.035)		-0.025	(0.056)		-0.032	(0.050)	
Pharmaceuticals	0.077	(0.045)	*	-0.011	(0.040)		0.045	(0.064)		0.005	(0.057)	
Chemical end products	0.063	(0.036)	*	0.074	(0.031)	**	0.115	(0.049)	**	0.073	(0.043)	*
Plastics	0.042	(0.035)		0.010	(0.031)		0.080	(0.049)		0.076	(0.042)	*
Basic metals	-0.024	(0.042)		-0.036	(0.039)		0.007	(0.059)		-0.002	(0.052)	
Fabric. metal products	-0.012	(0.028)		-0.012	(0.025)		0.037	(0.040)		0.044	(0.035)	
Machinery	0.036	(0.027)		0.084	(0.024)	***	0.113	(0.038)	***	0.080	(0.033)	**
Electrical	0.061	(0.033)	*	0.072	(0.028)	**	0.128	(0.045)	***	0.085	(0.039)	**
Automobile and transport	0.067	(0.039)	*	0.063	(0.034)	*	0.083	(0.055)		0.056	(0.048)	
Independent variables												
Licensing-in	0.037	(0.021)	*	0.050	(0.018)	***	-0.006	(0.029)		-0.005	(0.025)	
Outsourcing	0.032	(0.016)	**	0.013	(0.014)		0.036	(0.022)	*	0.054	(0.019)	***
Cooperation	0.031	(0.017)	*	0.046	(0.014)	***	0.045	(0.023)	**	0.034	(0.020)	*
Acquisition	-0.030	(0.032)		0.019	(0.027)		0.076	(0.042)	*	0.076	(0.036)	**

Table 3.4. Continued.

Model	Model 1	Model 2	Model 3	Model 4
Year	2000	2000	2004	2004
Dependent variable	Incremental innovation	Radical innovation	Incremental innovation	Radical innovation
Model parameters				
Number of observations	686	686	686	686
Uncensored observations	553	332	378	280
Left-censored observations	130	353	298	403
Right-censored observations	3	1	10	3
Chi^2 statistics	67.63 ***	102.1 ***	76.4 ***	69.01 ***
ML Cox-Snell (Pseudo) R2	0.094	0.138	0.105	0.096

[a] S.E.: Standard error.
[b] * $P<0.10$; ** $P<0.05$; *** $P<0.01$.

Table 3.5. Tobit regressions with in-house innovation explaining innovation performance.

Model	Model 5 2000 Incremental innovation			Model 6 2000 Radical innovation			Model 7 2004 Incremental innovation			Model 8 2004 Radical innovation		
Year of dependent variable / Dependent variable	Coefficient	S.E.ᵃ	b	Coefficient	S.E.ᵃ	b	Coefficient	S.E.ᵃ	b	Coefficient	S.E.ᵃ	b
Control variables												
Constant	0.164	(0.042)	***	-0.124	(0.038)	***	-0.170	(0.06)	***	-0.178	(0.053)	***
Size (LN employees)	-0.003	(0.006)		0.018	(0.006)	***	0.015	(0.009)	*	0.008	(0.008)	
Innovation intensity	0.063	(0.029)	**	0.032	(0.023)		-0.024	(0.050)		-0.007	(0.040)	
Firm part of group	-0.015	(0.018)		0.007	(0.016)		0.046	(0.026)	*	0.059	(0.023)	**
Search breadth	0.016	(0.005)	***	0.006	(0.004)		0.025	(0.007)	***	0.013	(0.006)	**
Food and drink	-0.025	(0.028)		-0.002	(0.025)		0.045	(0.038)		0.035	(0.034)	
Textiles	0.012	(0.045)		0.014	(0.040)		0.063	(0.061)		0.072	(0.052)	
Paper	-0.041	(0.035)		0.022	(0.031)		0.057	(0.049)		-0.045	(0.048)	
Printing and publishing	-0.022	(0.037)		-0.047	(0.035)		-0.048	(0.055)		-0.020	(0.048)	
Petrol	0.024	(0.076)		0.142	(0.064)	**	-0.047	(0.110)		-0.133	(0.116)	
Chemical basic products	-0.039	(0.039)		-0.034	(0.035)		-0.024	(0.056)		-0.034	(0.050)	
Pharmaceuticals	0.076	(0.045)	*	-0.013	(0.041)		0.051	(0.064)		0.012	(0.057)	
Chemical end products	0.056	(0.036)		0.076	(0.031)	**	0.129	(0.049)	***	0.084	(0.043)	*
Plastics	0.038	(0.035)		0.006	(0.032)		0.082	(0.049)	*	0.078	(0.042)	*
Basic metals	-0.025	(0.042)		-0.032	(0.039)		0.013	(0.059)		0.001	(0.053)	
Fabric. metal products	-0.012	(0.028)		-0.011	(0.026)		0.039	(0.040)		0.046	(0.035)	
Machinery	0.033	(0.027)		0.081	(0.024)	***	0.114	(0.038)	***	0.081	(0.034)	**
Electrical	0.067	(0.033)	**	0.082	(0.028)	***	0.134	(0.045)	***	0.088	(0.039)	**
Automobile and transport	0.057	(0.039)		0.050	(0.034)		0.081	(0.055)		0.054	(0.048)	
Independent variable												
Inhouse (no external linkages)	-0.045	(0.015)	***	-0.047	(0.014)	***	-0.060	(0.021)	***	-0.067	(0.019)	***

Table 3.5. Continued.

Model	Model 5	Model 6	Model 7	Model 8
Year of dependent variable	2000	2000	2004	2004
Dependent variable	Incremental innovation	Radical innovation	Incremental innovation	Radical innovation
Model parameters				
Number of observations	686	686	686	686
Uncensored observations	553	332	378	280
Left-censored observations	130	353	298	403
Right-censored observations	3	1	10	3
Chi^2 statistics	60.37***	88.921***	72.133***	63.381***
ML Cox-Snell (Pseudo) R2	0.084	0.122	0.100	0.088

[a] S.E.: Standard error.
[b] * $P<0.10$; ** $P<0.05$; *** $P<0.01$.

Proposition 3 stated that there is a negative relationship between in-house innovation and a firm's innovation performance. Models 5-8 provide strong support for this proposition (see Table 3.5). This result implies that firms that do not engage in any strategy for knowledge acquisition (licensing-in, outsourcing, cooperation, or firm acquisition) perform worse on both incremental and radical innovations, both at the short- and long-term. Thus, Proposition 3 is confirmed.

Table 3.6 summarizes the results of the analysis focused at the proposition testing. Now, we discuss the control variables. First, firm size has no impact on innovation performance measured as sales from new products, except for short-term radical innovations. In Model 7 firm size was positively related to the long-term performance of incremental innovation (significant at 10%). Whereas previous studies using CIS data found no relationship between firm size and innovation performance (e.g. Faems *et al.*, 2005; Mohnen and Dagenais, 2002; Raymond *et al.*, 2006), our study suggests that in the short term, large firms perform better in radical innovation than smaller firms. Large firms are more likely to have structural R&D and deep pockets for realizing radical innovations quicker.

Table 3.6. Outcomes of the analysis (proposition testing).

Propositions	Innovation performance 2000		Innovation performance 2004	
	Incremental innovation	Radical innovation	Incremental innovation	Radical innovation
P1a – Licensing-in positively related to innovation performance	Confirmed	Confirmed	Not confirmed	Not confirmed
P1b – Outsourcing positively related to innovation performance	Confirmed	Not confirmed	Confirmed	Confirmed
P1c – Cooperation positively related to innovation performance	Confirmed	Confirmed	Confirmed	Confirmed
P2 – Acquisition of a firm negatively related to innovation performance	Not confirmed	Not confirmed	Rejected (positive)	Rejected (positive)
P3 – In-house innovation negatively related to innovation performance	Confirmed	Confirmed	Confirmed	Confirmed

Second, there is a significant, positive relationship between innovation intensity and the short-term performance of incremental innovation (Model 1), which does not occur in the other models. Apparently, dedicating a substantial part of the firm to innovation is not enough for a consistently high innovation performance.

Third, interestingly, there is a significant, positive relationship between being part of a group and long-term innovation performance (see Models 3 and 4). Firms that belong to a conglomerate are able to draw on innovation resources from or activities carried out in, for instance, a sister firm, which enables them to innovate more consistently.

Fourth, the search breadth variable is significantly and positively related to innovation performance in most models, in particular for incremental innovations. Search breadth is positively, though not significantly, related to short-term performance of radical innovation. The overall positive relationship between search breadth and innovation performance confirms that successful innovating firms are externally oriented, open to useful information that is available outside the firm (Laursen and Salter, 2006). This does not automatically imply that firms can just stick to searching for information that is available to anyone. All eight models show that if firms really want to benefit from external knowledge and technologies, they have to establish formal linkages with other firms in the form of either licensing-in, outsourcing, inter-organizational cooperation, or acquiring other firms.

Lastly, the sector dummies show some significant relationships. Most notably out of the total of 15 sectors, we found that the chemical end-products, machine manufacturing, and electronics are the sectors that are consistently positively associated with the share of sales from new products.

3.5 Discussion and conclusions

3.5.1 Conclusions

In this chapter we analyzed the impact of different knowledge acquisition strategies on a firm's innovation performance. A unique contribution of our study is that, instead of analyzing one period only (e.g. Laursen and Salter, 2006), this study considered both the short- and long-term impact of knowledge acquisition strategies on innovation performance. Using a large cross-section of industrial innovative firms in the Netherlands we estimated the direct impact of the knowledge acquisition strategies, on both short-term and long-term innovation performance. Moreover, we analyzed the impact of the different knowledge acquisition strategies on incremental and radical innovations performance, measured as the share of sales from products new to the firm only and products new to the market, respectively. The differences are managerially relevant. Moreover, we contribute to a recent stream of literature that investigates innovation processes of firms in an inter-organizational context (Chesbrough, 2003b; Laursen and Salter, 2006; Rothaermel and Hess, 2007; Van de Vrande, 2007).

Our study shows that different knowledge acquisition strategies are positively related to the innovation performance of innovating firms, and this relation differs among the different strategies. First, our results provide new insights into the impact of licensing-in on innovation, something which has so far hardly been studied. For example, Tsai and Wang (2007) found that in electronics licensing-in had a positive impact on a firm's added value, as long as the firm has sufficient internal R&D to absorb the knowledge at stake. We found new and more wide-ranging evidence, using the cross-section of Dutch industrial innovative firms, that licensing-in positively contributes to the short-term innovation performance. In the case of licensing-in, an innovative firm buys knowledge and technologies that are relatively rapidly applicable for creating innovations. However, we found that in the longer run licensing-in turned out to have no impact, probably because the knowledge at stake may also be available to other organizations (Granstrand *et al.*, 1992). The first thing that firms should learn from our results is that licensing-in may bring temporary but not sustainable competitive advantages.

Second, our study indicates that outsourcing is a successful way to improve innovation performance. This finding is in conflict with the finding by Fey (2005) that among large R&D-intensive firms outsourcing was negatively associated with R&D performance. The positive impact of outsourcing was most clear for short-term performance of incremental innovation and long-term performance of radical innovation. This result could be an indication that firms have two distinct outsourcing strategies. Outsourcing (e.g. to suppliers) for quick improvements on existing products, and outsourcing of more basic research (e.g. to knowledge institutions) for radical innovation, or for monitoring new or emerging technologies. Further research is needed to gain better understanding of the multifaceted knowledge acquisition strategy of outsourcing.

Third, firms gain from inter-organizational cooperation for both incremental and radical innovations, which is in line with most existing studies on the impact of cooperation on innovation performance (De Man and Duysters, 2005; Rothaermel and Hess, 2007; Sampson, 2007; Van de Vrande, 2007). But our study adds to this literature by showing that cooperation also has a positive impact on innovation performance on the long-term. Firms may therefore cooperate with other firms to achieve both short-term and long-term goals. Taking the results with regard to licensing-in, outsourcing and cooperation together leads us to conclude that open innovation holds significant potential for improving the innovation performance.

Fourth, this study leads us to the conclusion that acquiring a firm has a positive impact on innovation performance, providing original and important, industry-wide evidence on the impact of M&As on the innovativeness of acquirers. To date, most studies on the impact of M&A on innovation performance found a neutral effect at best, or even negative effects (De Man and Duysters, 2005). Studies found a positive relationship between M&A and innovation performance only in specific circumstances, for instance, in high-tech sectors with moderate relatedness between the merging firms, or when the acquirer has sufficient experience with M&As (e.g. Ahuja and Katila, 2001; Cloodt *et al.*, 2006; Hagedoorn and

Duysters, 2002a). In contrast, our analysis of a cross-section of industrial firms shows that the acquisition of a firm has a substantial, positive impact on long-term radical and incremental innovation performance. Apparently, it takes a considerable time to integrate a firm, let alone the innovation function (Gerpott, 1995; Schweizer, 2005), but when the integration is complete, there are considerable innovative gains. Our results also suggest that firm acquisition has, compared with other knowledge acquisition strategies, the strongest impact on long-term innovation performance. So for firms in doubt as to how to formalize the external knowledge acquisition this research shows that although acquisitions can be demanding and expensive, they can really bring substantial innovation benefits in the longer term.

Fifthly, the results of this study show that in-house innovation, i.e. firms that do not engage in any of the knowledge acquisition strategies studies here, has a highly negative impact on the innovation performance of innovating firms. This does not imply that firms should not conduct any innovation activities in-house. Substantial levels of R&D are important for innovating firms to maintain sufficient absorptive capacity (Cohen and Levinthal, 1990), which is essential to recognize and absorb knowledge residing in other organizations. Our results suggest, however, that firms should not rely exclusively on in-house innovation, but instead should complement internal R&D and other innovation activities with knowledge and capabilities.

Finally, the results of this study strongly suggest, like Laursen and Salter (2006), that being open to external knowledge from different types of sources can be very beneficial to firms. However, considering the positive relationships found between the knowledge acquisition strategies and innovation performance, we can amend this conclusion to reflect the fact that searching for information for innovation is more effective when specific knowledge acquisition strategies are used.

3.5.2 Limitations and suggestions for further research

Obviously, our study is subject to several limitations. The first limitation regards the problem that comes with subjective firm-level data. The data used in our study are self-reported and have limited levels of sophistication. Therefore, we agree with Laursen and Salter (2006) that (preferably in-depth) case studies are needed to investigate how organizations manage innovation given different knowledge acquisition strategies. Furthermore, driven by the CIS data, we distinguished between only four, clearly identifiable and fundamentally different, knowledge acquisition strategies. Further research may also investigate sub-forms of inter-organizational cooperation, such as (non-) equity alliances or Joint Ventures, or other strategies, such as Corporate Venture Capital (CVC) investments. Both from a managerial and scientific point of view it would be interesting to investigate the impact of different knowledge acquisition strategies on innovation performance at the project level. Another limitation is that we did not investigate how firms manage the portfolio of external relationships needed for innovation. In this respect, studies of best practices as well as lessons from failures could complement our research, and could contribute to the existing knowledge on external knowledge acquisition strategies. A limitation of a different kind is the way we selected firms for the longitudinal dataset from the original CIS-3 sample of innovating firms. We explained in Section 3.3.1, for instance, that the longitudinal sample consists of significantly larger firms than the original CIS-3 sample, although both samples are similar in terms of the dependent and independent variables. A suggestion for further research would be to analyze the impact of different knowledge acquisition strategies on the innovation performance within samples of different size categories. Cooperation may be, for instance, especially beneficial for SMEs, whereas licensing-in could be a preferred strategy for large firms. Such an approach requires substantially large datasets, with a sufficient amount of innovating firm in each of the size classes.

Finally, restricted by the CIS data, our study focused on how external knowledge and capabilities enter the firm. Future research may also focus on how internal sources of innovation leave the firm, for instance how firms (can) profit from ideas or knowledge developed in-house that are further developed and implemented in other organizations.

3.5.3 Concluding remarks

In discussing the main findings of our study, we came across a number of interesting results, such as the consistently negative relationship between in-house innovation and innovation performance, and the positive impact of large M&As especially on the radical innovation performance. The results of our study may be of interest for managers of innovating firms. In view of the rapid growth in inter-organizational linkages for the sake of innovation, this study may guide managers when choosing the appropriate knowledge acquisition strategy. For instance, firms can learn from our results that licensing-in may bring temporary but not sustainable competitive advantages, whereas cooperation with other firms is beneficial for achieving both short-term and long-term goals. Managers intending to acquire another firm with the (sub) aim of improving the innovativeness of the firms should realize that it can take a substantial time before a positive impact is felt.

Finally, there is an important message for innovating firms that have so far not been engaged in external knowledge acquisition, and that have relied exclusively on internal knowledge and capabilities. These firms should ask themselves whether they are pursuing the best innovation strategy. In the current highly dynamic business landscape, where technological progress is rapid, firms must promote partnerships with other organizations or other knowledge acquisition strategies in order to profit from the knowledge and capabilities available there. Firms for which external knowledge acquisition is a new strategy, could set up training programmes for innovating in an inter-organizational context. In addition, these firms can try to valorize the learning from organizations that have experience in pursuing external knowledge strategies (see, for instance, Chapter 4 which presents the case of innovation brokers that assist inexperienced SMEs to innovate in a network).

Part II
Qualitative analyses

4. Orchestrating open innovation. The case of innovation brokers in agri-food SME Innovation Networks

4.1 Introduction

Chapter 4 presents an in-depth study on the orchestration of open innovation within SME innovation networks[11]. The study was primarily set up to analyze how innovation brokers orchestrate SME innovation networks in the context of the agri-food sector.

RQ3: How do innovation brokers orchestrate SME innovation networks in the agri-food sector?

In recent years EU, national and regional policy makers have focused on enhancing the innovativeness of their economies by stimulating inter-organizational cooperation by Small and Medium-sized Enterprises (Freel, 2003; Howells, 2005; Oughton *et al.*, 2002). Small and Medium-sized Enterprises (SMEs) often lack the essential knowledge and capabilities to successfully innovate exclusively by means of in-house activities (Narula, 2004; Nooteboom, 1994), making inter-organizational networks essential for SMEs that want to innovate. Nevertheless, when SMEs want to establish and benefit from innovation networks, they face several obstacles (Hoffmann and Schlosser, 2001; Kaufmann and Tödtling, 2002; Van Gils and Zwart, 2004).

The literature that employs the Systems of Innovation perspective (Dosi *et al.*, 1988; Malerba, 2002; Nelson, 1993) increasingly pays attention to several types of innovation intermediating organizations that support SMEs by eliminating obstacles for cooperation and innovation while stimulating and facilitating these processes (Howells, 2006; Smits and Kuhlmann, 2004; Winch and Courtney, 2007). For instance, innovation brokers may support SMEs by identifying their innovation needs, articulating their knowledge demands, setting up partnerships and managing the inter-organizational cooperation processes (Howells, 2006). The literature on this topic has provided an overview of the functions that these organizations may fulfil (Howells, 2006; Johnson, 2008; Pollard, 2006; Winch and Courtney, 2007), how they are organized in terms of funding, organizational model, mandate and scope (Klerkx and Leeuwis, 2008b; Kolodny *et al.*, 2001; Van Lente *et al.*, 2003; Van Looy *et al.*, 2003), and how they are embedded within SME networks and the innovation system (Huggins, 2000; Klerkx and Leeuwis, 2008a; Laschewski *et al.*, 2002). However, as Sapsed, Grantham and DeFillippi (2007) and Pollard (2006) state, more empirical and theoretical knowledge is needed on what defines a useful innovation broker in terms of its organization-level impact on

---

[11] This Chapter is based on: Orchestrating Innovation Networks: The Case of Innovation Brokers in the Agri-Food Sector. Batterink, M.H., Wubben, E.F.M., Klerkx, L and S.W.F. Omta. Forthcoming in Entrepreneurship and Regional Development.

the innovation process. Moreover, in their review of SMEs and innovation networks, Pittaway *et al.* (2004) concluded that the role of such 'third parties' in innovation networks has been under-researched.

Besides the Systems of Innovation literature, management literature has also focused attention on network orchestration processes aimed at innovation (e.g. Dhanaraj and Parkhe, 2006). These studies typically take the position of the commercial firm as the focal actor in knowledge acquisition processes, and in the establishment of R&D consortia (e.g. Doz *et al.*, 2000). Yet, research still has to *tease out the unique contributions a 'network orchestrator' makes, despite its lack of hierarchical authority* (Dhanaraj and Parkhe, 2006). Or as Winch and Courtney (2007) stated, the question is still open *to identify how innovation brokers operate, and under which conditions they function most effectively.* Therefore, in this chapter we aim to analyze *how* innovation brokers orchestrate SME innovation networks.

In order to analyse the network orchestration processes of innovation brokers, this chapter presents four in-depth case studies of innovation brokers, specifically in the agri-food sector. In the agri-food industry, firms capable of networking are associated with a larger innovative capacity (Bertolini and Giovannetti, 2006; Gellynck *et al.*, 2007; Pannekoek *et al.*, 2005). As in other sectors which have a high share of SMEs, agri-food firms face typical constraints when it comes to innovation. Moreover, Costa and Jongen (2006) pointed at some general barriers to agri-food innovation, such as a lack of concrete knowledge on how to organize the innovation process, especially in an inter-organizational setting. Other studies concluded that economic considerations and insufficient innovation competencies are important barriers to innovation in the agri-food sector (Batterink *et al.*, 2006; Garcia Martinez and Briz, 2000). It is perhaps therefore not surprising that intermediary organizations like innovation brokers can play a crucial role in the innovation networks of SMEs and agricultural entrepreneurs (Dons and Bino, 2008; Klerkx and Leeuwis, 2008b; Vanhaverbeke *et al.*, 2007).

The remainder of this chapter is organized as follows: Section 4.2 reviews the relevant literature on innovation in SMEs, elaborating on the inter-organizational context of innovation. As such, we discuss the importance of SME-driven innovation networks, how these networks are managed and the role of innovation brokers in these management processes. Then, in Section 4.3, the data and methodology of the empirical research is described. This section introduces the four innovation brokers that are investigated, and describes in detail how the data was collected and analyzed. Section 4.4 discusses the findings from the cases and derives research propositions. These findings are structured according to three main orchestration processes conducted by innovation brokers: innovation initiation, network composition, and innovation process management. Finally, Section 4.5 provides the discussion of the study, and draws the main conclusions, as well as suggestions for further research.

4.2 Theoretical background

4.2.1 Innovation in SMEs: an inter-organizational process

This chapter deals with the formation and operation of innovation networks of SMEs. As the research does not focus on specific innovations, we use the broad definition of innovation as given in Chapter 1, i.e. the *exploitation of new ideas to produce new products, processes, services or business practices* (in Pittaway *et al.*, 2004). With networks we are referring to *cooperative relationships between firms and other actors in which organizations retain control over their own resources, but jointly decide on their use* (Brass *et al.*, 2004). SMEs are enterprises that employ fewer than 250 people, have an annual turnover below €50 million, and/or an annual balance sheet which does not exceed €43 million (European Commission, 2005).

The topic of innovation in SMEs has received a great deal of attention from scholars (for a review see Edwards *et al.*, 2005). An obvious reason for this attention is that there are many differences in the way that large firms and SMEs deal with cooperation and innovation (Hoffmann and Schlosser, 2001; Nooteboom, 1994; Rogers, 2004). Nooteboom (1994) addressed a number of characteristics of SMEs that can be considered either strengths or weaknesses for their innovation processes. Well-known strengths of SMEs are motivated management and labour, effective internal communication and little bureaucracy (Nooteboom, 1994). Weaknesses of SMEs include limited absorptive capacity (Menrad, 2004), lack of innovation funding (Caputo *et al.*, 2002; Kaufmann and Tödtling, 2002), lack of functional expertise, diseconomies of scale and the short-term perspective of management (Bessant and Rush, 1995; Kaufmann and Tödtling, 2002; Nooteboom, 1994). These weaknesses are typically cited as a justification for establishing relations with external actors.

Research shows that some SMEs experience positive effects from cooperation to achieve innovations, but other SMEs experience major problems. The positive effects of cooperative innovation include increased turnover, higher profit rates and expansion of the product range (De Jong and Vermeulen, 2006; Van Gils and Zwart, 2004). Nevertheless, there are several reasons why many SMEs find it difficult to establish and benefit from inter-organizational innovation projects. First, SMEs are often managed by their owners. These entrepreneurs are accustomed to operating independently and within a certain region. Cooperation with other organizations does not come naturally to them (Wissema and Euser, 1991). Second, cultural differences and the lack of joint research experience hamper cooperation (Hoffmann and Schlosser, 2001). For instance, most SMEs are unfamiliar with research organizations (Caputo *et al.*, 2002; Kaufmann and Tödtling, 2002). Third, smaller firms cannot enforce their will upon others. Therefore, SMEs must be confident that the results of cooperative efforts will be allocated fairly (Van Gils and Zwart, 2004). Fourth, typically for SMEs, knowledge may unintentionally spill over to other organizations, while intended efforts for knowledge valorization may remain underutilized. Finally, inter-organizational innovation projects may involve organizations with divergent institutional and cultural backgrounds. An increase in the number and diversity of the organizations involved adds to the complexity within the project, which in the absence of related expertise among the SMEs, quickly lowers the success rate of an inter-organizational innovation project.

There have been several studies investigating the critical success factors for innovation in SMEs (Edwards *et al.*, 2005) and the related inter-organizational cooperation between SMEs. Most notable is a study by Hoffmann and Schlosser (2001) of 164 Austrian SMEs, which identified the following key success factors for inter-organizational cooperation in SMEs:

- precise definition of rights and duties;
- each partner contributes specific strengths;
- required resources are established;
- alliance objectives are derived from business strategy; and
- speedy implementation and fast results.

Typically, most key success factors relate to the early stages of the cooperative endeavour (Hoffmann and Schlosser, 2001). Another key success factor is the need for both roughly equal and non-conflicting interests in the project (Wissema and Euser, 1991). SMEs, however, often lack the capability to fulfil such key success factors for successful coordination and network management (Hoffmann and Schlosser, 2001). So how are such networks managed, and who is driving them?

4.2.2 Innovation networks

Innovation networks can be viewed as cooperative relationships between firms and other actors who seek innovation. We have focused on a subset of innovation networks in which a 'network orchestrator' (Dhanaraj and Parkhe, 2006) or 'network broker' (Snow *et al.*, 1992) is the primary actor engaged in the design and management of the innovation network. We adopted the framework of Dhanaraj and Parkhe (2006) who defined 'network orchestration' as the set of deliberate actions undertaken by a network orchestrator as it seeks to create value with and extract value from the network. The framework of network orchestration processes focused on innovation networks that are characterized by a small number of participants. Keeping the orchestrator in mind, we must distinguish between network design activities and ongoing network management activities and processes (Dhanaraj and Parkhe, 2006; Snow *et al.*, 1992). In terms of designing a network (the network recruitment process), the network orchestrator has to detail the following three aspects (Dhanaraj and Parkhe, 2006): network membership, network structure and network position. Network membership is specified by the size of the network (number of firms) and the diversity of its participants (a homogeneous or heterogeneous group). Network structure is typified by the density of the networks and their autonomy. Network position relates to the centrality of a firm and its status.

Once the network has been created, the orchestrator may deploy orchestration processes to realize network output. They do this by (1) managing resource mobility, (2) managing value creation and appropriation, and (3) managing network stability and development (Dhanaraj and Parkhe, 2006). Managing resource mobility, especially knowledge, includes processes of knowledge absorption, network identification, reinforcing a shared identity (Dyer and Nobeoka, 2000) and inter-organizational socialization in order to increase social and relational capital. Through exchange forums and formal and informal communication channels, a network orchestrator can enhance socialization and promote knowledge mobility within the network. Managing value creation and appropriation relates to the idea that in the innovation network equitable distribution of value must be ensured and the related concerns must be mitigated. A network orchestrator can facilitate these processes by focusing on trust, procedural justice and joint ownership (Uzzi, 1997). Therefore, organizations engaged in network orchestration must provide leadership in building trust levels and in communicating clear, pre-established sanctions for trust violation. Managing network stability refers to preventing isolation, migration, cliques and attrition. A network orchestrator can enhance a network's stability by using its reputation, by lengthening the shadow of the future, and by building multiplexity (Dhanaraj and Parkhe, 2006).

Although Dhanaraj and Parkhe (2006), in detailing their useful framework, had in mind an orchestrator that takes the position of a so-called commercial hub firm, we would like to show that their framework of innovation network orchestration processes also fits other facilitative intermediary organizations that are not part of the original network, i.e. specialized independent innovation brokers. These innovation brokers may facilitate the design and management of innovation networks.

4.2.3 The rise of specialized innovation brokers

In management literature, the firms that are described as fulfilling a role as network orchestrator are typically large and dominant firms, e.g. the hub firm that is part of the original network. In the context of innovating SMEs, the situation is rather different as SMEs do not have all the relevant capabilities for fulfilling an orchestrating role successfully. Systemic brokers as network orchestrators have been studied from an innovation systems and network perspective. From a network perspective, for instance, systemic brokers can be considered important for SMEs for they may enable the exploitation of opportunities that arise from 'weak ties' (Granovetter, 1973; Granovetter, 1985), or because they may provide brokerage in cases of a lack of connections in or between networks, i.e. exploiting 'structural holes' (Burt, 2004). Existing studies on systemic brokers cover inter-organizational SME networking and clustering (e.g. Cooke and Wills, 1999; Major and Cordey-Hayes, 2000; Malecki and Tootle, 1996), and the interaction between research institutes and SMEs (Isaksen and Remøe, 2001; Izushi, 2003; Johnson, 2008; Kaufmann and Tödtling, 2001; Kolodny et al., 2001). Such systemic brokers have been labelled, for example, as bridging organizations, third parties, brokers, technology transfer brokers, infrastructures or organizations, and boundary organizations. By way of synthesizing the various definition terms, Howells (2006, p. 720) proposed the broad term 'innovation intermediary', defined as *an organization or body that acts as an agent or broker in any aspect of the innovation process between two or more parties.*

Although innovation intermediation and network orchestration can also be fulfilled as a side rather than a core activity (Howells, 2006), the literature indicates that in recent years there has been a rise in the number of intermediaries who concentrate exclusively on network orchestration (Smits and Kuhlmann, 2004; Van Lente *et al.*, 2003; Winch and Courtney, 2007). In this study we follow Winch and Courtney (2007: 751), who coined the term innovation broker for this dedicated type of innovation intermediary, which they defined as *an organization acting as a member of a network of actors in an industrial sector that is focused neither on the organization nor the implementation of innovations, but on enabling other organizations to innovate.* Such dedicated and independent innovation brokers, which principally focus on facilitating innovation by fulfilling the role of broker or mediator between cooperating SMEs, are also a growing phenomenon in the innovation arena of agri-food SMEs (Dons and Bino, 2008; Hartwich *et al.*, 2007; Klerkx and Leeuwis, 2008b).

Although the literature has outlined several detailed functions of innovation brokers (see e.g. Howells, 2006; Snow *et al.*, 1992; Winch and Courtney, 2007), there appear to be three basic, aggregate functions for innovation brokers (Klerkx and Leeuwis, 2008b; Van Lente *et al.*, 2003): demand articulation, network composition and innovation process management. Demand articulation comprises diagnosis and analysis of problems and articulation of the needs (latent or otherwise) of SMEs (Boon *et al.*, 2008; Howells, 2006). Network composition refers to making external relations available to SMEs (Cooke and Wills, 1999), i.e. scanning, scoping, filtering and matchmaking of sources of complementary assets such as knowledge, materials and funding (Howells, 2006; Kaufmann and Tödtling, 2002; Kolodny *et al.*, 2001). Innovation process management primarily relates to enhancing communication, learning, and other forms of interaction and alignment among partners, facilitate intellectual property rights attribution and commercialization of innovation outcomes (Klerkx and Leeuwis, 2008b).

As regards the roles of such an innovation broker in the network of SMEs, the literature identifies a number of central 'values' or 'design requirements' that are needed to obtain and maintain a good and credible position in the network. A key premise of the facilitator role of innovation brokers is an impartial and independent position (Hanna and Walsh, 2002; Hassink, 1996; Isaksen and Remøe, 2001), i.e. one that does not adhere to certain 'preferred suppliers' or 'preferred development strategies'. In the context of the provision of innovation intermediation services to SMEs, Kolodny *et al.* (2001) formulated a number of design requirements that seem essential for proper functioning of innovation brokers: (1) visibility and accessibility to SMEs, (2) trustworthiness for SMEs, (3) access to appropriate sources of knowledge and information relevant to the innovation process, (4) credibility of the innovation broker with these sources, (5) quick response to the requests of SMEs, and (6) complementarity to the weaknesses of the SMEs it serves.

4.2.4 Towards a research framework

Our research framework was inspired by the innovation network orchestration framework of Dhanaraj and Parkhe (2006), which was primarily developed with a so-called 'hub firm' as the network orchestrator. In this study we are concerned with the network orchestration processes of innovation brokers.

The set of network design activities, as defined in the network orchestration framework, corresponds to the network composition function of innovation brokers. It is here that strategic, complementary partners are scanned and selected, a partnership is developed and procedures and tasks are established. Therefore, we included this process in our research framework. However, we refer to it as the function of network composition, because it emphasizes the specific function of getting the suitable organizations willing to cooperate within a new network.

In addition, Dhanaraj and Parkhe (2006) referred to the innovation network management process, which comprises the facilitation of knowledge mobility, innovation appropriability and network stability. In this manner, the innovation network management process corresponds to the innovation process management function of an innovation broker (Klerkx and Leeuwis, 2008b; Van Lente *et al.*, 2003). Innovation process management is the process of creating an atmosphere that stimulates knowledge sharing and learning (knowledge mobility), enabling a fair distribution of the costs and benefits between innovation network members (innovation appropriability) and anticipating and resolving conflicts between the members (network stability).

Demand articulation was not put forward as a network orchestration process by Dhanaraj and Parkhe (2006), although it is evidently one of the most important functions of innovation brokers (Howells, 2006; Klerkx and Leeuwis, 2008b). It appears to be a core task of such organizations to independently validate new ideas (Winch and Courtney, 2007) and to present good options for SMEs. Therefore, we included demand articulation in our research framework of network orchestration processes and will refer to this as innovation initiation.

In total, we arrive at three main functions of network orchestration that we include in our research framework: innovation initiation, network composition, and innovation process management. The underlying assumption of the research framework is that innovation brokers must have excellent practices for those three functions when they want to orchestrate innovation networks successfully.

4.3 Data and methods

Because the question under study – how do innovation brokers orchestrate SME innovation networks in the agri-food sector – is a recent one, a detailed approach is called for. Miles and Huberman (1994) suggested that researchers should use qualitative research designs when there is a clear need for in-depth understanding, local contextualization, causal inference, and exposing the points of view of the people under study. More specifically, Hoang and Antoncic (2003) argued in favour of more qualitative, inductive research into the development of networks of entrepreneurs to stimulate further work by introducing new theoretical ideas. As a consequence, we chose a qualitative and inductive approach in order to arrive at theoretical propositions (Eisenhardt, 1989) and to identify best practices of innovation brokers.

The sampling of the case studies is generally regarded as a crucial element in the case study method (Eisenhardt, 1989; Yin, 2003). Our first selection criteria was that stimulating innovation (through cooperation) and economic development of SMEs was a prime objective of the innovation broker. The comparability of our cases was enhanced by two additional features of the sample: all of the innovation brokers are mainly active in the agri-food sector and are relatively similar in size (between 5 and 9 Full Time Equivalents, FTEs). Given these selection criteria, we further relied on a convenient sampling strategy. Some innovation brokers that we approached declined participation because of firm policy and time pressures.

Furthermore, by their nature, innovation brokers are involved in several and sometimes many inter-organizational processes. By accessing these brokers, we were able to extract tacit knowledge from the people with ample experience in inter-organizational cooperation, involving more than 100 inter-organizational innovation projects of SMEs. The general characteristics of the four innovation brokers in our analyses are provided in Table 4.1. See Appendix 3 for a more detailed description.

Internal validity was handled by conducting multiple iterations and follow-ups during the analyses. We addressed the problem of reliability by drawing up detailed case study protocols and by following the required documentation and transcription standards. External validity was increased by studying multiple organizations and analyzing multiple findings. To enhance the external validity further, we investigated the processes and practices of innovation brokers from different EU countries: two from the Netherlands, one from France and a German-Dutch cross-border organization. Construct validity was enhanced by triangulation of the data sources. We therefore conducted 18 in-depth interviews (using semi-structured questionnaires) with key actors (innovation brokers, project leaders, and technical experts). We interviewed at least the director or general manager of the organization, and two other employees who act in the innovation networks as innovation brokers. In doing so, we were able to get both an in-depth and a broad picture of the organization, and to contrast views from within one organization. The first interview with each innovation broker – in all cases the interview with the director or general manager – had a much more open character than

Table 4.1. Description of the innovation brokers comprising the sample.

Innovation broker	Year of initiation	Region	Size in FTE	Legal status	Main source(s) of funding	Type of projects	Number of interviews
KnowHouse	2003	Southeast Netherlands	9	Public-private	Starting loan from shareholders. Currently operating entirely on the earnings from projects	Very diverse. There is cooperation between several organizations	4
my eyes	2005	Mainly the Netherlands, not officially limited to one region	5	Private	Basic capital collected through share emission. Most earnings are directly from projects, many of which have transaction-based business models	Very diverse. Projects in 'new commerce', partnership development, entrepreneurial innovation, start-ups, etc.	5
GIQS	2001	Mainly German-Dutch border region	5	Public-private, cross-border	Hardly any structural funding. Most funding is public, mainly based on large EU framework projects	Mainly application-based R&D. Relatively large projects, often subdivided into work packages or sub-projects	4
PEACRITT	2001	Rhone Alpes (France)	7	Public	Funding by the region and state (85%) and the EU (15%)	Individual projects aiming at starting innovation at firms; OPTIréseaux - for stimulating knowledge transfer to food processing SMEs; EU projects	5

the follow-up interviews, normally with the project leaders and technical experts active in the innovation networks. The more structured follow-up interviews allowed better comparison between the cases (Yin, 2003). The interviews lasted for about 1 to, in some cases, 2 hours. In addition to the interviews, we collected internal documents, annual reports, information from the websites, newsletters, etc. For the analysis of the innovation brokers, we combined interview data with collected documents. All interviews were tape recorded and fully transcribed. For each innovation broker a detailed within-case description was developed, drawing from the interviews and collected documents. After this, the cross-case analysis utilized a matrix technique for comparative analysis. In these matrices, exemplary quotes and other research findings from the cases were sorted per topic. Doing so enabled us to visually identify differences and similarities in the processes of innovation brokers. In order to provide in-depth understanding and contextualization, we have included examples from the data in Tables 4.2-4.8. These tables provide information on each case from the created matrices beyond that outlined in Table 1 and serve as the basis for the case discussion in the next section.

4.4 Results

This section primarily deals with the results from the cross-case analysis, but it also provides relevant information on all the individual cases. We focus on how innovation brokers create and extract value from their networks by trying to detect commonalities and differences in organizational characteristics and their roles and practices in the innovation networks. As such, the following sections present results from the qualitative data analysis to explain best practices of innovation brokers in orchestrating their innovation networks. The experiences of the innovation brokers found in this study form the basis for the formulation of the propositions. Our results focus on three main functions of innovation brokers from our research framework (see Section 4.2.4): innovation initiation, network composition, and innovation process management.

4.4.1 Innovation initiation

Incorporating innovation needs of SMEs

There are several ways innovation can be initiated. A fundamental aspect is the *prime driver* of a project. An innovation project involving SMEs can be driven by the entrepreneurs, by the availability of certain technologies following research, or by the availability of sources of funding. Hence, innovation projects can be characterized as 'SME driven', 'research driven', or 'subsidy driven'. In particular, research-driven and subsidy-driven projects have several drawbacks, most notably that they deliver solutions without a real market potential.

Both *my eyes* and *KnowHouse* acknowledge the importance of what they call the 'dream stage' (see Table 4.2). During this stage, SMEs or entrepreneurs can independently develop their ideas without being immediately influenced by limitations and restrictions imposed by

Table 4.2. Examples from the data for innovation initiation and incorporating SME's innovation needs.

Case	Quotes and other findings
KnowHouse	'There is this example of a programme commission who had to decide about some 40 innovation projects, proposed by an applied research institute. They divided the money between 30 projects, which meant that all projects needed to be downsized, making them ineffective. Now with *KnowHouse*, the ideas come straight from the sector, and we reduced the number of projects to only a few, but these projects or programmes really answered a question from the sector.'
	'We help them (the entrepreneurs) in their 'dream stage'.'
	'Entrepreneurs must be enthusiastic. We are not going to pull endlessly.'
my eyes	'In traditional innovation projects the first step of an innovation is missing... in our projects we take the time for what we call the 'dream phase' to better conceptualize the initial ideas of the entrepreneurs.'
	'We always look at the 'sense of urgency' of an entrepreneur.'
	'We appreciate novel ideas of entrepreneurs and try to keep them authentic. Many advisory companies try to standardize everything according to their own business models, with the result that the end product is also standard.'
GIQS	'We actively ask firms to get involved in projects. Sometimes that is difficult. We visit them... ask to take a look at the new initiative and ask if they are willing to take part in this project. Or, we ask them if they have new ideas for projects. So it basically goes from both sides.'
	'They [the SMEs] also need to invest in the project (as with other EU 6th framework programmes, only 50%, of the funding is from the EU). So they really must be willing to do it, because it is partly their own money.'
	'We have the comfortable situation that at the beginning of a project, we don't exactly know what we will do. We more or less have a topic and a partner structure. Then we have about six months to define, analyze and plan the pilot project. That is very nice, because there are so many demands, especially since business has different problems than science. And these two worlds have to be brought together. My task is to manage this whole process from the idea stage, to match science and business.'
PEACRITT	'PEACRITT provides situation analysis by a technical expert at the entrepreneurial firm, free of charge, in order to identify the company-specific problems and related knowledge needs.'
	'It costs little or nothing for entrepreneurs to get involved in potential projects.'
	'We help entrepreneurs to develop new ideas.'
	'The added value of the innovation must be self evident for SMEs, it should focus on benefits for the companies.'

funding bodies (governments), research institutes or other organizations. The four innovation brokers pointed at the need to assess whether the SME possesses a sufficient 'sense of urgency' to engage in the innovation. This enables the SME to commit to the innovation network and be open to the necessary changes.

In some innovation projects it can work differently. For instance, many projects of GIQS are part of large EU programmes (such as INTERREG) on a specific theme or topic. Within such a theme, several sub-projects are initiated by intensively discussing the options within the GIQS network. The content of these projects results from iterative talks and negotiations between the private and public organizations involved in the project. Then, as the overall project progresses, more specific innovation needs of SMEs are included.

We must conclude that each innovation broker in our study is actively concerned with incorporating the needs of SMEs in a project idea. They do this by assisting entrepreneurs or SMEs with demand articulation, i.e. problem diagnosis and specification, articulating innovative ideas, and translating them into knowledge needs and other factors needed for innovation. We argue that innovation projects that involve SMEs must truly be SME driven, which implies that the needs and problems of SMEs must be the point of departure for any innovation project. Therefore we have formulated the following proposition:

Proposition 1a
P1a: To orchestrate initiating innovation, innovation brokers should focus on the needs of SMEs.

Embeddedness of innovation brokers

Crucial for initiating innovation networks that work on a problem relevant for SMEs is that innovation brokers interact with the entrepreneurs. Innovation brokers should also make sure that they are sufficiently visible for innovating SMEs (Kolodny *et al.*, 2001). Indeed, the innovation brokers in our study organize diverse events in order to meet with SMEs and agricultural entrepreneurs, like innovation cafés, workshops or partnership days, and use several promotional means (see Table 4.3). Besides, to meet the SMEs the innovation brokers rely on the networking capabilities of their staff. As a result, the innovation brokers become truly embedded in the networks of SMEs targeted.

The respondents explained that, in addition to identifying specific innovation needs of SMEs, maintaining a large network helps them to identify 'common problems', observe connections with those that could provide complementary assets (e.g. knowledge, funding) and make the necessary links with other actors. For instance, GIQS organizes workshops and meetings with several stakeholders to discuss a common problem. Such a problem could be one that is of interest for the whole sector and that serves the public as well (e.g. food safety). GIQS then uses this information to develop more specific ideas for new projects.

Table 4.3. Examples from the data for innovation initiation and network embeddedness.

Case	Quotes and other findings
KnowHouse	'We meet the entrepreneurs at all kinds of events (social or otherwise) in the region in order to understand their problems and needs.'
	'We organize 'innovation cafés', where entrepreneurs gather and engage in networking.'
	'For entrepreneurs, innovation-related activities take place after office hours, in the evenings… KnowHouse visits these companies, also in the evenings.'
my eyes	'We organize partner days, where we meet different entrepreneurs, but also other types of actors.'
	'Sometimes we hear something from two different people in our network and think they could be brought together.'
GIQS	'Especially the director and the other people in the board have a very good network. They are able to speak directly to the right individuals.'
	'We have two people at GIQS who travel a lot and talk to our members and other stakeholders to search for new ideas or to find motivated partners for existing ideas.'
	'We sometimes visit trade fairs and other expert events where we meet businesses, but also scientific people.'
	'We organize idea generation workshops where we invite business partners and scientific partners and we have an annual meeting where we try to launch a specific topic or theme.'
	'We organize a big workshop in September, with all stakeholders. But these activities are limited to two or three times per year, due to the lack of structural funding.'
	'We are also becoming more and more involved in newsletters or events organized by other organizations. Through these events, where we meet many business partners, new ideas reach our organization.'
PEACRITT	'Many means are used to get SMEs interested in our services, such as PR, newsletters, fact sheets, our website, exhibitions and conference days.'
	'PEACRITT organizes a platform day for sharing ideas. This so-called OPTIréseaux day is seen as a good opportunity for exchange that encourages enterprises to formulate ideas and share them with other enterprises, experts and the regional authorities.'

Consequently, to be able to properly articulate the innovation demands of SMEs, innovation brokers must be well embedded in the local business and social networks of the SMEs, as well the networks of other stakeholders. We therefore argue that the degree of embeddedness of an innovation broker in the SME's social and business network, and the network of other stakeholders is essential for successful innovation initiation. This brings Proposition 1b:

Proposition 1b
P1b: To orchestrate innovation initiation, innovation brokers should be embedded in the social and business network of local SMEs.

4.4.2 Network composition

The second main function for the innovation broker is network composition. We explained in Section 4.2.4 that network composition entails scanning and selecting complementary actors, and establishing the procedures and tasks for the partnership.

Connecting with complementary actors from the innovation broker network

Many SMEs find it hard to connect with providers of knowledge (technological and otherwise) by themselves. It seems therefore that innovation brokers can be most valuable to the innovation process if they have access to and credibility with those sources of knowledge (Kolodny *et al.*, 2001). Indeed, all innovation brokers in the study maintain a strong network with several suppliers of knowledge, often the research organizations who are also a member or even one of the founders of the innovation brokers (e.g. in *KnowHouse, GIQS*, see Table 4.4). The respondents noted that they put a lot of effort into maintaining an extensive network, which enables them to quickly connect to other actors and set up goal-oriented innovation networks. Moreover, the innovation brokers do not limit their networks to the region or the core sector; they also make connections outside the agri-food sector when they are thought to be useful. In addition, during the interviews it came to the fore that the innovation brokers also maintain strong ties with public authorities, such as local government.

From the above data, we have ascertained that in order to make the right connections for composing an innovation network, the innovation broker must possess a large and heterogeneous network. Therefore, we formulate the following proposition:

Proposition 2a
P2a: To orchestrate network composition, innovation brokers should maintain a large and heterogeneous network.

Furthermore, the case findings suggest that network membership is not enough for composing a successful innovation network. The worlds of research, authorities and industry often have different cultures and priorities and are therefore not always easy to connect and keep connected (Johnson, 2008; Rasmussen, 2008; Winch and Courtney, 2007). Being in a position between the different stakeholders, the innovation brokers play a crucial role here.

Table 4.4. Examples from the data for network composition.

Case	Quotes and other findings
KnowHouse	'Our foundation is 'a knowledge portal' for entrepreneurs. Wageningen University and Research Centre (WUR) is also one of the founders. It is impossible to have a holistic picture of all relevant sciences, but our network is far reaching, and then it is easy to make phone calls' 'We often see a broader scope than entrepreneurs, and we see connections... then we know somebody and include them.' 'With research institutions it is important that we already know them... some researchers just cannot work together with entrepreneurs.' 'It can be fruitful to bring entrepreneurs from different sectors together. Since they are not competitors, and they don't need to cope with status, these entrepreneurs are much more open towards each other, which in turn results in new ideas.'
my eyes	'We have a multidisciplinary approach, and we understand all components. We also have a strong network with specialists for those components. We can bring things together, that is our holistic approach.' 'Sometimes we hear something from two different people in our network and think they could be brought together.'
GIQS	'We have good connections to people from other departments. But also our connections with public authorities are important. It is not difficult for us to find the specific people.' 'At a higher level we also participate in a formal (national) network, called 'Kompetenznetze' (competence network), so we are also visible to business and academia through this network. Organizations search these networks for partners in projects.' 'GIQS has excellent access to knowledge sources, especially to sources at the universities of Bonn, Wageningen, and Götingen.' 'You really have to know the people, and from the people you know the connections continue.' 'In North Rhine-Westphalia, we also have good links to government, such as the Ministry of Agriculture and the Ministry of Science.'
PEACRITT	'PEACRITT is well connected to many regional research centres.' 'As an broker organization, we are closer to the industrial world than most research organizations, so we can mediate between industry and research.' 'SMEs usually look for ways to improve economic performance, e.g. consolidation or growth of turnover and jobs. In contrast, academic researchers aim at publication in scientific journals, which requires a partnership with enterprises that are outstanding in the scientific field. An organization like PEACRITT can bridge the gap between the two worlds.' 'We are a kind of 'door opener' for SMEs to collectively analyze a problem and facilitate a linkage to technical support.'

The innovation brokers in this study seem to be aware of the fact that many innovation problems require multiple disciplines. The respondents emphasized the importance of possessing the skills and the absorptive capacity to understand complex problems, and to find experts on each discipline and link up with them. In this respect, innovation brokers can be especially valuable when connecting different types of actors who have different interests and cultural backgrounds. Previous research also suggested that innovation brokers add value by linking up complementary partners, so that each partner contributes specific strengths (Hanna and Walsh, 2008). Thus, we formulate the following proposition:

Proposition 2b
P2b: To orchestrating network composition, innovation brokers should link up complementary actors.

Coordination mechanisms

Before an inter-organizational innovation project gets started, appropriate coordination mechanisms (e.g. procedures, tasks and property rights) must be settled in order to prevent members from shielding off valuable knowledge, and to avoid free riding (Dekker, 2004; Dyer and Nobeoka, 2000). SMEs are often unfamiliar with inter-organizational projects, especially regarding the appropriate coordination mechanisms, so this is an area where innovation brokers can typically be valuable.

It was put forward during the interviews that, in contrast to the SMEs, innovation brokers have ample experience with earlier innovation projects and often have explicit ideas and even templates for setting up appropriate coordination mechanisms, such as contracts (see Table 4.5). For instance, *KnowHouse* and *my eyes* perceive a contract as a necessary backup, but they also note that in the case of innovation not too many details should be settled in advance. An overly detailed contract would decrease the level of freedom and creativity, which is perceived as detrimental to innovation. Interestingly, in some projects, *my eyes'* solution to this problem is to include a small number of scenarios in the contract: a best case, a normal case and a worst-case scenario. This enables the firms to have a better idea of where they may end up in different scenarios. Confidentiality is a common issue often addressed by the SMEs that must be settled up-front by the innovation broker. SMEs seem to be afraid that sensitive information will leak out through the network.

According to the respondents, formulating contracts can require a lot of effort, especially when they comprise many details. This effort can be disproportional to the size of the project. Evidently, SMEs are not keen on doing such a job. Moreover, when innovation networks are (co-) funded by large bodies, such as the EU, there are many formal issues that need to be settled up front. Innovation brokers such as *GIQS* and *PEACRITT* typically have the capability to deal with the formal coordination and administration procedures imposed by large subsidy providers. In this way, innovation brokers make larger EU projects accessible to SMEs.

Table 4.5. Examples from the data for network composition and coordination mechanisms.

Case	Quotes and other findings
KnowHouse	'We have our own standard confidentiality agreements. When it concerns more financial aspects of the project, we ask for advice from a legal expert.' 'Contracts are not very important in our projects, as they are typically rather small.' 'I never refer to the contract during projects.' 'Planning related issues is not part of these contracts, we also do not formalize the method and frequency of communication.'
my eyes	'In most projects we set up the contract. We have some templates, which can be supplemented with requirements from other participants.' 'Many entrepreneurs don't feel like writing a contract themselves. They lack the experience to do so, and we have templates so we can do it quicker' 'If it is useful for the process, then it could be necessary to define planning-related aspects. When a lot of uncertainty is involved, and interactivity and open communication is key, then you should not have too many protocols.' '… it is impossible to work without a contract; the examples I have seen of projects without contracts are not the successful ones… The mobility of people in firms is very high nowadays. So personal agreements are also temporary. Therefore you need a safety net.' 'With new things (innovations) it is always difficult. Together with our partners we make sure there is a worst case, best case and normal case scenario. When things go wrong, you know where you stand.'
GIQS	'GIQS often takes the lead in this process. We write the contracts and set up the administrative procedures, the project plan, etc.' 'We are familiar with the complexity that comes with large-scale EU framework projects. SMEs don't like the extensive administration that is often required, GIQS makes it easier for them.' 'The contracts include issues of property rights, patents, publication, the reporting procedures and financial issues.'
PEACRITT	'We provide the enterprises with administrative and financial engineering, which is really important and time consuming for the SMEs (who are always in a rush).' 'PEACRITT brings professionalism to the innovation process of agri-food SMEs.' 'We focus on the process, other actors are responsible for the content.' 'Confidentiality has to be settled in a formal way.' 'PEACRITT simplifies the administrative framework imposed by funding bodies on the firms.' 'We promote group autonomy, by stimulating co-responsibility and joint decision making.'

To summarize, the innovation brokers in our study often take the lead in setting up the coordination mechanisms for the innovation network. We learned from the cases that compared with other actors in the network, especially SMEs, an experienced innovation broker should be capable of establishing the most suitable coordination mechanisms. They know what a successful cooperation requires and are consequently best placed to set up appropriate arrangements (Hanna and Walsh, 2008). Therefore, innovation networks take the lead in setting up the coordination mechanisms, so that innovation networks are less likely to face, or will become better prepared for potential problems. Altogether, we arrive at the following proposition:

Proposition 2c
P2c: To orchestrate network composition, innovation brokers should take the lead in setting up coordination mechanisms.

4.4.3 Innovation process management

The interviews clearly showed that all four innovation brokers are involved in innovation process management. The innovation brokers are primarily concerned with the cooperative aspects of the innovation process, for instance by resolving conflicts between participating actors. Apart from typical cooperation-related issues in innovation process management, innovation brokers also take care of other activities of innovation process management, such as gate keeping and standard project management and administration. In the context of this study, we are primarily interested in innovation process management issues that are typical in the inter-organizational context, such as handling conflict, and the stimulation of network interactions.

Conflict handling

Managing the stability of the network is an important element in managing the inter-organizational innovation project (Dhanaraj and Parkhe, 2006; Wissema and Euser, 1991). Ideally, projects and networks are composed in such a way that conflicts are unlikely to occur (see Section 4.4.2). But when conflicts do occur, it is suggested that innovation brokers can play an important role in handling them (Johnson, 2008; Klerkx and Leeuwis, 2008b; Winch and Courtney, 2007).

The four innovation brokers in our study consider solving problems and conflicts in their innovation networks as one of their core activities (see Table 4.6). For instance, *KnowHouse* sees conflict handling in innovation networks as the most valuable service it has to offer. It is especially when conflicts occur, that *KnowHouse* comes further to the fore in the network, trying to steer the project in the right direction.

Table 4.6. Examples from the data for innovation process management and handling conflicts.

Case	Quotes and other findings
KnowHouse	'Solving problems is actually our core task… we mainly use common sense in that we do not use specific models… although we seem to have our own approach as well.'
	'We approach people personally, bilaterally, and sometimes tell them they should change their attitude.'
	'If there are problems in the cooperation process, we pull towards a solution. But if they really want to stop, we will just stop. But if this is a relational problem, and we still see opportunities for the project, we try to solve these problems.'
	'You really have to look at what is the real reason of a conflict… often there is some distrust. People always expect the other partners to have hidden agendas … I have the feeling that conflicts are more about something like that, rather than about costs and benefits.'
	'You really have to understand why people participate in a project.'
	'In some circumstances, when everyone agrees, we change the contract. The contract often states how and under which conditions things can be modified. Consensus is not always required, as long as nobody is against it.'
my eyes	'This is the essence of *my eyes'* working method, a kind of mediation. You have to show people the common goals in order to get them back together.'
	'We can be an outsider, which can make it – the innovation network – more stable.'
	'For example, a recent conflict was caused by different expectations. You first have to determine that this is the underlying cause of a conflict, and then by mentioning the different expectations, you can try and resolve it'
	'We also use the concept of dynamic consensus. That means that you should make decisions in a democratic way, but you also have to listen to everybody who has a different opinion. Even if it is a conflicting opinion, they have it for some reason and you have to understand that reason. You have to find out which fear or experience is fundamental to the way they act, and why someone has a different opinion.'
	'You always have to find a solution when there is a conflict, but when a company wants to stop, you just have to.'
	'If a partner is dissatisfied about something and there are fair reasons for this dissatisfaction, then we change elements in the contract to improve the long-term relationship. However, if it is just a matter of shifting the 'pain' towards others or to us, then we cannot accept that.'
	'There is a large project in which I sometimes refer to the contract, but I realize it can look 'childish' to use it…'

Table 4.6. Continued.

Case	Quotes and other findings
GIQS	'In my project, two partners work together who also worked together in a previous project. During that previous project they had a conflict. But they tried working together again in this new project. We first tried to find out what went wrong, what was the problem exactly, without pointing directly at who was responsible. And now in this project we try to organize it differently in order to avoid that problem.'
	'A typical conflict is that you have defined a different output in the project. It is often difficult to get every output from every partner.'
	'Sometimes partners don't really know what they should do, and then they need more support to define the specific output. We give them such support.'
	'We have to deal with that conflict, because it is also our responsibility that the projects end successfully'
PEACRITT	'We realize that the objectives of SMEs and researchers are different. In particular, very small enterprises do not look for fundamental or complex innovations, but instead look for technical solutions already approved and tested.'
	'It is important in a collective setting to have a common problem, so we try to direct the projects towards a common objective.'

In the case of conflicts between the other parties innovation brokers are typically an outsider (Hanna and Walsh, 2008; Johnson, 2008). In this outsider role, innovation brokers can be considered as a stabilizing factor in the cooperation process. Moreover, it became clear during the interviews that when handling conflicts, innovation brokers draw from their experience and 'lessons learned' from previous projects.

In conflict handling, the innovation brokers emphasize the importance of a personal approach, which means that one should focus not on formal organizations, but on their people. For instance, *my eyes* uses techniques such as mediation or dynamic consensus in order to arrive at a setting with minimal conflicts. One respondent of *my eyes* explained that it is important to listen carefully to any opinion and to try to understand why people say certain things, or have a strong opinion. These techniques help to solve conflicts.

Some respondents experienced that many problems and related conflicts occur due to the existence of hidden agenda's, different expectations, or a lack of motivation. Partners sometimes find it difficult to do tasks that are not primarily in their own interest. In the case of conflicts *PEACRITT* carefully takes into account the goals of entrepreneurs on the one side and the research institutes on the other side. It may be a challenge to identify and emphasize common goals of the project, but this is typically something in which *PEACRITT* takes the lead.

In line with earlier studies, we conclude that innovation brokers take the lead in handling conflicts. Furthermore, we conclude that innovation brokers are able to do so, because they have ample experience with previous innovation networks and because of their neutral position in the network innovation broker.

Proposition 3a

P3a: To orchestrate the innovation process, innovation brokers should take the lead in handling conflicts between the network members.

Enhancing transparency

In addition to structural, motivational, and formal mechanisms, informal mechanisms also play an important role in preventing conflicts (Dekker, 2004). In the informal context, issues like trust, transparency and openness become apparent. Trust is a phenomenon often considered as one of the basic requirements for successful cooperation in inter-organizational relationships (Bstieler, 2006; Nooteboom, 1999a; Uzzi, 1997; Zaheer *et al.*, 1998). Trust can be defined as *a psychological state comprising the intention to accept the vulnerability based upon the positive expectations of the intentions or behaviour of another* (Rousseau *et al.*, 1998). Several facilitators of trust exist, such as social interactions and transparency between network partners (Bstieler, 2006). In this study, transparency refers to timely, accurate, open and adequate communication among the people in the network, in order to develop a shared understanding, to improve the atmosphere of the relationship and to foster commitment.

The respondents stated that transparency in all processes and openness towards all partners are important factors for the stability of innovation networks (see Table 4.7). As the director of *my eyes* put it, *problems in innovation networks occur due to differences in expectations (caused by an unintended lack of transparency about the expectations), hidden agendas (a deliberate lack of transparency) or because of 'unasked questions' (lack of openness due to dependencies).*

The innovation brokers in this study deal with transparency in innovation networks in several ways. According to one of the respondents of *KnowHouse*, persons that fulfil the role of innovation broker should be open-minded towards everyone in the network, clearly say what he or she thinks, and inform others about what is on his/her mind. In doing so, also the other network actors are stimulated to enhance transparency. In addition, *KnowHouse* facilitates transparency by making sure that all partners clearly state why they are participating in the project and by being open about situations (problems) not directly related to the project. It could explain why somebody acts in a certain way in a project. Sometimes a neutral setting (which could be at the location of the innovation broker) stimulates entrepreneurs to be more open as well.

KnowHouse believes that the internal organization should also be transparent. According to one respondent, the colleagues at *KnowHouse* are also very open towards each other. Also in the

Table 4.7. Examples from the data for innovation process management and enhancing transparency.

Case	Quotes and other findings
KnowHouse	'It is always important that at an early stage parties communicate explicitly why they are participating in the project, but normally that takes quite some time. That also makes it easier to settle the financial issues.'
	'There was this example in a project where somebody often changed his standpoint, without clearly explaining why...we thought it had to do with the company succession (father-son). But it was incredibly difficult for this guy to explain something like that in the group (with other entrepreneurs). We addressed that issue in the group. That helped.'
	'Only by being open towards each other, can you trust each other. You must be able to discuss anything, including personal things. As a consequence, we have a working method that we included in our projects. But if you want to work like that in external projects, you must make sure this openness is also present inside your organization,'
	'It starts with people. We are very transparent in everything we do, and we always keep our word. You must also trust the other people, that means that you have to present yourself in an open way. Being open and transparent means that you have to say what you think. Also when we see or hear something strange in a meeting, we ask about it straightaway.'
my eyes	'Unasked questions sooner or later result in problems.'
	'Projects often fail, or fail to get started, because of hidden agendas...it is a challenge to be open and fair'
	'If something goes wrong in a project you should look at yourself first to see if you have a role in this... And when things go well, people assume it is due to their efforts,... but is it really? You should be honest with yourself... but this goes against the nature of most people.'
	'You should be able say what you want (in a cooperative project), similar to the situation where you are the boss. Often, however, dependence is created between the participant with the idea and the financer. That is deadly for a project. The one with the idea cannot say what he/she really thinks, which limits the potential of the idea.'
GIQS	'I ask a lot of questions, because I don't understand everything. Sometimes that seems stupid to them, but with my questions, they also know at the end what the problem is. So it helps to define problems as well.'
PEACRITT	'In the collective efforts it is important that there is a situation where individual problems are openly discussed.'
	'We try to valorise success stories by systematically presenting results from projects.'
	'In our framework of collective projects, there are visits to participating companies or study trips. The companies become more aware of the possibilities that come with the project, and they experience that the project is becoming more realistic.'
	'In reporting as well, you need to be open and honest.'

projects – each run by one of the co-innovators - the participants should share their problems because this leads to new ideas and solutions. In a similar vein, one of the respondents of *my eyes* states that transparency is also about being fair about what you do yourself. If a project appears to be going into the wrong direction, anyone should have the courage to acknowledge his/her own role in this situation. Similarly, in the case of success one should consider whether he/she can really take credit, or whether it was due to something or someone else.

Transparency can also be facilitated by asking questions during project meetings. For instance, by asking many questions *GIQS* forces the various partners to really think about the project and explicitly state why they do certain things in certain ways. In this way, *GIQS* tries to make it clear if there are problems, hidden or otherwise.

Finally, transparency also refers to previous acts and achievements. The innovation brokers stated that in ongoing projects it is important to present results at an early stage. By visiting test sites, (early) results can be made visible to everyone in the network. Moreover, some innovation brokers structurally include small, go/no-go decision moments, which implies that the each decision moment concerns relatively little money. As a result, these small go/no-go decision moments make the components of innovation effort in innovation networks transparent and comprehensive enough for each member. In this way, little-by-little, trust will be enhanced just enough to go one step further. At a later stage, when there is more trust, entrepreneurs will be more willing to invest, since the partners will have more confidence in the overall project.

To summarize, the cases revealed that innovation brokers can play a crucial role in the innovation process by enhancing transparency in the actions of individual partners and the joint innovation activities. Based on the above findings, we have formulated the following proposition:

Proposition 3b
P3b: To orchestrate the innovation process, innovation brokers should focus on enhancing transparency between the network members.

Network interactions

In innovation networks, the way partners interact and communicate is said to be another important factor for success, because interaction between network partners enhances trust (Bstieler, 2006; Ring and Van de Ven, 1994). Innovation brokers may be very helpful in mediating between the two worlds of industry and research, who have different mindsets, expectations and time frames. In this regard, innovation brokers may act as a translator or mediator (Johnson, 2008; Klerkx and Leeuwis, 2008b) to facilitate a situation that enhances knowledge mobility (Dhanaraj and Parkhe, 2006) and subsequent learning.

The innovation brokers in our study play a leading role in the interactions within the inter-organizational innovation networks (see Table 4.8). First, the innovation brokers all acknowledge the importance of having face-to-face meetings in the innovation networks. These meetings are often organized by the innovation brokers. Face-to-face meetings are needed to exchange information in such a way that everybody in the network is up to date, so that the more important decisions can be made. In addition, *KnowHouse*, for instance, calls in all participants for a meeting if there is a specific problem in the cooperation process.

During the innovation network meetings, innovation brokers often play the role of moderator. This role comes naturally to them, because innovation brokers often have a neutral position in the network. Sometimes another independent party is included to chair the meeting, and sometimes an external expert is included, who can add a new perspective to the project.

According to several respondents, because meetings take a lot of time, and travel is often required, they should not be held too often and be complemented with other mechanisms. Meetings must be planned very carefully, with clearly defined goals. Moreover, innovation brokers use many other means of communication in the innovation networks, such as telephone, e-mail, digital document sharing, video conferencing, or workshops. *My eyes* has developed specific services and tools that facilitate inter-organizational cooperation, based on ICT. *KnowHouse's* main means of communication remains the telephone, since this seems to be most appropriate when dealing with the entrepreneurs. Both *GIQS* and *PEACRITT* note that it is important that an innovation broker responds quickly to the SMEs, whereas to research institutes, the interaction may take more time. It appears that innovation brokers are aware of the different practices between different types of partners in communication and interaction. Consequently, they are in a good position to stimulate the interaction so that there is a good platform for learning.

To conclude, from the cases we have ascertained that innovation brokers are very concerned with interaction processes in the innovation networks and that they take the lead in facilitating interactions between the network members, who often represent different types of actors with different timeframes and cultures.

Proposition 3c
To orchestrate the innovation process, innovation brokers should focus on facilitating interaction within the network.

Table 4.8. Examples from the data for innovation process management and interaction.

Case	Quotes and other findings
KnowHouse	'Meetings are about synchronizing, about making some decisions… many things can be settled on the phone, but sometimes you just have to sit around the table.'
	'There are regular meetings about the progress, and there are meetings when there are problems… then, the agendas and the objectives are totally different.'
	'We just use the telephone a lot… that just seems to work best'
	'Depending on the project, the frequency differs… also, when there are problems we make contact several times per day, but if a project runs well, once per week may be sufficient.'
	'When a researcher from a research institution is included, he/she needs to participate in the process with the entrepreneurs.'
my eyes	'We use all kinds of interactive means of communication: video, individual, workshops, games – whatever may be necessary. In general we have an informal way of communicating, but we also realize that formal communication is needed, especially with the feedback.'
	'Real physical meetings are also very important, but this requires a lot of time as well. You need to find a balance.'
	'Project meetings should always have a goal, which we determine beforehand. It can really benefit the meeting if there is an independent party who leads or chairs the meeting.'
	'My eyes developed ICT tools especially to facilitate inter-organizational cooperation.'
GIQS	'You have to respond quickly to SMEs, but you should also be careful with potential information overload.'
	'Business partners have a lack of time, so it is really hard to contact them. Often I call them on their mobile phone and ask about the project, and I e-mail them.'
	'To a certain extent, I can guide the discussion so that progress is made during the meetings. I take minutes, I organize the agenda and the topics, and I try to moderate the meetings, to keep the overall aim of a meeting in mind.'
	'It is very important that partners physically meet each other. It is not easy to build trust by only communicating by e-mail and telephone. For us it is important to have a meeting with all partners at least every six months, so that everybody knows what is going on, what the problems are and so on. They just share their knowledge better that way.'
	'You can't compel trust, it grows in time. Meetings and social events are important, and it is quite important that all the partners visit each other. But it is sometimes complicated to meet each other all together, people need to travel.'

Table 4.8. Continued.

Case	Quotes and other findings
PEACRITT	'The ideal is to answer the SMEs within three days of their request. But it depends on the time of year. Some times are more problematic for us than others.' '…save time for training and mutual knowledge exchange.' 'Peacritt offers a platform in which different types of actors interact, analyse common problems and consider joint solutions.' Our role of 'translator' is very important in complex partnerships that comprise a varied set of actors from different worlds… We build a bridge between those worlds and try to develop a 'common language.'

4.5 Discussion and conclusions

This chapter addressed the problem SMEs have in finding successful ways to innovate in a partnership. In particular, we concentrated on the question as to how innovation brokers orchestrate SME innovation networks in the agri-food sector (RQ3). Networks are increasingly becoming important for the innovation activities of agri-food firms (Batterink *et al.*, 2006; Bertolini and Giovannetti, 2006; Gellynck *et al.*, 2007; Pannekoek *et al.*, 2005), but especially SMEs have difficulties to profit from it (Hoffmann and Schlosser, 2001; Kaufmann and Tödtling, 2002; Van Gils and Zwart, 2004).

Based on three main functions for innovation brokers in orchestrating innovation networks – innovation initiation, network composition, and innovation process management – eight propositions were developed, each accompanied by best practices and rich insights identified from the cases. Our results indicate that innovation brokers successfully orchestrate innovation networks when they engage in a number of network orchestration processes (see our framework in Figure 4.1). Innovation brokers orchestrate innovation initiation by incorporating the actual innovation needs of SMEs in the innovation project (Proposition 1a) and by being strongly embedded in the social and business networks of the SMEs (Proposition 1b). Innovation network composition can be successfully orchestrated when innovation brokers maintain a large and diverse network (Proposition 2a) and by the extent to which an innovation broker is really capable of connecting with complementary actors (Proposition 2b). Moreover, when orchestrating network composition, innovation brokers take the lead in setting up the coordination mechanisms (Proposition 2c). After innovation networks are created, innovation brokers play an important role in innovation process management. Innovation brokers should take the lead in handling conflicts that accompany the inter-organizational processes, thereby orchestrating the actual innovation process (Proposition 3a). Additionally, innovation brokers

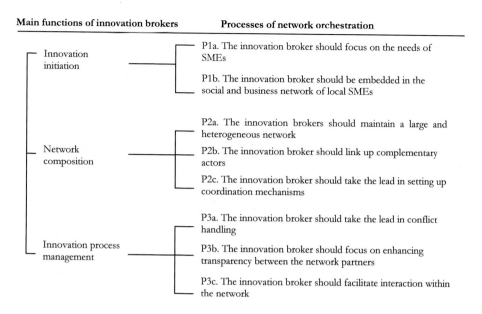

Main functions of innovation brokers	Processes of network orchestration

Figure 4.1. Framework for successful network orchestration by innovation brokers.

orchestrate the innovation process in networks by enhancing transparency (Proposition 3b) and facilitating interaction between network members (Proposition 3c).

4.5.1 Limitations and suggestions for further research

The present study has a number of potential limitations. First, it should be noted that our theoretical framework for orchestrating innovation networks by innovation brokers may not be conclusive. The four in-depth case studies could have overlooked important elements of innovation network orchestration. However, our results do confirm the findings from existing literature on innovation networks and innovation brokers. For example, we found that innovation brokers help to initiate innovation networks by helping SMEs to articulate their knowledge demand, by searching for, delineating, filtering and matching cooperation partners, and by guiding the actual cooperation during the innovation process. This corresponds with the findings from other studies of innovation brokers (e.g. Boon *et al.*, 2008; Klerkx and Leeuwis, 2008a; Sapsed *et al.*, 2007).

Second, the generalizability of the propositions is limited by the relatively small size and scope of the sample, which is inherent to this type of exploratory study. Larger-scale empirical research is necessary to statistically assess the relationships presented here and to help define the contexts in which these relationships vary. Moreover, the results of this study could be context specific and vary between different regions and different institutional settings. However, we investigated innovation brokers from different European countries, and the results suggest that there are many similarities in the way innovation brokers orchestrate innovation networks. An area for further research could be comparing innovation brokers from different countries and/or institutional settings. Possible issues are, for instance, how to orchestrate innovation networks in more developing countries? Or how does country culture affect orchestration processes among innovating firms?

Third, in our study on network orchestration we concentrated on the innovation brokers and were unable to, for instance, interview the SMEs or other members of the networks. Evidently, SMEs may have a different view on the role of an innovation broker in network orchestration processes. Nevertheless, SMEs would only be able to reflect on one or just a few projects, whereas the innovation brokers in our study have experience with a large number of innovation projects.

We make a special plea for quantitative studies on innovation brokers, both at the level of innovation networks (comparing networks that are being orchestrated by an innovation broker with networks that are not) and at the level of the innovation broker (comparing different types of innovation brokers and the impact of their specific tools and instruments, and certain organizational characteristics on performance). Moreover, the way in which innovation brokers function in different types of innovation networks (with respect to structure: density, centrality and size) is another theoretical issue that should be investigated further, since the structure of a network may impact the network orchestration process (Dhanaraj and Parkhe, 2006).

4.5.2 Concluding remarks

Our in-depth study of four innovation brokers makes a welcome contribution to the existing literature on innovation networks and innovation brokers for it answers the call for studies of the actual practices of successful innovation brokers (Sapsed *et al.*, 2007; Winch and Courtney, 2007). In addition, our study on orchestrating open innovation has a number of implications. First, the study has made explicit several ways in which innovation brokers can help SMEs to overcome the typical barriers to innovation as we outlined in Section 4.2.1. In line with other studies (e.g. Hanna and Walsh, 2008), we conclude that due to their experience with previous inter-organizational processes, innovation brokers have a clear understanding of what a successful cooperation requires. As a result, innovation brokers can assist SMEs that are inexperienced with inter-organizational processes, so that the SMEs can profit from the knowledge and capabilities of other organizations. In addition, innovation brokers can make large capital funding available to SMEs by making the strict administrative procedures imposed by large subsidy providers more comprehensive for the SMEs.

Second, the results suggest several ways in which SMEs can improve the performance of innovation networks themselves. For example, SMEs must act in an open way, i.e. they must be explicit about why they are participating in the project and must be open about situations (problems) not directly related to the project. This is how they can add to an open and positive atmosphere that is essential for learning and innovation in an inter-organizational setting.

Third, policymakers can take into account the best practices identified in our study when they stimulate SME-driven innovation networks. They may consider investing in innovation brokerage as an important instrument for stimulating innovation of SMEs, regional or otherwise. Our case study findings are derived from a number of successful innovation brokers from different European regions with rich experience in inter-organizational processes. The insights provided by this study could therefore serve as a starting point for establishing a new innovation broker, especially if focussed on SMEs in the agri-food sector. However, one should be careful when using a general template. As was explained during one of the interviews: *If you want to set up something similar to our organization in a different region, you should make sure it is independent from how it is set up here. You really have to consider the dynamics of the region and set it up accordingly.* This corresponds with arguments forwarded by Tödtling and Trippl (2005) that simply copying a successful recipe for innovation support is unlikely to be feasible, and that context-specific interventions must be designed.

To conclude, further research into the multi-faceted orchestration processes in innovation networks of SMEs remains essential if we want to fully understand why innovation networks succeed or fail.

5. The impact of technological relatedness on innovation synergy realization. An in-depth study of 10 large high- and medium-tech M&As in the life sciences

5.1 Introduction

Chapter 5 is concerned with how firms profit from external knowledge and capabilities by acquiring or merging with another firm[12], and was set up to answer the following research question:

RQ4: What is the role of technological relatedness in realizing innovation synergies in M&As?

Mergers and acquisitions (M&As) are often cited as an important strategy for firms to gain access to technological knowledge and engineering capabilities and to improve a firm's innovativeness (Chakrabarti *et al.*, 1994; Coff, 1999; Graebner, 2004; Granstrand *et al.*, 1992; Hitt *et al.*, 1996). Over the years, however, M&As often have been associated with high failure rates (Cartwright and Schoenberg, 2006; King *et al.*, 2004; Mueller, 1985; Ravenscraft and Scherer, 1987; Schenk, 2006; Seth, 1990) and with high levels of uncertainty when it comes to realizing innovation synergies (Bannert and Tschirky, 2004; Chakrabarti and Souder, 1987; Chatterjee, 1986). In fact, most empirical studies showed that on average firms engaging in M&As experience a neutral effect at best on their innovativeness (De Man and Duysters, 2005; Hall, 1989; Hitt *et al.*, 1991, 1996; Ikeda and Doi, 1983). Only recently, research found that M&As can have a positive impact on innovation (e.g. see the result of our quantitative analysis in Section 3.5). The overall disappointing results of M&As are often attributed to a poorly designed and implemented Post M&A Integration (PMAI) process (Bakker and Helmink, 2000; Epstein, 2004; Gerpott, 1995; Haspeslagh and Jemison, 1991; Jemison and Sitkin, 1986; Schweiger, 2002). However, there are also strong indications that good integration management can dramatically improve the likelihood of achieving integration and improve innovativeness as well (Chakrabarti *et al.*, 1994; Chakrabarti and Souder, 1987; Gerpott, 1995).

In addition to the literature on post M&A integration, there is a growing body of research on the impact of M&As on innovation which emphasizes that certain context characteristics, such as various forms of relatedness between the involved firms, may impact the likelihood

---

[12] Parts of this chapter are based on: (1) Batterink M.H., Wubben E.F.M., Simonse L.W.L. and Omta S.W.F., Realizing innovation synergies through Mergers and Acquisitions, paper presented at AoM Annual conference 2007, Philadelphia, 3-8 August 2007; and (2) Wubben, E.F.M., Batterink, M.H., Simonse, L.W.L. and Omta, S.W.F. Realizing innovation synergies through Post Merger Integration, RADMA conference in Bremen, 4-6 July 2007.

that an M&A leads to better innovation performance (e.g. Ahuja and Katila, 2001; Cloodt *et al.*, 2006; Hagedoorn and Duysters, 2002a; Prabhu *et al.*, 2005). For instance, for high-tech M&As there seems to be a curvilinear (inverted u-shape) relationship between technological relatedness and post M&A innovation performance (Ahuja and Katila, 2001; Cloodt *et al.*, 2006). This would imply that firms that are moderately related in terms of the knowledge and technologies involved have the most positive effect on the post M&A innovation performance.

However, these studies concentrating on the M&A context characteristics in explaining post M&A innovation performance, e.g. on the role of technological relatedness, consider the process of synergy realization (i.e. through post M&A integration) as a black box. With this study, we aim to open this black box of innovation synergy realization in M&As by concentrating on the M&A context characteristics as well as the post M&A integration process. The mixed results from existing studies on the relationship between M&As and innovation, make it even more necessary to investigate in what specific situations innovation synergies can be expected from M&As, and how these synergies are realized in terms of integration mechanisms and instruments.

The study builds on the premise that in order to realize innovation synergies in large M&As, managers need to apply a dedicated integration approach, which may be different from the overall post M&A business integration. A dedicated approach would be in line with recent findings by other scholars who have investigated R&D integration in different high tech settings. For instance, Schweizer (2005) concluded that large pharmaceutical companies apply a hybrid approach when integrating biotech companies, i.e. a quick integration of most business functions and a slower integration and more autonomy for the more specific biotech R&D. Moreover, the findings of Purunam *et al.* (2006) in their study of small technological acquisitions by large firms, suggests that acquired firms primarily involved in exploration should be kept autonomous as much as possible in order not to disrupt ongoing innovation activities, whereas for acquired firms mainly involved in exploitation, less autonomy and more integration is favorable. Although these studies have come up with important knowledge on what kind of integration strategy to choose for the R&D function, they have concentrated on relatively small technologically motivated acquisitions by large established firms. When large firms acquire or merge with other large firms, the situation can be much more problematic. What is the best R&D integration strategy in large M&As, involving firms that are active in both exploration and exploitation, and in which technology and innovation is only one aspect of the deal? In addition to improving the capacity for exploitation and exploration, large M&As in particular may offer substantial potential for optimization, for instance through the exchange of best practices.

This study is based on 10 in-depth case studies and analyzes the post M&A integration of large (medium) high-tech firms in the life-science industry and develops a conceptual model of innovation synergy realization. The high-tech industry setting is especially relevant for studying innovation synergy, because (medium) high-tech firms focus significant attention on innovation and R&D, and because research found that especially technologically motivated high-tech M&As improve the innovation performance (e.g. Ahuja and Katila, 2001). The study specifically concentrates on the role of technological relatedness in, and on the R&D integration mechanisms responsible for innovation synergy realization in large horizontal (medium) high-tech M&As. In this respect, the study builds on the findings from the study by Cassiman *et al.* (2005), who linked technological relatedness with specific integration efforts and subsequent changes in the R&D function.

The remainder of this chapter is organized as follows. Sections 5.2 provides a theoretical background on innovation synergy realization. This section sets out conceptually what innovation synergies are in the context of M&As, discusses the literature on the M&A context characteristics that may influence the potential for innovation synergy realization, as well as the literature that has investigated the post M&A integration processes within the innovation setting. Altogether, the findings from the literature study are integrated into a research model (see Figure 5.1). Then, section 5.3 describes the approach of the qualitative research, i.e. the data collection and analysis method. In Section 5.4 the results of the empirical investigations are presented, with a special focus on technological relatedness and the integration mechanisms responsible for realizing innovation synergies. Moreover, Section 5.4 elaborates on a number of key success factors for R&D integration in M&As. Section 5.4 closes with an R&D integration framework for large high-tech M&As. Finally, Section 5.5 details conclusions and suggestions for further research.

5.2 Theoretical background

5.2.1 Innovation synergies in M&As

Synergy is the term used to describe a situation where the final outcome of a system is greater than the sum of its parts. The broadest types of synergy associated with M&As that can be distinguished are financial synergy, collusive synergy, and operational synergy (Chatterjee, 1986; Larsson and Finkelstein, 1999; Lubatkin, 1983). Financial synergy refers to reductions in the costs of capital, e.g. through coinsurance and risk diversification (Lubatkin, 1983; Seth, 1990). Collusive synergy is the result of an increase in market power and the ability to dictate prices (Chatterjee, 1986; Singh and Montgomery, 1987). Operational synergy relates to efficiencies in functional areas such as production, marketing, R&D, and administration, mainly through economies of scale and scope (Harrison *et al.*, 1991; Seth, 1990; Singh and Montgomery, 1987) and skill transfer (Harrison *et al.*, 1991; Haspeslagh and Jemison, 1991). Larsson and Finkelstein. (1999) also identified managerial synergy, but we regard this type of synergy already covered by the other types of synergy. These three types of synergy encompass all M&A-related synergy effects.

We define innovation synergy as the innovation outcomes that can only be realized when two firms are combined. M&A-induced innovation synergies are a form of operational synergies, although some of the synergistic innovation effects that will be discussed are based on diversification and therefore could be considered as financial synergy. To realize operational synergies, a certain level of integration is required and resources and capabilities must, to a certain extent, be transferred (Haspeslagh and Jemison, 1991). We discard collusive, i.e. market power related, synergies in this study, because this type of synergy does not require transfer or integration. In contrast, collusive synergy is an externally located appropriability benefit, that is extensively investigated in industrial organization literature. Although collusive synergies may co-exist with innovation synergy realization, we here exclude it from consideration in detail (see for some discussions on the relationship between market dominance and innovation: Blundell et al., 1999; Cabral and Polak, 2004; Firth and Narayanan, 1996). Instead, we want to focus primarily on straightening out and conceptually model the yet underexplored field of innovation synergy realization in terms of actions that can be undertaken by integration managers.

So far, the literature on M&As and innovation has not yet defined or made explicit M&A-related innovation synergies. Different scholars, however, suggested a number of M&A-related innovation benefits, such as reduction of innovation costs, innovation lead-time reduction, and the realization of more large and more risky innovation trajectories (Cassiman et al., 2005; Cloodt, 2005; De Man and Duysters, 2005; Gerpott, 1995; Grimpe, 2007; Hagedoorn and Duysters, 2002a). Drawing from an extensive literature study, we identified three main categories of innovation synergy: (1) innovation cost synergy, (2) innovation process synergy, and (3) a new growth platform (Batterink et al., 2007).

Innovation cost synergy

The first type of innovation synergy is innovation cost synergy. The existing literature suggests that innovation cost synergies are mainly realized by means of resource re-allocations related to economies of scale and scope. Economies of scale can be achieved by eliminating duplicate innovation activities (Röller et al., 2006). This can be realized by closing R&D labs, terminating R&D programs and firing employees (Cassiman et al., 2005). Savings may also be attributed to utilizing more intensively the given expensive innovation related resources, such as laboratory resources, computer resources, and libraries (Henderson and Cockburn, 1996), but also in the administration functions of R&D. Existing resources can be allocated to alternative innovation trajectories at little or no additional costs. This case can be regarded as economies of scope (Henderson and Cockburn, 1996; Seth, 1990). Scale economies can also be realized when a given cost for innovations are spread over a larger sales base (Cassiman et al., 2005; Cockburn and Henderson, 2001). In other words, when two firms are combined, there is a larger customer base that may be reached with the same innovation, so that it is easier to recoup innovation costs. This is, for instance, the case when the merging firms had been active on geographically separate markets.

Innovation process synergy

The second type of innovation synergy identified is innovation process synergy. This is innovation synergy related to optimization of the innovation processes, which may in turn bring both costs reductions and revenue enhancements. By sharing complementary competences and best practices in innovation management the innovation processes can be brought to a higher level, resulting in increased productivity (De Man and Duysters, 2005; Griffin, 1997). Moreover, M&As increase the possibilities to reorganize R&D teams, especially in terms of further specialization in R&D tasks (Cassiman *et al.*, 2005). Furthermore, state-of-the-art technologies that are present in the merging firms can be shared, enabling incremental innovations and/or shorter innovation lead times (Harrison *et al.*, 1991). In addition, due to combined innovation-related resources, there is potential for parallel development trajectories, better allocation of R&D specialists across projects, reducing innovation lead times (Omta, 1995). In sum, via this path of optimizing innovation processes, M&As may help firms to overcome innovation related weaknesses (Harrison *et al.*, 1991) and leverage its competencies and capabilities. Optimization of the innovation process may result in both new products being introduced on the market earlier, and additional improvements in existing products (Griffin, 1997).

New growth platform

The third type of innovation synergy to be recognized is the establishment of a new product platform, creating a growth platform. A growth platform can be seen as a new technology development trajectory oriented at creating new products and/or new markets. Such a growth platform enables the realization of a breakthrough innovation, followed by a continuous flow of new products within the same product family (Meyer *et al.*, 1997; Wheelwright and Clark, 1992). A growth platform can be realized in different manners. First, by combining and integrating complementary knowledge-based resources and capabilities integrated firms may develop new knowledge that would otherwise simply not have been developed (Bresman *et al.*, 1999; Ranft and Lord, 2002). When complementary knowledge bases are integrated, the new firm may start projects that have become feasible in terms of having available the right pool of technological capabilities and knowledge. The second way of realizing a growth platform through M&As is when the two combined firms overcome a threshold level in terms of scale and scope. M&As enable specific innovation projects with relatively higher costs and/or higher risks, that were beyond the reach of the individual original firms (Henderson and Cockburn, 1996). This is an example of how innovation synergy can be regarded as financial synergy. Evidently, for certain types of R&D or other innovation related activities, most notably in pharmaceutics, a substantial level of input is required, a minimum efficient scale or threshold level (Omta, 1995). Ultimately, the result of a growth platform may be radical or breakthrough innovations, which would otherwise (without the combination of firms) not have been realized or realized much later, and subsequent incremental innovations.

Empirical evidence for the existence of innovation synergies in M&As

Although we have identified a number of innovation synergies that could possibly be realized in a merger or acquisition, whether on average innovation synergies are actually realized in M&As remains unclear. For instance, a literature review by De Man and Duysters (2005) revealed that empirical studies on the direct impact of M&As on post M&A innovation input and output show at best a neutral, or a negative relationship between M&As and innovation performance, suggesting there is no evidence for innovation synergy realization. More specifically, the relationship between M&As and innovation input (e.g. R&D expenditures) seems to be inconclusive. Hall (1989), for instance, in a sample of 2500 firms, found that firms involved in acquisitions seemed to experience permanent declines in their R&D expenditures relative to other firms in the industry. In a sample of 22 Japanese manufacturing firms active in M&As, most firms increased absolute R&D expenditures following the M&A, although with R&D expenditures relative to sales the results were mixed (Ikeda & Doi, 1983). For a subset of the 11 largest mergers the results were similarly mixed (Ikeda and Doi, 1983). However, a decrease in R&D expenditures does not necessarily cause a decrease in innovation performance, as decreases in R&D expenditures may result from economies of scale in R&D or other productivity gains (i.e. innovation cost synergy). Due to the limitations of input indicators for innovation performance, other studies used innovation output indicators, such as patents or the number of new products introductions. For instance, in a cross-industry study of 191 acquisitions, Hitt *et al.* (1991) found a negative impact of M&As on both R&D expenditures and patent intensity. These authors conclude also that diversifying acquisitions in particular negatively affect patent intensity. Apparently, M&As pursuing a diversification strategy are detrimental for post M&A innovation performance. In addition, Hitt *et al.* (1996) found in a study of 250 M&As a negative relationship between M&As and internal innovation (a variable composed of R&D intensity and new product announcements). More recently, Van de Vrande (2007) found in a sample of 105 pharmaceutical firms that acquisitions have a positive effect on innovation performance measured as patent counts, but a negative effect when patents referred to radical innovations or so-called pioneering technologies. Finally, in Chapter 3 we found a positive impact of acquisition on the performance of especially radical innovation, measured as the share of sales from new products new to the market, even when controlled for other knowledge acquisition strategies. In sum, empirical research brings us to the conclusion that there is mixed evidence at best on the relationship between M&As and both innovation input and output indicators, whereas until recent date researchers found a prevailing negative relationship between M&As and innovation output indicators. The mixed results may be illustrative of the complexity of the relationship between M&As and innovation performance in general and innovation realization in particular.

5.2.2 M&A context characteristics determining innovation synergy realization

There is a growing stream of research that focuses on the M&A context characteristics determining post M&A innovation performance. M&A context characteristics can be defined as *general attributes of the acquiring firm, the target, or the relation among them that may affect the amount of value creation potential that exists in a transaction* (cf. Gerpott, 1995). Examples of M&A context characteristics are absolute and relative size of the M&A, different types of relatedness, and previous experience in M&A. We also include M&A motives as an M&A context characteristic, because there is an evident link between the M&A motives or objectives and the amount of attention (top) management devotes to realizing them.

M&A motives

Obviously, not all M&As are undertaken for the same reasons. Among often cited motives for M&As are (Bakker and Helmink, 2000; Chakrabarti *et al.*, 1994; Chakrabarti and Souder, 1987):
- access to new markets;
- broadening the customer base;
- increasing market share;
- product line expansion;
- access to new technologies and skills;
- reduction of cost;
- diversification of risks.

It may be evident that technology motivated acquisitions in particular provide potential for improving innovation synergy realization (Ahuja and Katila, 2001; Cloodt *et al.*, 2006). In general, however, motives associated with innovation (e.g. access to technologies) ranks in the middle in terms of importance, with market-related motives prevailing (Cassiman *et al.*, 2005; Chakrabarti and Souder, 1987). Moreover, the extent to which innovation is a motive may vary per industry. For instance, especially high-tech industries and other industries in which technological development progresses fast, are associated with technology-motivated acquisitions. In other industries, such as pharma, the costs for innovation may be very high, which may focus M&A in this sector on enlarging the scale and scope of R&D and increasing the productivity in R&D (Henderson and Cockburn, 1996). Still, even with M&As that are not undertaken primarily for reasons of innovation, *management nevertheless mostly faces the challenge to ensure some form of synergistic coordination of both firms' R&D resources* (Gerpott, 1995).

Absolute and relative size

The second context characteristic is the size of the M&A. Several studies showed that the absolute and relative size of M&As are a relevant factor in explaining post M&A innovation performance. Absolute size refers, in the case of an acquisition, to the firm size or knowledge base size of the target firm. Relative size refers to the firm or knowledge base size of the target relatively to the acquiring firm, or in the case of a merger to the firm size or knowledge base size of one firm, relative to the merging partner. With respect to absolute size of the target firm, it is argued that, generally speaking, the larger the absolute size, the more technological knowledge and innovation capabilities are obtained. Hence, M&As with larger absolute sizes should offer more potential for synergy realization and improving the innovation performance. Indeed, several studies found, in general, a positive relationship between the absolute size of the acquired firm (in terms of sales or the size of the knowledge base) had a positive impact on post-M&A innovation performance (Ahuja and Katila, 2001; Chakrabarti *et al.*, 1994; Cloodt *et al.*, 2006; Prabhu *et al.*, 2005).

With respect to relative size it is argued that the larger the relative size of the acquired target, the more effort it will take to integrate the target into the acquirer, the more likely this will disrupt ongoing (innovation) activities, and hence the less likely it is to be successful (Chakrabarti *et al.*, 1994; Haspeslagh and Jemison, 1991). Indeed, some studies showed that the relative size of the knowledge bases has a negative influence on innovation output, which means that the larger the knowledge base to be integrated, relative to the acquiring firm's knowledge base, the more negative the impact is on post-M&A innovation performance (Ahuja and Katila, 2001; Cloodt *et al.*, 2006). On the other hand, it is also argued that similarity in terms of firm size may be an indication of organizational fit, and may thus foster synergy realization. In a study of 35 M&A-active firms in the computer industry Hagendoorn and Duysters (2002a) found that the degree of similarity between the merging firms in terms of firm size (which corresponds to a large relative size), have a positive impact on post M&A innovation performance. Furthermore, Gerpott (1995) found a positive association between a large relative size and R&D integration success. We must therefore conclude that the relationship between relative size and innovation performance can be two-fold.

Relatedness

The relatedness between the two firms involved in the M&A is the third context characteristic. In fact, studies into the relationship between M&A and innovation have investigated various kinds of relatedness between the merging firms, of which technological (or knowledge) and market relatedness seem to dominate. Technological relatedness refers to the overlap or similarity in firm-specific aspects such as technological disciplines and engineering capabilities, and to the technological overlap in the knowledge bases of the merging firms (Ahuja and Katila, 2001; Cloodt *et al.*, 2006; Prabhu *et al.*, 2005). The empirical literature seems to be consistent in its findings with respect to technological relatedness: firms with moderate technological relatedness produce more innovations from M&As than firms with very high or very low technological relatedness (Ahuja and Katila, 2001; Cloodt *et al.*, 2006; Prabhu *et al.*, 2005). Apparently, there is an inverted u-shape relationship between technological relatedness and post M&A innovation performance. Such a relationship can be explained by the argument that with strong technological relatedness, compared to moderate relatedness, relatively little new or complementary knowledge is acquired (Rindfleisch and Moorman, 2001). As a consequence, there will be little potential for new opportunities and learning. With low technological relatedness an M&A brings relatively more novel knowledge, but the knowledge bases may be too distinct, resulting in absorption and integration problems (Ahuja and Katila, 2001; Cohen and Levinthal, 1990). More specifically, Cassiman *et al.* (2005) found that merged firms that are technologically complementary, maintain or increase R&D inputs, while merged firms which are technologically substitutive decrease their R&D inputs after an M&A. Finally, some other studies have also looked at other types of relatedness, for instance the relatedness in terms of products and markets. Hagendoorn and Duysters (2002a), for example, found a positive relationship between market relatedness and the number of patents applied for, although they only tested linear relationships. In addition, Keil *et al.* (2008) found that only acquisitions that can be regarded as intra-industry acquisitions (i.e. implying high market relatedness) have a positive impact on a firm's innovation performance, whereas less related acquisitions had a significant negative impact. In addition, if the merging firms are rivals (which implies high product-relatedness) there are more clear reductions in R&D than if they were non-rival (Cassiman *et al.*, 2005).

Previous M&A experience

From an organizational learning perspective it can be argued that firms that have experience with integrating the innovation functions following M&As become better able to integrate subsequent acquisitions. However, the literature investigating M&A experience in explaining post-M&A innovation performance shows somewhat mixed results. Although experience in M&A determines the likelihood of firms to enter into subsequent M&As (Hagedoorn and Duysters, 2002b; Haleblian *et al.*, 2006), surprisingly, additional acquisition experience does not automatically result in better general M&A performance (Bakker and Helmink, 2000; Barkema and Schijven, 2008; Finkelstein and Haleblian, 2002; Zollo and Singh, 2004). Instead, Zollo and Singh (2004) found that M&A experience only contributed to post M&A performance when the acquirer tactically accumulates and explicitly codifies M&A experience in manuals, systems and other acquisition-specific tools. In addition, M&A experience with similar types of targets seems to positively affect subsequent acquisition performance (Finkelstein and Haleblian, 2002; Haleblian and Finkelstein, 1999), which also suggests that routines and practices built up in prior comparable M&As can be transferred to subsequent acquisitions. Surprisingly, however, in his study of R&D integration within 92 acquisitions between German firms Gerpott (1995) found that M&A experience negatively influences R&D integration success. An explanation for a negative relationship may be that experienced firms tend to develop a standardized, often formalized, PMAI approach, with non-dedicated management and/or overconfident management which underrates individual and situational challenges (Chakrabarti *et al.*, 1994).

5.2.3 The role of Post M&A integration in innovation synergy realization

Having discussed the studies concentrating on the M&A context characteristics determining post M&A innovation performance, we now turn to a second stream of research on M&As and innovation. This second stream of research claims that Post M&A Integration (PMAI) itself is an important factor in explaining the performance of M&As (Bakker and Helmink, 2000; Grimpe, 2007; Haspeslagh and Jemison, 1991; Jemison and Sitkin, 1986; Larsson and Finkelstein, 1999; Schweiger, 2002; Wubben *et al.*, 2007).

We define Post M&A Integration (PMAI) as a temporary process, comprising primarily of strategic and tactical management decisions and related activities with the aim of fostering the integration of two firms, following the formal closure of the deal until it is business as usual again. Moreover, post M&A integration should be regarded as *an interactive and gradual process in which individuals from two organizations learn to work together and cooperate in the transfer of strategic capabilities* (Haspeslagh and Jemison, 1991: 106). Thus, PMAI is a temporary process of organizational change. It is during this process that much of the (expected) synergy is created, and (too often) a lot of value is destroyed (Bannert and Tschirky, 2004; Haspeslagh and Jemison, 1991). Therefore, PMAI is claimed to be an important factor in explaining the performance of M&As (Bakker and Helmink, 2000; Haspeslagh and Jemison, 1991; Jemison and Sitkin, 1986; Larsson and Finkelstein, 1999; Schweiger, 2002). Depending on the different characteristics of the M&A and the different strategic goals, different integration levels and integration approaches are suggested (Epstein, 2004; Haspeslagh and Jemison, 1991; Schweizer, 2005). In line with other studies on the PMAI of the R&D function (e.g. Bannert and Tschirky, 2004), our study considers that PMAI (i.e. both the design and the implementation) has an important influence on the ultimate success of the merger or acquisition.

Haspeslagh and Jemison (1991) distinguish between four corporate integration approaches: (1) preservation, (2) absorption, (3) symbiosis, and (4) holding. An absorption integration approach implies a unilateral process where one firm is assimilated into the processes, culture, and other organizational characteristics of the other firm with the eventual goal of full consolidation. With preservation both firms continue to operate autonomously so that their processes, culture, and other organizational characteristics remain intact and independent. Symbiosis integration requires some degree of initial change to various aspects of both firms' organizational design and processes, as both firms' leading practices are gradually blended together. A symbiosis can be seen as the most complex approach to integration, as considerable resource transfers are necessary in both directions. The fourth integration approach, the holding, implies that the acquired firm remains autonomous, i.e. like a separate division in a holding firm. With a holding integration the firms have no intention of integrating and creating value except for financial transfer and risk sharing (Haspeslagh and Jemison, 1991: 146). Which of the 4 integration approaches is most appropriate depends mainly on two factors (Haspeslagh and Jemison, 1991): (1) the need for organizational autonomy, and (2) the need for strategic interdependence. Based on 35 M&As, Grimpe (2007) concluded that the symbiosis and absorption approaches are most beneficial for post M&A innovation performance. Apparently, in order to fully realize the potential benefits from M&As, substantial integration between the two firms is required.

More specifically, R&D integration can be defined as the changes in R&D and other innovation activity arrangements, organizational structures, systems, and cultures, following an M&A until it is business as usual again (adapted from Gerpott, 1995). As said in the introductory section, it was concluded in several studies that the success of innovation synergy realization can be significantly influenced by management interventions concerning R&D integration (Chakrabarti *et al.*, 1994; Chakrabarti and Souder, 1987; Gerpott, 1995). Therefore, PMAI of the R&D functions should be considered if we want to understand why some firms are better than others in realizing innovation synergies. In this respect, we are especially interested in the integration mechanisms and integration instruments and key success factors that are relevant for R&D integration.

Integration mechanisms

We define integration mechanisms as organizational changes and resource re-allocations in the firms involved following an M&A that are aimed at fostering integration and synergy realization. Innovation integration mechanisms can include elements of structural linking, standardization of systems, and process re-design (Grimpe, 2007). Structural linking refers to connecting (R&D) units to provide a basis for synergy realization. Structural linking relates to the arrangements for collaboration and transfer, ranging from liaison offices, cross-firm project groups, process integrators (e.g. project, brand, program, account managers), up to fully integrated departments (Galbraith, 1974; Nadler and Tushman, 1997). Next, standardization of systems refers to the harmonization of information, reporting, and control systems, as well as career incentive systems, and the employment of expert databases to locate knowledge in the new organization (Grimpe, 2007). Finally, process re-design refers to a change within the R&D function as well as to the coordination with other business functions and often involves reorganization at both firms, including for instance centralization of research and technology tasks, or decentralization of development (Grimpe, 2007). Often, process re-design associated with M&As include rationalization processes, i.e. the closing of R&D departments or research sites (Cassiman *et al.*, 2005; Röller *et al.*, 2006). Moreover, elements of structural linking and systems standardization are often part of a process re-design in R&D, i.e. it would be hard to specialize and consolidate R&D on one site, without applying structural linking and/or systems standardization. Based on 35 M&A cases Grimphe (2007) concluded that structural linking and systems standardization were positively associated with post M&A innovation success. Process re-design, the most far-reaching integration mechanism, may disrupt ongoing R&D so much that innovation synergy is not realized at all. In this respect, it is generally acknowledged in the literature that high levels of integration seem to foster the potential for synergy realization, whereas low levels of integration (a high level of autonomy) are beneficial for not disrupting ongoing innovation activities, especially those of an explorative kind (Puranam *et al.*, 2006; Ranft and Lord, 2002; Schweizer, 2005). Firms that aim to realize innovation synergies in a merger or acquisition, have to cope with this dilemma.

Integration instruments and success factors

Within the PMAI literature there have been several studies examining specific factors and integration instruments associated with successful integration of R&D functions (Wubben *et al.*, 2007). For instance, some studies showed that R&D integration success can be fostered when the PMAI process is extensively planned upfront including R&D integration (e.g. Bannert and Tschirky, 2004; Gerpott, 1995). Next, the speed and timing of PMAI implementation as an important factor for success (e.g. Angwin, 2004; Bakker and Helmink, 2000; Bresman *et al.*, 1999; Homburg and Bucerius, 2006). However, the results regarding speed and timing are ambiguous: some researchers emphasize the importance of doing the integration fast (e.g. Angwin, 2004; Gerpott, 1995), whereas others point at the importance of taking the PMAI process slowly, for instance when the merging firms are very different in terms of management style and corporate culture (Homburg and Bucerius, 2006), or when the intention is to transfer and combine tacit knowledge (Ranft and Lord, 2002). Furthermore, the establishment of a dedicated PMAI team is regarded as an important instrument in the PMAI (Bakker and Helmink, 2000; Epstein, 2004; Gerpott, 1995; Schweiger, 2002). The PMAI team is involved in executing the PMAI process, based on the integration design and integration strategy (Epstein, 2004), so that the ongoing activities of important business functions such as R&D are hindered as little as possible. The next factor is the retention of key employees, as their retention will foster the preservation of the acquired firm's technologies and capabilities that are based on tacit and/or socially complex knowledge (Narin and Breitzman, 1995; Ranft and Lord, 2002). Next, PMAI success can be fostered when the PMAI has a focus on preventing a culture clash in the new organization (Epstein, 2004). Resistance to changes in structure and to the adaptation of different practices and cultures by employees of the firms involved are important obstacles to synergy realization (Birkinshaw *et al.*, 2000; Jemison and Sitkin, 1986; Weber and Camerer, 2003). Finally, open communication at all levels of the organization (e.g. Birkinshaw *et al.*, 2000; Gerpott, 1995), and stimulating interaction between employees by organizing cross-firm teams of managers, joint R&D teams, job rotation, frequent face-to-face meetings, and holding and attending various informal and social events turned out to be important factors for successful innovation integration (Birkinshaw *et al.*, 2000; Bresman *et al.*, 1999; De Noble *et al.*, 1988; Gerpott, 1995; Ranft and Lord, 2002).

5.2.4 Research framework

By integrating the insights from the literature, we can arrive at a research framework for innovation synergy realization in M&As. The main constructs of the framework include (1) M&A context characteristics, (2) R&D integration mechanisms, (3) integration instruments and success factors, and (4) innovation synergy realization. From the literature review we may derive that the first three constructs are all related to innovation synergy realization. However, key in our mode is the assumption that M&A context characteristics, technological relatedness in particular, determine the potential for innovation synergy realization. Based on this synergy potential, specific integration mechanisms are put in place to realize specific

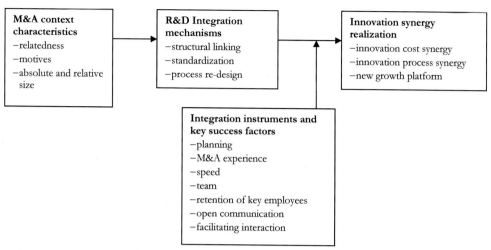

Figure 5.1. Research framework.

innovation synergies. Moreover, whether these integration mechanisms actually lead to synergy realization, depends on the key success factors of the integration process. The framework is presented in Figure 5.1.

5.3 Data and methods

Since the relationship between M&As and innovation performance is a complex one, a detailed empirical research approach is called for. An in-depth and integrated analysis of innovation synergy realization in the context of M&As may add to a better understanding of how M&As are related to innovation performance. Miles and Huberman (1994) suggested that researchers should use qualitative research designs when there is a clear need for deep understanding, local contextualization, causal inference, and exposing the points of view of the people under study. In earlier research on M&As, Larsson and Finkelstein (1999) concluded that investigating a complex and multidimensional process like synergy realization requires rich and extensive data that the case study method can produce. The use of a case study method is in line with several other studies of M&A implementation and PMAI (e.g. Birkinshaw *et al.*, 2000; Ranft and Lord, 2002; Schweizer, 2005). Hence, we opt for a case study method (Yin, 2003) to analyze the types of innovation synergies realized through M&As of R&D intensive firms and the related integration mechanisms and integration instruments.

The sampling of the case studies is crucial, because the choice of sample influences the results of a study (Miles and Huberman, 1994). Eisenhardt (1989) suggest theoretical sampling as a base for case selection in order to focus research efforts in theoretically useful cases. In addition, for reasons of reproducing logic for external validity, the cases should be sufficiently comparable. First, we selected cases within one industry category, the life-science industry. The life-science industry comprises sub-sectors such as agriculture, food processing, agrochemicals, biotech, pharmaceutics, and health and medical systems. Within the life-science industry, we selected companies from medium high-tech and high-tech industries. In (medium) high-tech industries firms typically focus on innovation with substantial levels of R&D activities. Second, we focused on large horizontal M&As. The researched firms, except one, are multi Billion Euro firms and most deal sizes exceeded 0.5 billion Euro. In addition, many of these M&As were subject of investigation by European and US merger regulators. This implies that the acquisitions can be regarded as typical horizontal acquisitions and that they were not marginal but substantial. Especially intra-industry acquisitions seem to be beneficial for innovation synergy realization (Keil *et al.*, 2008). Third, to make sure innovation and R&D was an issue in the M&As, the sample comprises of acquisitions with each of the merging firms having a substantial R&D function. Finally, all the selected M&A cases, except one, were implemented at least three years, but in most cases more than five years ago. This time frame was chosen because it normally takes some time before the innovative advantages of the M&A become evident (Ahuja and Katila, 2001). Selecting M&As with a substantial R&D component, and a time frame of more than 3 years enabled us to identify the integration mechanisms that have resulted in innovation synergies.

Taking into account the aforementioned selection criteria, we further relied on a convenient sampling strategy. One has to realize that the post M&A integration activities and especially the (re) organization of R&D activities are highly sensitive topics that are often the subject of restrictive information policy (Grimpe, 2007). Moreover, firms typically do not want to interfere with ongoing R&D activities. When contacting and informing a substantial number of large life-science firms in high-tech industries in the EU, many firms declined participation, or declined participation in research at the detailed level we aimed for. In total 5 firms were willing to participate, through which we gained access to 10 M&As. Most acquisitions exceeded €1 Billion deal size (see Table 5.1). The smallest acquisition had a deal size of about €110 Million, the largest was larger than €15 Billion in size. The 10 high-tech M&As selected were from life-science sectors ranging from agro chemicals, and pharmaceuticals, to medical systems. It turned out that the generally perceived overall success of the M&A cases differs between moderately successful to very successful. In each of these successful M&As at least to some extent innovation benefits were achieved as a result of the M&A. We were able to investigate both 3 isolated acquisitions, and two series of acquisitions carried out by individual firms. Including series of acquisitions in this study enabled the researcher to identify how a firm learns from its experience in other M&As. The first series was over a six-year period and the second was in a shorter period. In this second series, much of the PMAI of the

Table 5.1. Overview of the merger and acquisition cases.

M&A	Deal size	Industry	Year of transaction	M&A status 2008	Interviews
Case 1a	€7.3 billion	Agricultural chemicals	2001	Firm successfully integrated	2
Case 1b	€2.3 billion	Health care	2004	Firm successfully integrated, even better and faster than expected	1
Case 1c	€16 billion	Pharmaceutics	2006	Firm successfully integrated	2
Case 2	Merger (combined sales >€20 billion)	Pharmaceutics	2000	Firms successfully integrated, but in the beginning PMAI looked a disaster	4
Case 3	€2.3 billion	Food ingredients and fine chemicals	2002	Firm successfully integrated and is an independent division	2
Case 4a	€2.0 billion	Health industry	2001	Firm successfully integrated, forming a BU[1] with 4c	6 *
Case 4b	€1.2 billion	Health industry	2001	Firm successfully integrated, forming a BU[1] with 4d	5 *
Case 4c	€0.7 billion	Health industry	1998	Firm successfully integrated at the level of sales and business (service) systems, like IT, finance and logistics	5 *
Case 4d	€0.5 billion	Health industry	2000	Firm successfully integrated at the level of sales, other business remained autonomous	6 *
Case 5	€0.11 billion	Chemicals and life sciences	2004	Acquired firm still running as an independent division, but now increased linking and interaction	2

* In total 8 interviews carried out in firm 4, which covered the total set of acquisitions. The minimum coverage per M&A was five interviews.
[1] Business Unit.

individual M&As was part of an overall integration process as the firms were integrated almost simultaneously[13].

Before we started investigating the cases, we carried out 6 pilot interviews with M&A experts (consultancy and academic experts) in order to test and adapt our a priori research framework and subsequent interview questions. These interviews focused on the motives of M&As, the possible impact of M&As on post M&A innovation performance, and the post M&A integration process of R&D.

To investigate the M&As, we carried out 21 semi-structured in-depth interviews, with both innovation managers, integration managers, and general managers. These managers had sufficient seniority to have a profound knowledge of the PMAI and they were often knowledgeable about more than one M&A in the set. A list of the main questions used in the interviews can be found in Appendix 4. The interviews, typically taken by two interviewers from the research team, lasted for 1 to 2 hours and were recorded and fully transcribed to capture subtleties in the qualitative data. Transcripts were offered to the interviewees for review. Transcripts were analyzed through cyclic reading and rereading. Although most interviews concentrated on one specific acquisition case, often comparison with, and illustrations from other acquisitions were provided. One possible weakness in the design is that respondents have to report on actions and processes that took place a number of years ago, which could lead to the problem that informants may not be able to recall the past, that informants try to present a socially desirable picture of themselves or the firm, or that informants distort information to fit previously held beliefs and preferences (Miller *et al.*, 1997; Schmidt and Calantone, 1998). On the other hand, taking a time lag will reduce direct stakes in M&As, which can make interviewees more reflective and open minded. Furthermore, in order to improve the internal validity we used triangulation in sources and methods as we collected other data, such as annual reports, articles from the business and trade press, press releases and internal documents (e.g. presentation slides), which stemmed mainly from the period of M&A announcement and implementation. The analysis of the various data sources resulted in the identification of the M&A context characteristics, a detailed picture of the PMAI (in terms of integration mechanisms and the key success factors) and, finally the innovation synergies, which are the main constructs of our conceptual model that formed the basis for the within- and cross-case analysis. Then, for each M&A case a detailed within-case description was developed. After this, for the cross-case analysis we utilized a matrix technique for comparative analysis (Miles

---

[13] It should be noted that one acquisition within this second series was left out the analysis. In this acquisition, the acquirer managed to acquire only 70% of the shares. As a consequence, the acquirer could not start the intended integration and subsequent innovation synergies were not realized. Moreover, employees from the target were very resistant to the (perceived) hostile takeover. Together with some additional (legal) problems with the acquired firm (that were unrelated to the acquisition) this situation caused that acquirer to divest the firm in 2008, resulting in substantial depreciations. As a consequence, this acquisition did not deliver any useful information for our analysis of how innovation synergies are realized in terms of integration mechanisms and integration instruments.

and Huberman, 1994). The resulting matrices allowed visual identification of differences and similarities in the cases.

In our study we concentrate specifically on the role of technological relatedness in, and on the R&D integration mechanisms responsible for innovation synergy realization in large horizontal (medium) high-tech M&As. As we will see in the next section, such M&As are by definition large in terms of absolute and relative size (in contrast with small acquisitions of, for instance, biotech companies). Moreover, in such large M&As, innovation and/or access to new knowledge is often one of the motives for the merger or acquisition. As a consequence, we found these M&A context characteristics were neutral in our study, whereas technological relatedness will be a key variable in which the cases differ substantially.

5.4 Results

5.4.1 M&A context characteristics

In detailing the methods and data (see Section 5.3) a number of general attributes of the M&As were already provided (see also Table 5.1). In this section, we set the scene of the analysis in more detail by discussing the most relevant M&A context characteristics: M&A motives, relative and absolute size, relatedness and M&A experience.

M&A motives

The first M&A context characteristic in our study was the M&A motives. Initial questions asked in each interview were used to identify the prime motives of the M&As. The motives stated by the interviewees were compared with the objectives stated in the annual reports and official press releases of the firms. The most prominent motives for the M&As in our study turned out to be strategic repositioning of the business, access to new markets, and completing the product portfolio (see Table 5.2). Improving R&D, enhancing innovation or access to knowledge and technologies were mentioned in six cases as an important motive for the acquisition. Especially in the M&As from sectors in which the costs to develop innovations are enormous (e.g. pharma and agricultural chemicals), lowering the (relative) costs of R&D by increasing the scale and scope and by improving R&D productivity were important drivers for the M&As. In the cases that did not explicitly mention innovation enhancement in the initial M&A announcements (e.g. in press releases), the interviews and/or additional documentation clarified that innovation enhancement was or became a relatively important aspect of the M&A. For instance, for firm 4, it was a precondition for the acquisitions that the target firms had a high-end R&D-function. In general, innovation enhancement was an important aspect in the 11 cases, though not the dominant motive, which is in line with previous studies (e.g. Cassiman et al., 2005). As a consequence, we can conclude that each of the M&As has the potential for innovation synergy realization.

Table 5.2. M&A context characteristics.

Case	Formal motives for merger or acquisition	Technological relatedness	Market relatedness[1]	Relative size[2]
Case Ia	Access to new markets; towards more complete product portfolio; increase R&D scope	high	3-digit	equal
Case Ib	Towards more complete product portfolio; better regional coverage in markets; increase R&D scope	high	3-digit	equal
Case Ic	More balanced product portfolio; better filled new product pipeline, improve R&D productivity; increase R&D scope	high	3-digit	equal
Case 2	To anticipate rapid advances in science and technology (increase R&D scope); increase market power	high	3-digit	equal
Case 3	Strategic repositioning, access to new markets / business; increase R&D scope	moderate	3-digit	medium
Case 4a	Expanding product portfolio; entering new markets	moderate	3-digit	medium
Case 4b	Expanding technology and product portfolio; establishing new market positions	moderate	3-digit	medium
Case 4c	Expanding technology and product portfolio; establishing new market positions	low	3-digit	medium
Case 4d	Expanding product portfolio; increase customer bases	low	3-digit	medium
Case 5	Access to new markets; access to R&D resources	low	3-digit	medium

[1] NACE classification: The EC statistical office (Eurostat) classification scheme of economic activities. SBI is the Dutch equivalent for NACE. For instance, within the 2-digit sector 'production of chemical products' there are several 3-digit sectors, such as 'production of agricultural chemicals' (242) and 'pharmaceutics' 244.
[2] Equal relative size indicates a sales ratio of >70% at the time of the deal. Medium refers to a sales ratio of between 10% and 70%.

Absolute and relative size

The second and third M&A context characteristics are absolute and relative size. With respect to absolute size, it was already stated in Section 5.3 that our sample comprises of relatively large M&As, especially when compared to existing studies on acquisition implementation (e.g. Gerpott, 1995; Ranft and Lord, 2002; Schweizer, 2005). Only Case 5 is substantially smaller than the others (see Table 5.1), although still exceeding €100 Million in deal size. Moreover, considering the fact that we investigated M&As in (medium) high-tech life science, in which innovation plays a substantial role, the M&As involved large knowledge bases.

In our assessment of relative size we have concentrated on the size of the acquired firm relative to the related division of the acquirer, rather than to the total acquiring firm. The reason for this is that in fact, most M&As did not affect other business units or divisions of the acquirer. Cases 1a, 1b, 1c, and 2 were more or less equal in size in terms of sales (see Table 5.2). The size in terms of the total sales of these acquired firms was at least 10% of that of the acquiring or other firm. In comparison with other studies using relative size as an indicator (e.g. Ahuja and Katila, 2001; Cloodt *et al.*, 2006; Gerpott, 1995), our sample comprises of large relative sized M&As. Taking the learning from the literature study, we can conclude that the (medium) high-tech M&As in this study are large in terms of absolute and relative size, so that relatively large knowledge bases are acquired, and that the M&A and PMAI have a relatively large impact on the acquiring firm. In addition, as the set of M&As are relatively similar in terms of size, the involved firms should be relative compatible in terms of organizational fit. In that respect, our sample differs from samples in other studies that typically include small acquisitions and absorption integration (e.g. Puranam *et al.*, 2006; Ranft and Lord, 2002; Schweizer, 2005).

Relatedness

The third M&A context characteristic in this study is relatedness. In line with previous studies (see Section 5.2.2), we concentrate on market and technological relatedness. In order to determine the market-relatedness of the M&As, we have looked at the NACE sector classification. In all cases, the involved firms were operating in the same sector at 3-digit level (see Table 5.2), so they can be classified as horizontal M&As. In that sense, most M&As involved the combination of rivals. However, during the interviews it became apparent that, although the firms were operating in the same (3-digit) markets, most of the products were not direct competitors. This was further demonstrated by the fact that although about half of the M&As were subject to in-depth investigations by anti-trust authorities in the EU, only in four M&As did some products have to be divested. The impact of these divestments were relatively small on average (except for Case 2, in which the product divestments amounted to €0.4 billion turnover, which is still relatively little compared to the business sizes of the merging firms). In addition, with some M&As the involved firms were active with similar products, but in different regions. Since high market-relatedness was positively associated with post-acquisition performance of firms (Hagedoorn and Duysters, 2002a; Keil *et al.*, 2008), we may expect that the cases in our sample may potentially realize innovation synergies.

Interestingly, there was substantially more variation with respect to technological relatedness (see Table 5.2). It should be noted that it can be difficult to determine the level of technological relatedness between two large firms involved in a merger or acquisition, because these large firms from (medium) high-tech industries are often specialized in a number of technological areas simultaneously. During the interviews we discussed the most important technological areas and R&D trajectories of the involved firms. Similar to the research by Cassiman *et al.* (2005), we cross-checked this interview information against publicly available information, and had our research team resolving any conflict through careful re-examination of the available information. Nevertheless, it was not possible to eliminate all subjectivity in determining the technological relatedness, although we are, as Cassiman *et al.* (2005), quite confident that the information we used is more reliable than the variables based on quantitative data, like patents. Examples of technological areas and R&D trajectories are magnetic resonance imaging and drug development in oncology respectively. Although the firms involved in the Cases 1a, 1b, 1c and 2, were specialized in specific technologies, in general many of the technologies in place were strongly related – though not comparable. Moreover, the innovation processes in those firms were organized in a relatively similar way, which can point to high internal relatedness (Homburg and Bucerius, 2006). Therefore, these cases were categorized as M&As with a relatively high technological relatedness. In the Cases 3, 4a and 4b a substantial part of the technologies were completely new for the acquirer. There was only substantial overlap in a specific technological field. Consequently, these cases were categorized as M&As with moderate technological relatedness. Finally, in comparison with the other cases, Cases 4c-d and 5 showed the lowest level of technological relatedness. For instance, with the acquisitions of 4c and 4d firm 4 acquired technologies that were almost completely new to them. In one technological area, firm 4 had some related technologies at its disposal, but these were not as advanced as those of the acquired firm 4c. For the acquiring firm in Case 5, innovation mainly concerned process innovation, dominated by engineers, and focused on cost efficiency to serve the commodity market. In contrast, the acquired firm had a strong innovation center oriented at developing new technologies to serve the high-end markets. In that respect, R&D and the technological knowledge possessed by the two firms were relatively unrelated. Consequently, Cases 4c, 4d and 5 were categorized as M&As of low technological relatedness.

On the matter of relatedness we can conclude that, although in all cases the firms involved were active in the same 3-digit markets, in terms of technological-relatedness, the firms involved sometimes differed significantly, and our sample shows substantial variation.

5.4.2 Post M&A integration

Corporate and integration approach

The M&As in this study show substantial variety with respect to the corporate integration approach (Haspeslagh and Jemison, 1991) and the general R&D integration approach. It appeared that 4 cases (1a-c, 2) can be characterized as a merger of equals and as a symbiosis integration (with related division). Cases 1a-c were actually acquisitions (only Case 2 was a formal merger of equals), although the M&A was only relevant for a related division. At the divisional level, these acquisition could be better characterized as mergers. In these cases, substantial levels of organizational integration were realized, with the new organization (or division) drawing from the 'best of both worlds'. Case 5 can be best described as a sequence of a preservation and symbiosis integration. The acquired firm was initially kept as a separate division (preservation), with only specific functions, such as finance, sales and IT being slowly harmonized and integrated with the dominant firm. With Case 3, the integration approach was activity specific. A new division was created, comprising predominantly of the newly acquired business, although certain parts of the target were fully absorbed by the acquirer. For the four acquisitions of Firm 4 (Cases 4a-d), which involved one division and which occurred in a relatively short time period, a 4-fold integration approach was used, starting right after the final acquisition (Case 4b). The marketing and sales departments of the four firms were integrated (centralized) with that of the related division, as well as some other business functions such as Human Resources and IT. For R&D, however, a different integration approach was used (see next paragraph).

It should be noted that due to the integration in other business functions, especially in sales and marketing, innovations were introduced on the target's market and vice versa. This was, for instance, relevant in the cases where the merging firms had been active in geographically separate markets (e.g. Case 1b, Case 5, Cases 4b, 4c and 4d). As a result, by combining each other's markets, there was a larger customer base that could be served with the same innovation. This type of economy of scale can be realized when the given cost for an innovation can be spread over a larger sales base (Cassiman *et al.*, 2005; Cockburn and Henderson, 2001). The respondents perceived this type of synergy more as a market/sales synergy, as it was not specifically the result of integration within the R&D functions, but in sales and marketing.

R&D integration approach

In 5 cases (Cases 1a, 1b, 1c, 2 and 3) the idea was to integrate and link the R&D functions of the organizations involved, because from the start the intention was to achieve synergistic gains in R&D. In contrast, in three cases (Case 4a combined with Case 4c, and Case 5) the idea was to keep the acquired R&D autonomous and separate from the acquirer's R&D. The primary reason for doing so was that the acquiring firm did not want to intervene in the ongoing R&D activities. In fact, after the acquisition of Case 4c, which was technologically moderately related

Table 5.3. Key findings with respect to R&D integration mechanisms and innovation synergies.

Case	Technological relatedness	Main R&D integration mechanisms
Case 1a	High	Re-design of R&D, focused on specialization and eliminating duplicate R&D Integration at the department level (physically) Standardization in R&D practices going in both directions incorporating best of both worlds
Case 1b	High	Region-driven re-design of R&D, specialization / consolidation of R&D at 2 sites Gradual change of the (R&D) organization structure Standardization in R&D incorporating best of both worlds
Case 1c	High	Re-design of R&D, specialization and consolidation of R&D to 3 sites Elimination of (many) duplicate jobs and innovation trajectories, mainly in research (limited at development) Integration at the department level (physically) Standardization incorporating best of both worlds
Case 2	High	Complete re-design of R&D, specialization into 6 dedicated entrepreneurial research centers Duplicate R&D eliminated (projects stopped) Integration at the department level (physically and virtually) and virtually integrated teams, cross departmental Standardization incorporating best of both worlds
Case 3	Medium	Department level integration only for new R&D areas Ongoing R&D stayed separate (preservation) Impose best practices in R&D (management) of acquirer to the target's ongoing R&D (new organizational structure, more business driven, also new approach in R&D in target) Employees (mainly management) from acquirer to target
Case 4a	Medium	Standardization of (innovation) management (systems and reporting) Integration of R&D with the (related) 4c R&D (integrated management team (with 4c), single design manager, and employee exchange Adoption of project management from acquirer to target R&D budget of acquired BU's directed to central Research Duplicate R&D activities were stopped

Innovation synergies

Lower innovation costs through cuts in R&D
More efficient and effective innovation process, through mutual exchange of best practices and tools
New breakthrough products resulting from combined technologies
New product/market combinations
Increased critical mass for structural R&D

More critical mass for structural R&D
Benefit from combining capabilities for marketing innovations and product innovations
Some innovation cost synergies

Lower innovation costs through cuts in R&D
More critical mass for R&D
Streamlined R&D, mainly in basic research

Significant cost savings due to cuttings in duplicate R&D
Substantial increase in the productivity in R&D
New innovation trajectories by combining knowledge and by more critical mass in R&D

More effective and efficient innovation process at target (more innovation-driven organization)
New R&D set up in new technological areas based on combining knowledge

Some (minor) innovation cost synergies by eliminating duplicate R&D activities
Exchange of state-of-the-art technologies resulted in improved products
Incremental and breakthrough innovations realized by combining knowledge

Table 5.3. Continued.

Case	Technological relatedness	Main R&D integration mechanisms
Case 4b	Medium	Standardization of (innovation) management (systems and reporting) Parts of R&D combined with 4d to one site Integrated R&D managers Some NPD team-level integration In a later stage, integration with corporate research of the acquirer
Case 4c	Low/medium	Initial preservation of the acquired R&D functions, only 'quick win' integration efforts Standardization of (innovation) management (systems and reporting) A small amount of duplicate R&D was stopped on the side of the acquirer After acquisition 4a: R&D budget of acquired BU's directed to corporate research of acquirer After the acquisition of case 4a, formal integration efforts in R&D with 4a to form a separate R&D organization R&D employees looking beyond their BU (across former firm boundaries) for solutions Focus on standardization of terminology and reporting in R&D, not specifically on the actual R&D practices Exchange of several state-of-the-art technologies, and re-design and standardization of products
Case 4d	Low	Initial preservation of the acquired R&D functions, only 'quick win' integration efforts Standardization of (innovation) management (systems and reporting) After acquisition 4b: R&D symbiotically integrated with 4b: integrated R&D management, and cross-company development groups Partial R&D integration with corporate research of acquirer – through an integrated management team R&D budget of acquired BU's directed to corporate research of the acquirer Focus on standardization of terminology and reporting in R&D, not specifically on the actual R&D practices Exchange of several state-of-the-art technologies, and redesign /standardization of products
Case 5	Low	Initial preservation of the acquired R&D functions. Only linking at the level of the top R&D management (one cross-company R&D manager) In a later stage (3 years), cross-company R&D teams formed After 3 years acquirer started to slowly adopt the R&D structure of the target and innovation management best practices were transferred from target to acquirer

Innovation synergies

Minor innovation cost synergies by eliminating some overlap in R&D
Improvement of quality of existing products due to complementary skills in R&D
Exchange of state-of-the-art technologies resulted in improved products
New innovation trajectories have been started up, using the combined know-how, which resulted in unique new products

Some (minor) innovation cost synergies by eliminating duplicate R&D activities
The exchange of state-of-the-art in technologies resulted in improved products with substantially more sales
New innovation trajectories by combining knowledge

The exchange of state-of-the-art in technologies resulted in improved products

Breakthrough innovations realized by combining knowledge, and by overcoming a threshold in R&D

Limited innovation cost synergies
More structured and effective R&D process and shorter time to market on acquirer side

to Case 4a, the R&D of Case 4a and Case 4c integrated and formed an autonomous R&D function. Similarly, after the acquisition of Case 4d, which was technologically moderately related to Case 4b, R&D integration of Case 4b and Case 4d took place, and was slowly integrated with Firm 4's corporate research. In some interviews (e.g. in Case 5) it was also stated that there was no initial awareness of any synergy potential in R&D, which would make integration unnecessary. There, the only integration aimed for was a little standardization of some innovation (management) practices and information and control systems.

5.4.3 Integration mechanisms

In the interviews a great deal of the focus was on the PMAI of the R&D functions, more specifically on the actual integration mechanisms at place, and on innovation synergy realization. Information on PMAI of the R&D functions is typically not available or only to a limited extent in more general company documents, such as annual reports. Table 5.3 summarizes the main R&D integration mechanisms and innovation synergies realized in the cases. In Section 5.2.3 we identified 3 general integration mechanisms relevant for R&D integration: i.e. structural linking, standardization of systems, and process redesign. We will first discuss the most far-reaching integration mechanism, i.e. process re-design, followed by structural linking and standardization of systems.

First we describe the process re-design in the R&D functions. In general, we found that in the M&As with high technological relatedness the most far-reaching R&D integration took place, which could be characterized as an intense re-design of the R&D process. In Cases 1a, 1b, 1c, 2 and 3 the focus in PMAI was to increase specialization. For instance, in Case 1a R&D was re-located in such a way that each remaining location would host one area of R&D (related to one business unit). A central issue in the PMAI in Case 1a was where to place Development. In the acquired company, Development was part of Marketing, whereas in the acquiring company, Development was part of Research. Initially, Development became a separate function, but later it was integrated in the research function. In Case 2, new specialized, de-centralized research units were created. The research units were supposed to organize the efforts of the more than 20 R&D sites across the globe, to work semi-autonomously and compete to attract financial resources from the head office and internal users. The research units were established to balance the small and large areas of research operations in order to enhance the productivity and output of R&D. The idea was to keep the research units small enough to be creative and innovative, without the dead-weight associated with the bureaucracy of a large company. In Case 3, a new department for R&D in new business areas was created, in which the two companies had related activities, combining their knowledge in that new business area in order to specialize on that subject.

Apart from specialization, another important aspect of process re-design is rationalization. In five cases rationalization processes took place, in the form of closing R&D sites or departments (especially in Cases 1a, 1c, and 2), stopping innovation trajectories/projects or firing employees (e.g. Cases 1a, 1c, 2, 4a, 4c). For instance, in Case 1c a number of research sites were closed, as R&D was consolidated in 3 remaining locations. Interestingly, in Case 4c, the (small amount of) related R&D activities at the acquirer were completely terminated and some R&D employees were transferred to the acquired firm. In contrast, in the cases with low technological relatedness, process re-design was not an issue, as there were no or hardly any integration efforts focused at specialization or rationalization (e.g. Cases 4d and 5). This finding is consistent with the study of Cassiman *et al.* (2005), who also linked a high technological relatedness with rationalization processes. Finally, the momentum of the M&A was often used to evaluate and re-assess the total innovation portfolio in order to scrap less promising projects, and reposition more promising projects (e.g. in Cases 1a, 1b, 1c, 2 and 3). Especially in Case 2, this type of assessment had led to a major short-term drop in pipeline projects.

Interestingly, the results teach us that technological relatedness appeared to be associated with the focus in the R&D integration. The data suggests that especially with M&As with a high level of technological relatedness, there will be substantial technological overlap and therefore much potential for cutting duplicate R&D, further specialization, and re-prioritization. M&As with high levels of technological relatedness show the most far reaching forms of integration, at the level of the department. It seems that such M&As consolidate their R&D activities into a smaller number of R&D sites, often specialized in a particular technological area. These integration mechanisms are typical examples of process re-design. With M&As with moderate and especially M&As with low technological relatedness, R&D integration is not, or is to a much lesser extent focused on process re-design. Accordingly, we formulate the following proposition:

Proposition 1a
P1a: With a high level of technological relatedness, R&D integration is focused on process re-design.

In addition, M&As with a high level of technological relatedness and a focus on process re-design in R&D integration, seem to have realized the most apparent innovation cost synergies. Indeed, with regard to innovation cost synergy, our analysis (see Table 5.3) revealed that especially Cases 1a, 1b, 1c, and 2 reported significant innovation related cost savings. Some of these cases showed that innovation-related cost savings were transferred to other (new) innovation programs. In Case 1a, for instance, innovation cost savings due to elimination of overlap in R&D were used to increase the R&D budget in other areas. This was also evident in Case 2. In this way, cost savings may bring the firms on the road to new innovations that would have been out of reach without the M&A. Cases with a moderate level of technological relatedness also identified some innovation cost synergy, but in general to a lesser extent. Apparently, innovation cost savings are most likely to be realized when there is a strong relatedness between the two firms (Cassiman *et al.*, 2005). Moreover, the M&As with a high level of technological relatedness also demonstrated that they had realized innovation process synergies, mainly as a result of the process re-design (see Table 5.3) and standardization efforts as part of the process re-design. In 4 cases (i.e. Case 1a, 1b, 1c and 2), the process re-design in

R&D was set up to utilize the best R&D competences from both sides in the new combined R&D function. Thus, the process re-designs in those cases were typically a form of symbiotic integration.

Finally, we were also able to identify a number of new growth platforms in the M&As with a high level of technological relatedness (Cases 1a, 1b, 1c, and 2), especially as a result of reaching a threshold level in R&D. Apparently, process re-design is an integration mechanism that potentially leads to different innovation synergies.

Proposition 1b
P1b: Process re-design in R&D integration enables innovation cost synergy, innovation process synergy, and new growth platforms.

Second, we detail the structural linking identified in the cases. In each of the cases some kind of structural linking took place (see Table 5.3), although in the Cases 4c and 4d structural linking took place only after an initial preservation until the acquisitions of Cases 4a and 4b, and in Case 5 no structural linking took place initially either. Structural linking occurred at different levels in the organization. The most far-reaching level of structural integration identified was the permanent integration at the department level. In Cases 1a, 1c, 2, 3 and 4b at least a number of R&D departments were integrated. Whereas in most cases, departments were integrated and consolidated at one site, in Case 3 the integration was primarily virtual organizational. In other cases, structural linking took place primarily by means of integration at the R&D management level (Case 1b, 4a, 4b, 4c, 4d and 5). Furthermore, in some cases cross-company R&D teams were formed (Case 5 after 3 years, and 4b). Another form of structural integration identified in the cases was the re-allocation of (some) R&D budget from the acquired business to the acquirer's corporate research (Cases 4a,b,d,e). In doing so, the acquired businesses could determine research directions at acquiring company's research facility for parts of the research originally carried out within the acquired business. Although this integration mechanism was initially received with skepticism by the acquired firms' managers, it did facilitate integration and cooperation between the different R&D functions. Finally, in some cases there was sufficient freedom created for employees to move through the new organization, crossing the original organizational boundaries, in order to find solutions.

In the M&As with moderate technological relatedness, several forms of structural linking could be identified for those cases, whereas process re-design only took place to a limited extent. Moreover, in M&As with moderate levels of technological relatedness, integration mainly occurred at the R&D management level, or only for the real related technological areas at the level of the R&D department. In the latter case (e.g. Case 3), unrelated R&D of the acquired firm stayed separate from the acquirer's R&D. In M&As with low technological relatedness, there was only limited (or only in a later stage) focus at structural linking

Proposition 2a

P2a: With a moderate level of technological relatedness, R&D integration is focused on structural linking.

Interestingly, when evaluating the innovation synergies for the M&As with moderate technological relatedness, two types of innovation synergy dominate (see Table 5.3). First, structural linking (e.g. at the R&D management level) facilitated the exchange in best practices in R&D management, and of state-of-the-art technologies, which resulted in incremental innovations (e.g. Cases 3, 4a, and 4b) and a more effective innovation process (e.g. Case 3). In such cases, existing products from one firm could relatively easily be improved by incorporating the technologies from the other firm. Second, structural linking enabled combining knowledge and technologies in a new growth platform, leading to breakthrough innovations (see Table 5.3). Apparently, structural linking is an integration mechanism that facilitates innovation process synergy and new growth platforms. In contrast, innovation cost synergy could not specifically be linked to structural linking. Hence, we arrive at the following proposition:

Proposition 2b

P2b: Structural linking enables innovation process synergy and new growth platforms.

The third integration mechanism was the standardization of systems, e.g. the harmonization of information, reporting, and control systems. In the cases of more symbiotic-type integration, (R&D) systems standardization typically was an integrated part the process re-design, and was based on the best of both worlds (e.g. Cases 1a, 1b, 1c, 2). In other cases, system standardization was primarily a one-way street (e.g. Cases 3, 4a,b,c,d, and 5). Interestingly, whereas process re-design and structural linking occurred either not at all or only to a limited extent in the M&As with low technological relatedness, a minimum level of R&D integration was identified in the form of standardization of R&D management practices and systems. Such a type of integration can be regarded as preservation, followed (some years later) by slow symbiotic integration efforts. Consequently, we arrive at the following proposition:

Proposition 3a

P3a: With a low level of technological relatedness, R&D integration will initially be of a preservation type, and is focused on standardization of management and systems.

In addition, it seems that standardization of systems by itself, does not lead to concrete innovation synergies. The M&As with low levels of technological relatedness show, despite standardization efforts, no deliberate synergy seeking. Although substantial synergies were realized in other business functions (e.g. in sales and marketing), within R&D this was not or hardly the case. Nevertheless, Table 5.3 shows that there are a number of innovation synergies for the cases with low technological relatedness, but these innovation synergies were the results of more far-reaching integration efforts, i.e. occasional structural linking, mainly realized at a later stage (e.g. an integrated R&D manager in Case 5, who started to transfer the R&D

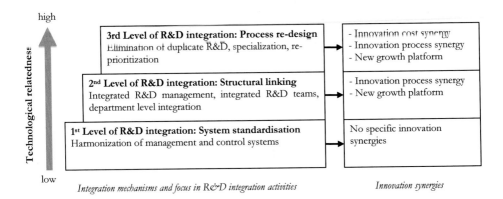

Figure 5.2. Post M&A Integration framework: a dedicated model for innovation synergy realization.

organizational structure from the acquired firm to the acquirer after a number of years). Consequently, we arrive at the following proposition:

Proposition 3b
P3b: Systems standardization does not enable significant innovation synergies.

5.4.4 Towards a R&D integration framework

Combining the results from the former sub-section on integration mechanisms leads to a Post M&A Integration framework for innovation synergy realization (see Figure 5.2). The results of the case studies suggest that within R&D integration three generic levels of integration can be distinguished. Depending on the level of technological relatedness, different integration mechanisms and related R&D activities are carried out. Finally, depending on the level of technological relatedness and the subsequent integration mechanisms, different types of innovation synergy are realized.

The first level of R&D integration encompasses the standardization of systems such as information, reporting, and control system, and is applied even in most M&As with low technological relatedness. In such situations, which are often acquisitions, R&D of the acquired business is preserved, while the acquiring firm imposes its systems on the acquired firm. It should be noted, however, that in our study, the M&As with low technological relatedness could not be classified as a preservation or holding (c.f. Haspeslagh and Jemison) entirely. In the M&As with low technological relatedness many of the other business functions became much more integrated (in contrast to the R&D function), which would be in line with a hybrid integration approach (Schweizer, 2005), identified for the specific situation of relatively small biotech acquisitions by large pharmaceutical corporations. This hybrid integration approach distinguishes between R&D and non-R&D-related business functions and suggests more autonomy for more specific biotech R&D, and more integration for more common biotech R&D, as well as other business functions (Schweizer, 2005). Finally, standardization of systems by itself should not be regarded as an integration mechanism leading to innovation synergies, although it can be seen as a prerequisite or key success factor for integration success (Grimpe, 2007).

The second level of R&D integration involves elements of the first level integration, although here it goes further with structural linking up to the level of an integrated R&D management team, or one cross-company R&D manager. In this way, R&D units are being linked so that knowledge and technologies can be exchanged. Management integration is often succeeded by cross-company teams focused on developing a new technology, drawing from the complementary knowledge residing in both original firms. This form of structural linking can be especially useful in M&As characterized by partially overlapping and complementary R&D, and partially unrelated R&D, which can remain autonomous, so that ongoing unrelated R&D activities are harmed as little as possible. Finally, structural linking is linked to innovation process synergy and new growth platforms, and not innovation cost synergy.

The third and most far-reaching form of R&D integration is process re-design, i.e. a substantial and disruptive re-organization at the R&D department level. This level of integration also includes the elements of the first two levels of R&D integration, but now includes consolidation and specialization. Especially in the M&As with high technological relatedness, there seems to be great potential for consolidation and rationalization processes. Duplicate or overlapping R&D is reduced for the sake of cost benefits, or re-allocated to other and/or new technological areas. This process leads to increased specialization and enables firms to increase the scale and scope of R&D, so that it reaches a threshold level for e.g. fundamental research or for new large and risky projects. Finally, process re-design can be linked to each form of innovation synergy.

It was also found that as integration moves from the first level towards the 3rd level, integration will become a more two-way process (i.e. symbiosis), utilizing the best practices and state-of-the-art technologies from both sides. In addition, process re-design in particular encompasses disruptive changes in the R&D function and organizational trauma, which may hamper ongoing innovation activities. Consequently, although process re-design may bring innovation synergies, it may also have a negative impact on the innovation capacity. This may be reflected in the inverted u-shape relationship between technological relatedness and post M&A innovation performance, found in a number of studies (e.g. Ahuja and Katila, 2001; Cloodt et al., 2006). Whereas in these studies this finding is attributed entirely to complementarity as a pre-requisite for innovation synergies, our findings suggest that an inverted u-shape relationship can be caused by the intensity in R&D integration, which is in turn caused by the technological relatedness.

5.4.5 Integration instruments and success factors in PMAI

Although it was not the prime focus in this study, in the interviews with integration and R&D managers we came across a number of factors and integration instruments that moderated the relation between R&D integration and innovation synergy realization, in our research framework labeled integration instruments and key success factors. As these key success factors and integration instruments are of great managerial importance, we will briefly discuss them here.

First of all, in a number of cases with substantial synergy realization (e.g. Cases 1a, 1b, 2 and 3) the respondents emphasized that even before the official deal, extensive data gathering of the target took place and a detailed integration plan was drawn up. Moreover, in these M&As, the management used the time required for the assessments of the anti-trust authorities to make a more detailed PMAI schedule. Officially, at such a stage the exchange of information is restricted to non-sensitive information. Firms typically used third parties (often consultants) and worked with coded information in order to make planning possible, without revealing sensitive information. In Case 1c detailed up-front planning was not possible as the acquiring firm had to act quickly as it came as a white knight after a hostile bid on the target by a competitor. However, as it took some time to squeeze out some last shareholders to reach the required level of acquired shares, PMAI managers could use this period to make an in-depth schedule for the PMAI process.

The second factor was PMAI pace and timing. Following early planning of the PMAI, the focus in the Cases 1a to 3 was on taking PMAI of R&D quickly. However, it should be noted that even in cases with a focus on rapid integration, the PMAI of R&D had a dedicated phasing, more or less independent from the PMAI of other business functions, which is in line with suggestions by earlier studies (e.g. Schweizer, 2005). In other cases (e.g. Cases 4c, 4d and 5), initially no R&D integration took place. Whereas, for instance, finance, sales and IT of Cases 4c and 4d were integrated into the acquirer, management decided not to integrate R&D, for the purpose of not disturbing ongoing R&D activities and to retain the R&D employees. At a (much) later stage, after the acquisitions of 4a and 4b, and when the firms got to know the new business and related R&D better, then attempts (in subsequent PMAI projects) were undertaken to slowly link or integrate the acquired R&D function. However, interviewees stated that the strong delay in R&D integration caused missing opportunities, and that in future they consider starting R&D integration some earlier.

The third key success factor was a dedicated PMAI team. Except for case 5, all M&As had a dedicated PMAI team. Such teams typically consisted of representatives from both sides, and in some cases an R&D representative was included as well.

Fourth, cultural issues dominated a number of M&As, which were tackled by a number of instruments. Although most M&As were international, the main cultural frictions encountered were at corporate level. Firms undertook many actions, such as cultural training to overcome cultural barriers and to build a new corporate culture. Furthermore, interaction between employees from the different firms was enhanced using integration instruments such as exchanging employees (e.g. Cases 1b, 3, 4b, and 5), team building and workshops (e.g. Case 1a) and setting up career paths exceeding the national and firm boundaries (Case 3). These instruments were perceived necessary to build a (new) integrated corporate culture and to satisfy and retain employees.

The fifth factor was communication. Cases 1a, 1b, 1c, 2 and 3 in particular paid a lot of attention to openly communicating about the PMAI process throughout the whole organization. For instance, in Case 1c, the open and positive communication by the top management of the acquired firm helped the employees cope with the new and uncertain situation. In addition, it was stated in the interviews that communication by top management in particular about the PMAI decisions was perceived as positive by the employees. In the four acquisitions of firm 4, communication to lower levels in the organization was delegated to the managers of the business units. The reason was that the perception in those cases was that PMAI was too much top-down organized.

The sixth factor was systematically utilizing and making explicit the experience from previous M&As. In at least 5 cases, the experience with previous M&As was used in tools and guidelines that were adjusted and improved with each subsequent M&A (e.g. cases 1a, 1b, 1c, 2 and 3). Case 3, for instance had been systematically analyzing all acquisitions from the previous 20 years in order to identify lessons learned and best practices. The learning was made explicit in an 'M&A and integration handbook', which includes templates, checklist and other tools for implementing M&As. It was stated in the interviews that this experience was an important factor in the successful and quick integration of Case 3. This finding is in line with what earlier studies suggest, i.e. that routines and practices built up in prior acquisitions can be transferred to subsequent acquisitions (Finkelstein and Haleblian, 2002; Haleblian and Finkelstein, 1999), and that the acquirer must tactically accumulate and explicitly codify acquisition experience in manuals, systems and other acquisition-specific tools (Zollo and Singh, 2004). It thereby conflicts with Gerpott (1995), who found that experience in M&As was detrimental.

A final important factor for the PMAI of R&D is the retention of key employees. Different instruments were used to satisfy and retain the employees. In some M&As the emphasize was on a fair selection of candidates for the new positions, without looking at the original firm (most notably Cases 1a, and 2). Moreover, the perception of fair and equal assessments of personnel was facilitated by having an external organization to do this job (e.g. Cases 1a-c, and 2). Moreover, in Case 2 it was decided to keep as many R&D locations open as possible, in order to retain key personnel. In Cases 4c, 4d and 5, retention of employees was one of the reasons for not integrating the R&D too early. Interestingly, financial rewards were rarely mentioned as a useful instrument to retain employees. Many managers did not believe in financial incentives or stated explicitly that nobody is indispensable.

5.5 Discussion and conclusions

5.5.1 Conclusions

In this study, we sought to understand how innovation synergies are realized in large horizontal M&As. Drawing on the concepts of M&A context characteristics, and the existing literature on post M&A integration, we argued that innovation synergy realization is influenced by the technological relatedness of the combined firms. In line with earlier studies (e.g. Schweizer, 2005), our findings show a clear need for a dedicated integration approach, which goes beyond simply integrating. Our findings suggest that firms in M&As must tailor the integration activities according to the innovation specific synergies sought, which is determined by the level of technological relatedness, a practice also suggested by Cassiman *et al.* (2005). The study links different levels of technological relatedness, with specific R&D integration mechanisms (Propositions 1a, 2a, and 3a), and subsequently with different types of innovation synergy (Propositions 1b, 2b, and 3b).

Furthermore, we identified three types of innovation synergy (innovation cost synergy, innovation process synergy, and new growth platforms) and described a number of integration instruments and other key success factors in the PMAI that may moderate innovation synergy realization through R&D integration. In doing so, we answered RQ4, and answer calls for more research into acquisition implementation and the resource re-allocations that lead to a positive performance of M&As (Capron *et al.*, 1998; e.g. Grimpe, 2007; King *et al.*, 2008).

5.5.2 Implications

The findings from our research amongst 10 large, medium- and high-tech M&As have implications for both research and practice. First of all, our study contributes to the academic debate on the relationship between M&As and innovation performance. Interestingly enough, whereas most of the empirical studies have found a negative or neutral impact of M&As on innovation (De Man and Duysters, 2005), the 10 cases from high-tech industries in our study revealed that various significant innovative gains can be achieved. It should be noted that our sample included (medium) high-tech M&As from life-science industries in which innovation had a certain relevancy. Earlier studies already pointed at a positive impact of M&As on innovation performance in such settings (Ahuja and Katila, 2001; Cloodt *et al.*, 2006).

Second, our study has made more explicit the relationship between M&A context characteristics, most notably technological relatedness, and innovation performance. Earlier studies concentrating on technological relatedness have mainly considered post M&A integration as a black box (Ahuja and Katila, 2001; Cloodt *et al.*, 2006; Keil *et al.*, 2008). Moreover, whereas Cassiman *et al.* (2005) introduced two categories of technological relatedness (i.e. same technological fields versus complementary technological fields), our findings suggest that there are three relevant categories, i.e. high (like same technological fields), moderate (like complementary technological fields) and low technological relatedness (which refers to only limited or no overlap). These three categories each relate to a different focus in the R&D integration process.

Third, our research suggests that studies investigating the impact of M&As on innovation performance should take into account the type of innovation synergies focused at, and their specific (innovation) performance consequences. For instance, innovation cost synergies may lead to reductions in R&D expenditures, but these savings may as well be re-invested in other R&D. In such situations, it is not likely that the overall R&D spending decreases, and hence, it can explain why it is sometimes difficult to quantify innovation cost synergy in M&As (e.g. Cassiman et al., 2005). In addition, researchers focusing on output indicators should be aware of the limitations of patent data in the context of M&As. If researchers use patents as a proxy for innovation performance (e.g. Ahuja and Katila, 2001; Hagedoorn and Duysters, 2002a; Keil et al., 2008), they miss an important attribute of the M&A, which is that innovations (including the ones already in the pipeline) become available for different markets. This diffusion of innovations may be improved primarily by the integration of the marketing and sales functions. Thus, in addition to the new knowledge created due to M&As, M&As are especially useful in increasing the market potential of new technologies as different markets are brought together or completely new markets are created. This is in line with some recent findings that with M&As, marketing and technology resources positively reinforce each other (King et al., 2008). Patents miss this element. Therefore, although patents may function as a good proxy for innovation performance in high-tech sectors (Hagedoorn and Cloodt, 2003), we opt for using indicators that also capture the commercial success of the innovations, such as the shares of sales from innovative products. In doing so, there will be a fairer assessment of the impact of M&As on innovation performance in different technology sectors (e.g. in low tech). The cases also suggest that optimizations in the innovation process (innovation process synergy) lead to quick wins and improved products in the market, which can boost sales of existing products. Again, patents would not capture such innovative gains. Instead, researchers should focus on developments with respect to R&D productivity and innovation lead times (time to market) or on the performance of new and incrementally improved products.

Our findings also have implications for practice. Innovation managers and integration experts alike may benefit from considering more precisely the different types of (innovation) synergy realization, and take the required decisions in order to realize them. Considering the high failure rates of M&A (Cartwright and Schoenberg, 2006; Schenk, 2006), and the seemingly small gains from M&As with respect to innovation (De Man and Duysters, 2005), there seems to be large potential to improve both the pre-M&A decision making and the post-M&A integration process. It is the task of managers *to be as explicit as possible about how, why, and where acquisitions can be reasonably expected to strengthen the firm* (King et al., 2004). Our conceptual model of innovation synergy realization that was depicted in Section 5.4.3 may be a good starting point for managers to develop and implement a dedicated PMAI strategy focused at the R&D function. Depending on the level of technological relatedness, integration managers could opt for different integration mechanisms. In the case of low technological relatedness, it is important not to disturb ongoing R&D activities, and the focus in R&D integration could be on systems standardization only. In the case of moderate relatedness, integration managers should consider which parts to structurally integrate (e.g. by means of an integrated R&D team) so that complementary knowledge can be combined. With high technological relatedness, integration managers might opt for process re-design, which can lead to innovation cost synergy. However, process re-design in particular may disrupt ongoing R&D activities significantly, subsequently leading to decreased innovation performance.

Finally, the cases provided examples of how firms can foster the PMAI process of the R&D function (see Section 5.4.5). For instance, in line with earlier research (e.g. Zollo and Singh, 2004) we found that firms really benefit from the previous M&As experiences in subsequent M&As by using the same (experienced) people in the new PMAI team, developing M&A handbooks and integration templates. Firms that lack this experience may choose not to integrate the R&D functions in the first stage, i.e. initial preservation, or use a so-called 'cool down strategy' (Bakker and Helmink, 2000). In the period of preservation the M&A does not harm or foster innovation and the acquirer can start to learn the acquired business including the R&D function. As time progresses, R&D managers can start to look across the original organizational boundaries and shop on both sides for new solutions, applying a more symbiotic integration approach. However, our results also suggest that acquiring firms should not wait too long with integrating R&D as they miss important opportunities.

5.5.3 Limitations and suggestions for further research

The study presented in this chapter also has a number of limitations. First, due to the small sample size, the generalizability of our findings is limited to large (medium) high-tech M&As in the life-science industry. For example, the extent to which our conceptual model and research propositions hold for smaller M&As (e.g. among medium-sized firms), or in low-tech sectors remains an empirical question. Larger-scale empirical efforts are necessary to statistically assess the relationships presented in our study and may help define the contexts in which these relationships are valid. In addition, although related to this issue, several factors in our research framework (Figure 5.1) were more or less constant for the cases in our study. Whereas our study focused on technological relatedness in particular, further research could concentrate more on (variations in) other context characteristics, most notably relative and absolute size. Relatively small acquisitions in particular may follow an absorption integration approach (Haspeslagh and Jemison, 1991), which was not found in our sample of large M&As.

Second, our study mainly relied on subjective assessments of the innovation synergies and integration mechanisms. Although this may raise questions concerning validity, it should be noted that as far as possible we triangulated our interview findings with formal company documents (e.g. annual reports) and we interviewed at least two managers (except for one case that did not allow us to). In most cases the interviewees represented both original firms, which further enabled us to critically analyze the M&As. Moreover, so far this subjective approach seems to be the only way of getting in-depth information on acquisition implementation and innovation synergy realization (e.g. Cassiman *et al.*, 2005; Grimpe, 2007).

5.5.4 Concluding remarks

With this study, we answered calls for more research into the intersection of M&As and innovation research (e.g. Cassiman *et al.*, 2005), and the impact of acquisition implementation on post M&A innovation performance (Capron *et al.*, 1998; Grimpe, 2007; King *et al.*, 2008). More in-depth investigations in particular were called for, to provide integration managers with more discretion to detail the actual decisions they make and to see how they affect the R&D function (Cassiman *et al.*, 2005; Gerpott, 1995). In summary, we help managers by making more explicit how, why, and where M&A-related synergies can be reasonably expected (King *et al.*, 2004) and by suggesting how to reach these synergies through a structured PMAI process.

6. Discussion and conclusions

In this chapter we will discusses the main findings of the different studies presented in this book. To do so, we recap in Section 6.2 how the studies have answered the research questions and formulate the main conclusions. Next, in Section 6.3 we summarize the main contribution to literature provided in this book. Finally, this chapter closes with Section 6.4 on the managerial implications.

6.1 Main findings and conclusions

The overall objective of this book is *to analyze how firms can profit from external knowledge, by using different knowledge acquisition strategies.* In order to meet this objective we addressed four research questions, which we tried to answer in the Chapters 2 to 5.

Part I presents two quantitative studies on the relevance of external knowledge acquisition for Dutch innovating companies. These studies use data of industrial firms from the Dutch Community Innovation Survey (CIS). The first quantitative study combines data from 5 subsequent surveys covering the period of 1994-2004 to analyze trends with respect to the adoption of open innovation. The second quantitative study is based on a statistical analysis of two Dutch community innovation surveys (CIS), from which we selected a large cross-section from Dutch industry (686 innovating firms) to analyze the impact of different knowledge acquisition strategies on a firm's innovation performance.

In Chapter 2 we have looked at how industrial firms profit from the knowledge and capabilities residing in other organizations. More specifically, we addressed the Research Question 1.

RQ1: To what extent do different types (size and technology classes) of innovating firms pursue an open innovation strategy?

For the Netherlands, we identified a trend that has seen, especially since the turn of the century, an increasing share of innovating firms pursue an open innovation strategy, i.e. using external knowledge acquisition strategies, such as cooperation, outsourcing, and licensing-in (see Figure 6.1, which is based on Table 2.1).

In addition, we found an increase in cooperation for different types of cooperation partners, such as suppliers, customers and research institutes. The most prevalent cooperation partners are actors from within the supply chain, i.e. suppliers and customers. Finally, the results in Chapter 2 show that in the period 2002-2004 on average innovating firms work together with more different innovation partners than in 1994-1996 (see Section 2.4.4, Table 2.3).

We conclude that there is a clear break in the trend in the application of open innovation around the year 2000. Interestingly, our longitudinal analysis showed that low- and medium-

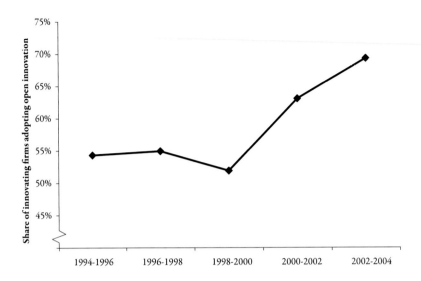

Figure 6.1. Adoption of open innovation in Dutch industry.

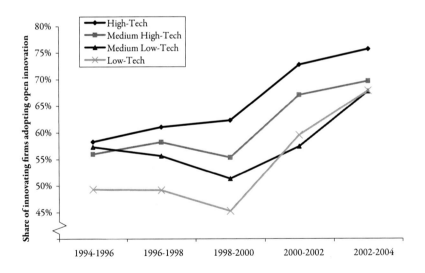

Figure 6.2. Adoption of open innovation in the Netherlands across technology sectors.

tech firms in particular are clearly catching up (see Figure 6.2, which is based on Table 2.1). That open innovation could also become an important strategy for firms residing in low-tech sectors has already been suggested by some qualitative studies (e.g. Chesbrough and Crowther, 2006), but it has never been tested in a large-scale, quantitative study before. Moreover, we concluded in Chapter 2 that SMEs increasingly pursue open innovation strategies. Yet, in general, large firms and firms from high-tech industries are still the most inclined to adopt open innovation strategies.

To answer Research Question 1, we conclude that the different knowledge acquisition strategies associated with open innovation are increasingly practiced, especially since 2000, amongst innovating firms from different size and technology classes. Most notable is the rise in adoption of open innovation strategies by SMEs and by firms from low- and medium-tech industries, and that cooperation has become the dominant open innovation strategy.

Chapter 3 concentrates on the performance consequences of different knowledge acquisition strategies. We concluded in Chapter 2 that open innovation has become more common, but is it also more successful? In Chapter 3 we addressed Research Question 2.

RQ2: What is the impact of different external knowledge acquisition strategies on the short-term and long-term innovation performance of innovative firms?

To answer this question, we first analyzed the impact of licensing-in, outsourcing, cooperation (each open innovation strategies) on the short-term and long-term performance of incremental and radical innovation. We found that firms that acquire knowledge and capabilities from other organizations perform better on innovation than companies that innovate exclusively in-house. More specifically, we found that licensing-in contributes significantly to short-term innovation performance of both incremental and radical innovations, but not to long-term innovation performance. Furthermore, we found that outsourcing has a positive impact on a firm's short-term performance of incremental innovations, and on the long-term performance of incremental, but especially radical innovations. Inter-organizational cooperation was found to have a positive impact on incremental and radical innovation, both in the short and long term. The results suggest that there may be several sub-modes of outsourcing and inter-organizational cooperation that facilitate innovation in different ways. For instance, in the case of outsourcing one strategy may be aimed at quick improvements on existing products (e.g. outsourcing to suppliers), whereas another outsourcing strategy may involve basic research for radical innovation, or monitoring new or emerging technologies (e.g. outsourcing to knowledge institutions).

In addition to the knowledge acquisition strategies associated with open innovation, we then looked at the performance consequences of major firm acquisitions and of in-house innovation. We concluded that the acquisition of a relatively large firm boosts the innovation performance significantly, but only after a substantial number of years. Apparently, it takes considerable time and effort to integrate the acquired firm in such a way that it improves the innovation performance. Several studies (e.g. Ahuja and Katila, 2001; Cloodt *et al.*, 2006; De Man and Duysters, 2005) already suggested that it normally takes considerable time before M&As impact the innovation performance positively. However, the results also indicate that, compared to other knowledge acquisition strategies, in the long run acquisitions have the biggest impact on radical innovation performance. Finally, exclusive in-house innovation turned out to be a sub-optimal strategy, as we found that exclusive in-house innovation had a consistently significant negative impact on the performance of both short and long-term performance of incremental and radical innovation.

In answer to Research Question 2 we conclude that knowledge acquisition strategies associated with open innovation have an overall positive impact on a firm's innovation performance, but that, in contrast to earlier findings, major acquisitions can also be beneficial for improving the innovation performance, though only in the long term. Exclusive reliance on in-house innovation is clearly an sub-optimal strategy for innovating firms.

Part II presents two qualitative studies of knowledge acquisition processes. In Chapter 4 we focus on cooperation processes in open SME innovation networks and asked Research Question 3.

RQ3: How do innovation brokers orchestrate SME innovation networks in the agri-food sector?

We concluded in Chapter 2 that innovating in an open setting is a fairly new phenomenon for SMEs, especially in low-tech sectors. In Chapter 3 we learned that inter-organizational cooperation has a positive impact on innovation performance. For SMEs, however, it can be a major challenge to cope with all the issues stemming from inter-organizational cooperation, such as cultural differences (e.g. between academics/researchers and entrepreneurs), appropriation concerns, motivational problems, leakage of sensitive knowledge, etc. (Caputo *et al.*, 2002; Hoffmann and Schlosser, 2001; Kaufmann and Tödtling, 2002; Van Gils and Zwart, 2004). Drawing from the rich experience of four innovation brokers in the agri-food sector, we substantiated the network orchestration processes that are important for successful innovation of SMEs (see also Figure 4.1 in Section 4.5). First, innovation brokers assist SMEs in the early stage of the innovation project, to develop ideas independently of large institutional actors, and to find complementary partners such as other SMEs, or research institutes. In contrast to an individual SME, an innovation broker can typically draw from a large and diverse network, in order to compose a network of complementary actors. Second, innovation brokers take the lead in setting up appropriate coordination mechanisms to facilitate the inter-organizational cooperation within the new innovation network. Third, innovation brokers often are involved in the network during the whole innovation trajectory, in order to manage the inter-organizational cooperation between the different parties. Especially in the case of conflict between the parties, innovation brokers are of added value in SME innovation networks. Being in a neutral position in an innovation network in which all other parties have a commercial stake, and having ample experience with inter-organizational innovation processes, enables innovation brokers to do so.

To answer Research Question 3, we refer to the above listed network orchestration processes and the illustrations provided in Section 4.4, which provide in-depth insights into best practices of how innovation brokers orchestrate SME innovation networks.

Chapter 5 addresses Research Question 4.

RQ4: What is the role of technological relatedness in realizing innovation synergies in M&As?

In Chapter 3 we concluded that major acquisitions have a positive impact on the long-term performance of radical innovation. In Chapter 5 we analyze *how* major M&As can contribute to innovation performance. To do so, we first conceptualized the M&A derived innovation synergies: innovation cost synergy, innovation process synergy, and new growth platforms. Some earlier studies already pointed at some potential innovative gains from M&As (e.g. Cassiman *et al.*, 2005; Cloodt, 2005; Gerpott, 1995; Grimpe, 2007; Hagedoorn and Duysters, 2002a), but these studies have hardly made explicit how these innovative gains are realized in terms of Post M&A integration (PMAI), and how these synergies are related to different M&A context characteristics. The case studies of large, medium- and high-tech M&As in life-science industries showed that these different innovation synergies are realized in different ways, and that synergy realization is determined by the level of technological relatedness between the involved firms.

The results suggest that depending on the level of technological relatedness, firms apply different integration mechanisms. In highly technological related M&As, firms focus R&D integration on process redesign, i.e. rationalization processes (eliminating duplicate R&D), specialization, and re-prioritizing of innovation projects. Process re-design is associated with each of the three types of innovation synergy, innovation cost synergy, innovation process synergy, and new growth platforms. In moderately technological related M&As, firms focus R&D integration mainly on structural linking, e.g. in terms of integrated R&D management, R&D teams, or even R&D departments. Structural linking turned out to be associated with innovation process synergy, new growth platforms, but not with innovation cost synergy. Finally, in the case of lowly technological related M&As, firms tend not to integrate the R&D functions, but focus on standardizing systems, such as the harmonization of information, reporting, and control systems. In principle, system standardization could not be associated with specific innovation synergies, although it can be regarded as an important success factor in the integration process. It should be noted that process re-design included also elements of structural linking and systems standardization, and structural linking included also elements of systems standardization. This suggests that there are three levels of R&D integration, starting with system standardization (in cases of low technological relatedness) up to the most far-reaching, and thereby most disruptive integration mechanism, process re-design (in cases of high technological relatedness).

On the issue of organizing the PMAI, we conclude that there are several factors that enhance innovation synergy realization. First, we found that the integration of the R&D functions often gets a dedicated PMI pacing. A considerable number of M&A scholars already suggested that firms should have dedicated approaches to the integration of different business functions/areas (e.g. Homburg and Bucerius, 2006; Puranam *et al.*, 2006; Schweizer, 2005). We found that especially in M&As with low technological relatedness, unlike other business function, the acquired R&D functions were preserved even for a few years to get to know the acquired R&D better, before they started some form of integration. Second, firms with a track record of similar acquisitions, draw explicitly from their experience by using dedicated PMAI tools and guidelines. These firms are likely to integrate the R&D functions more quickly than firms without relevant experience. Finally, we concluded that, although rewarding, integrating two R&D functions was difficult and time consuming.

To answer Research Question 4, we conclude that there are three prime innovation synergies and that these synergies require distinct integration mechanisms. In addition, these different integration mechanisms and innovation synergies are determined by the level of technological relatedness between involved firms.

6.2 Contributions to literature

In this book we present four empirical studies on how innovating firms profit from external knowledge. These studies have made six main contributions to literature.

First, our research showed that, especially since the year 2000, Dutch innovating firms are increasingly adopting an open innovation strategy. The general perception was that open innovation is especially important for large, and especially high-tech firms (Chesbrough, 2003b). Moreover, so far most of the empirical evidence was limited to (1) anecdotal evidence from a small number of case studies, (2) evidence from high-tech firms, and (3) evidence from large firms (e.g. Chesbrough, 2003b; Christensen *et al.*, 2005; Dittrich and Duysters, 2007). Our longitudinal research of cross-sectional CIS data of Dutch innovating firms quantified the relevance of open innovation for the first time on this scale. Open innovation turns out to be relevant across Dutch innovating firms. Moreover, our study clearly shows that open innovation is not only important for large firms and firms from high-tech industries, but also increasingly for SMEs and lower-tech firms. With our quantitative analysis of industrial firms in the Netherlands, the study has substantially advanced the external validity of the open innovation model.

Second, we were able to analyze the performance consequences of the different knowledge acquisition strategies in one integrated model, within the setting of a cross-section of 15 industries. Existing studies on this issue concentrated on one particular mode, or has limited the analysis to one (high-tech) industry (e.g. Fey, 2005; Rothaermel and Hess, 2007; Van de Vrande, 2007). The extension on knowledge acquisition strategies and industries brings research on open innovation to a higher level.

Third, our research showed that firms profit from licensing-in and outsourcing as we found significant positive relationships with innovation performance. So far, only a limited number of studies have looked at the performance consequences of licensing-in and outsourcing (Fey, 2005; Tsai and Wang, 2007). Whereas Tsai and Wang (2007) found that licensing-in has a positive impact on innovation performance, as long as the firm has sufficient capacity to absorb the knowledge, Fey (2005) found that outsourcing has a negative impact on a firm's innovation performance. Taking a cross-section of Dutch industry, we found that licensing-in has a short-term positive impact on a firm's innovation performance. A possible explanation for this finding is that licensing-in involves knowledge and technologies that are available on the market, also to competitors, so that it does not lead to a sustainable competitive advantage. In addition, we found that outsourcing has a positive impact on a firm's short-term performance in incremental innovation and long term performance in both radical and incremental innovations. This finding could be an indication that there are distinct outsourcing strategies, e.g. outsourcing to suppliers to improve existing products, and outsourcing of fundamental research to universities. Our empirical findings on the impact of licensing-in and R&D outsourcing on a firm's innovation performance can be regarded as another contribution to the literature on open innovation. However, further research is required in order to fully understand how licensing-in and R&D outsourcing contribute to the innovation performance

Fourth, taking a cross-section of Dutch industry, we found that major acquisitions have a positive impact on the long-term performance of radical innovations. Interestingly, so far, the majority of the empirical studies had found a neutral effect at best, or even a decline, in innovation performance (De Man and Duysters, 2005). Only in specific situations did researchers find that M&As had a positive effect on innovation performance (e.g. in the case of technology motivated M&As in high-tech sectors). An explanation for our surprising finding could be that we used a more suitable indicator to assess innovation performance in the context of M&As than previous studies. Whereas previous studies(e.g. Ahuja and Katila, 2001; Cloodt et al., 2006; Hitt et al., 1998, 1991) concentrated primarily on innovation input indicators (e.g. innovation expenditures), new product announcements, or technological performance (measured as patents counts), we used an indicator for innovation performance that also captures the commercial impact of innovations. With M&As, next to R&D, complementary business functions, such as marketing and sales, are also part of the deal and can enforce innovation synergy realization (King et al., 2008). Therefore, an indicator that captures the commercial impact of innovations seems to be more appropriate for analyzing performance consequences of M&As. To conclude, we believe we provided relevant insight into the ongoing discussion within the management literature on whether M&As are beneficial for innovation or not (De Man and Duysters, 2005).

Fifth, we substantiated the network orchestration processes of innovation brokers active in SME innovation networks. We discussed best practices that go one level deeper than codes and standard terms (e.g. trust) typically listed. Moreover, whereas research within the Systems of Innovation literate (e.g. Howells, 2006; Klerkx and Leeuwis, 2008b; Winch and Courtney, 2007) identified a number of functions and roles of innovation brokers in the innovation system, we have come up with more specific orchestration processes relevant at the network level.

Sixth and finally, in this book we have further opened the black box of innovation synergy realization in the context of M&As. We substantiated the concept of innovation synergies and linked them to technological relatedness and the relevant integration mechanisms. Most existing studies had either focused on the PMAI process (Bannert and Tschirky, 2004; Grimpe, 2007; Ranft and Lord, 2002; Schweizer, 2005), or on M&A context characteristics determining post M&A innovation performance (Ahuja and Katila, 2001; Cloodt *et al.*, 2006). In line with the ideas of Cassiman *et al.* (2005), we studied in-depth innovation synergy realization, considering both M&A context characteristics (e.g. technological relatedness) and the R&D integration mechanisms. In addition, our finding that there are diverse innovative gains have important ramifications for further quantitative studies concentrating on the relationship between M&As and innovation. So far these studies (e.g. Ahuja and Katila, 2001; Cloodt *et al.*, 2006) have concentrated on one single aspect of innovation performance (e.g. technological success measured as ex-post M&A patent counts), which may, as mentioned, provide a very partial analysis of M&As.

6.3 Managerial implications

The business landscape for modern firms has been subject to serious change in the last two decades. In today's business, firms face huge challenges arising from the fast technological developments, ever-changing customer demands, scarcity in resources, and changing regulations. Achieving innovation success is essential for firms that want to prosper in this new business landscape. From a managerial perspective it is then important to know how to improve the innovation performance. Based on the results from the different studies in this book several implications for managers are extracted.

First, it is important that firms take advantage of the knowledge and capabilities residing in other organizations. Managers of firms that have so far not been active in external knowledge acquisition should ask themselves whether relying exclusively on in-house innovation is the optimal innovation strategy. The results in this book clearly recommend to pursuing open innovation strategies i.e. building linkages with other organizations to complement in-house knowledge to maximize innovation and commercial performance. Firms must, however, be aware of the managerial challenges that come with innovation management in an inter-organizational context. Managing innovation in an inter-organizational setting requires specific capabilities that may be different from the capabilities required for managing in-house innovation. Firms that choose to pursue an open innovation strategy should therefore make sure they have specific capabilities for managing it, for instance particular influencing, trust building and negotiation skills (Du Chatenier *et al.*, 2008). To get such capabilities, firms could get involved in training, and set up specific recruitment criteria for new employees. As a result, employees would be better accustomed to innovating in an open setting, increasing their chances of competitive advantage. In addition, to get the adequate capabilities for open innovation, firms could reap the rewards of the experience and learning trajectories of other organizations. For instance, as we showed in Chapter 4, innovation brokers can complement SME innovation networks with typical open innovation capabilities.

Second, the following factors that improve the chances of success for cooperative innovation projects can be derived from the study of innovation brokers orchestrating open innovation in SME innovation networks:

Transparency: participants must be transparent in their processes and actions. For instance, firms must be explicit as to why they participate in a collaborative project, what they expect from it etc. This will increase the trust among the partners.

Complementary partners: an inter-organizational project should comprise of partners that truly add something to the project. In the case of SMEs this can equally be volume, in order to reach a minimal scale needed for the innovation.

Business-driven innovation: the starting point of any inter-organizational innovation project should be an idea or problem that is relevant for a commercial firm. Subsidy driven projects or innovation consortia led by researchers often lead to sub-optimal solutions from a commercial perspective.

Adequate governance mechanisms: for each innovation projects there should be tailored governance mechanisms set up for the inter-organizational project. Too many formal rules and procedures can be detrimental for innovation.

Third, when firms choose between different knowledge acquisition strategies, they must consider the different impacts they may have on the firm, especially on its innovation performance. For instance, the results in this book indicate that licensing-in can be beneficial for both radical and incremental innovation, but only for a temporary competitive advantage (see Section 3.4.2). On the long run, firms engaged in licensing-in do not perform better than firms that do not. This is probably, because the licensed-in knowledge is also available to competitors. Licensing-in should therefore be regarded as a strategy to keep pace with technological developments in the market, rather than a strategy to sustainably increase competitive advantage.

In strong contrast to licensing-in, our research has shown that M&As impact the innovation performance positively only after a considerable number of years. Firms should realize that acquiring or merging with another firm does not instantly result in innovative gains, even if the target has clear complementary knowledge and capabilities. Innovation synergies stemming from M&As are preceded by intensive integration efforts, i.e. process re design and structural linking, which are complex processes to manage. But, once the firms manage to integrate, the rewards may be great: more budget available for innovation, a leaner innovation process and ultimately breakthrough innovations that would not have been realized without the integration. Our R&D integration framework (Figure 5.2) may help managers to direct the integration activities. Firms that are inexperienced with M&As may opt for an initial preservation of the acquired R&D function, so that the two firms get to know each other better.

Fifth, in many M&As enhancing the innovativeness is not the prime motive. Nevertheless, we argue that firms should pay careful attention to integrating the R&D function. If not well managed, post M&A integration may hinder ongoing innovation activities, which may seriously delay new product introductions. Moreover, even without an initial focus on innovation synergies, firms must think about possible complementarities or overlaps in R&D. During our in-depth interviews with R&D and integration managers it came to the fore that M&As often offered substantially more innovation synergies than expected. As the synergies had a great strategic impact, managers regretted that they had not started dedicated R&D integration projects earlier.

Sixth and finally, our research should not be seen as a plea to simply reduce internal R&D and other innovation efforts. Although our study clearly shows that firms relying exclusively on in-house innovation perform significantly worse on innovation than firms that acquire external knowledge, firms should maintain substantial levels of internal R&D to posses sufficient absorptive capacity (Cohen and Levinthal, 1990). Only then will firms be fully able to profit from external knowledge.

References

Ahuja, G., 2000. The duality of collaboration: Inducements and opportunities in the formation of interfirm linkages. Strategic Management Journal 21 (3), 317-343.

Ahuja, G., Katila, R., 2001. Technological acquisitions and the innovation performance of acquiring firms: A longitudinal study. Strategic Management Journal 22 (3), 197-220.

Angwin, D., 2004. Speed in M&A Integration: The First 100 Days. European Management Journal 22 (4), 418.

Arranz, N., Fdez. de Arroyabe, J.C., 2008. The choice of partners in R&D cooperation: An empirical analysis of Spanish firms. Technovation 28 (1-2), 88-100.

Baker, W.E., Sinkula, J.M., 2005. Market orientation and the new product paradox. Journal of Product Innovation Management 22 (6), 483-502.

Bakker, H.J.C., Helmink, J.W.A., 2000. Successfully Integrating Two Businesses. Gower: Burlington, VT.

Bannert, V., Tschirky, H., 2004. Integration planning for technology intensive acquisitions. R & D Management 34 (5), 481-494.

Barkema, H.G., Schijven, M., 2008. How do firms learn to make acquisitions? A review of past research and an agenda for the future. Journal of Management 34 (3), 594-634.

Barney, J.B., 1999. How a firm's capabilities affect boundary decisions. Sloan Management Review 40 (3), 137-145.

Batterink, M.H., Wubben, E.F.M., Omta, S.W.F., 2006. Factors related to innovative output in the Dutch agrifood insdustry. Journal on Chain and Network Science 6 (1), 31-45.

Batterink, M.H., Wubben, E.F.M., Simonse, L.W.L., Omta, S.W.F., 2007. Realizing innovation synergies through Mergers and Acquisitions. Paper presented at the Academy of Management Annual Meeting, Philadelphia.

Becker, W., Dietz, J., 2004. R&D cooperation and innovation activities of firms - evidence for the German manufacturing industry. Research Policy 33 (2), 209-223.

Bertolini, P., Giovannetti, E., 2006. Industrial districts and internationalization: the case of the agri-food industry in Modena, Italy. Entrepreneurship and regional development 18 (4), 279-304.

Bessant, J., Rush, H., 1995. Building Bridges For Innovation - The Role Of Consultants In Technology-Transfer. Research Policy 24 (1), 97-114.

Birkinshaw, J., Bresman, H., Hakanson, L., 2000. Managing the post-acquisition integration process: How the human integration and task integration processes interact to foster value creation. Journal of Management Studies 37 (3), 395-425.

Blundell, R., Griffith, R., Van Reenen, J., 1999. Market share, market value and innovation in a panel of British manufacturing firms. Review of Economic Studies 66 (3), 529-554.

Boon, W.P.C., Moors, E.H.M., Kuhlmann, S., Smits, R.E.H.M., 2008. Demand articulation in intermediary organisations: The case of orphan drugs in the Netherlands. Technological Forecasting and Social Change 75 (5), 644-671.

Booz-Allen, Hamilton, I., 1968. Management of new products. Chicago.

Brass, D.J., Galaskiewicz, J., Greve, H.R., Tsai, W.P., 2004. Taking stock of networks and organizations: A multilevel perspective. Academy of Management Journal 47 (6), 795-817.

Bresman, H., Birkinshaw, J., Nobel, R., 1999. Knowledge transfer in international acquisitions. Journal of International Business Studies 30 (3), 439-462.

Brock, D.M., 2005. Multinational acquisition integration: the role of national culture in creating synergies. International Business Review 14 (3), 269-288.

Bstieler, L., 2006. Trust formation in collaborative new product development. Journal of Product Innovation Management 23 (1), 56-72.

Burgelman, R.A., Christensen, C.M., Wheelwright, S.C., 2009. Strategic Management of Technology and Innovation (5 ed.). McGraw-Hill: New York.

Burt, R.S., 2004. Structural holes and good ideas. American Journal of Sociology 110 (2), 349-399.

Cabral, L.M.B., Polak, B., 2004. Does Microsoft Stifle Innovation? Dominant Firms, Imitation and R&D Incentives. CEPR Discussion Papers 4577, C.E.P.R. Discussion Papers.

Capron, L., Dussauge, P., Mitchell, W., 1998. Resource redeployment following horizontal acquisitions in Europe and North America, 1988-1992. Strategic Management Journal 19 (7), 631-661.

Caputo, A.C., Cucchiella, F., Fratocchi, L., Pelagagge, P.M., Scacchia, F., 2002. A methodological framework for innovation transfer to SMEs. Industrial Management & Data Systems 102 (5-6), 271-283.

Cartwright, S., Schoenberg, R., 2006. Thirty years of mergers and acquisitions research: Recent advances and future opportunities. British Journal Of Management 17, S1-S5.

Cassiman, B., Colombo, M.G., Garrone, P., Veugelers, R., 2005. The impact of M&A on the R&D process - An empirical analysis of the role of technological- and market-relatedness. Research Policy 34 (2), 195-220.

CBS, 1998. Kennis en Economie. Centraal Bureau voor de Statistiek: Voorburg/Heerlen.

CBS, 2000. Kennis en Economie. Centraal Bureau voor de Statistiek: Voorburg/Heerlen.

CBS, 2002. Kennis en Economie. Centraal Bureau voor de Statistiek: Voorburg/Heerlen.

CBS, 2004. Kennis en Economie. Centraal Bureau voor de Statistiek: Voorburg/Heerlen.

CBS, 2006. Kennis en Economie. Centraal Bureau voor de Statistiek: Voorburg/Heerlen.

Chakrabarti, A.K., Hauschildt, J., Suverkrup, C., 1994. Does It Pay To Acquire Technological Firms. R & D Management 24 (1), 47-56.

Chakrabarti, A.K., Souder, W.E., 1987. Technology, Innovation And Performance In Corporate-Mergers - A Managerial Evaluation. Technovation 6 (2), 103-114.

Chandler, A.D., 1990. Scale and scope: the dynamics of industrial capitalism. Harvard University Press: Cambridge.

Chatterjee, S., 1986. Types of Synergy and Economic Value: The Impact of Acquisitions on Merging and Rival Firms. Strategic Management Journal 7 (2), 119.

Chesbrough, H., 2003a. The logic of open innovation: Managing intellectual property. California Management Review 45 (3), 33-+.

Chesbrough, H., 2003b. Open innovation. The imperative for creating and profiting from technology. Harvard Business School Press: Boston.

Chesbrough, H., 2004. Managing open innovation. Research-Technology Management 47 (1), 23-26.

Chesbrough, H., 2006. Open Innovation: A New Paradigm for Understanding Industrial Innovation. In: Chesbrough, H., Vanhaverbeke, W., West, J. (Eds.), Open Innovation: Researching a New Paradigm. Oxford University Press: New York.

Chesbrough, H., Crowther, A.K., 2006. Beyond high tech: early adopters of open innovation in other industries. R & D Management 36 (3), 229-236.

Chesbrough, H., Vanhaverbeke, W., West, J., 2006. Open Innovation: Researching a New Paradigm. Oxford University Press: New York.

Christensen, C.M., 1997. The Innovator's Dilemma. Harvard Business School Press: Bosten Mass.

Christensen, C.M., Suarez, F.F., Utterback, J.M., 1998. Strategies for survival in fast-changing industries. Management Science 44 (12), S207-S220.

Christensen, J.F., Olesen, M.H., Kjaer, J.S., 2005. The industrial dynamics of Open Innovation--Evidence from the transformation of consumer electronics. Research Policy 34 (10), 1533-1549.

Churchill, G.A., 1999. Marketing research: Methodological foundations. Dryden Press: Orlando, Florida.

Cloodt, M., 2005. Mergers and Acquisitions in High-Tech Industries. Dissertation, Universiteit Maastricht, Maastricht.

Cloodt, M., Hagedoorn, J., Van Kranenburg, H., 2006. Mergers and acquisitions: Their effect on the innovative performance of companies in high-tech industries. Research Policy 35 (5), 642-654.

Cockburn, I.M., Henderson, R.M., 2001. Scale and scope in drug development: unpacking the advantages of size in pharmaceutical research. Journal of Health Economics 20 (6), 1033-1057.

Coff, R.W., 1999. How buyers cope with uncertainty when acquiring firms in knowledge-intensive industries: Caveat emptor. Organization Science 10 (2), 144-161.

Cohen, W.M., Levinthal, D.A., 1990. Absorptive Capacity: A New Perspective on Learning and Innovation. Administrative Science Quarterly 35 (1), 128-152.

Cooke, P., Wills, D., 1999. Small firms, social capital and the enhancement of business performance through innovation programmes Small Business Economics 13 (3), 219-234.

Costa, A.I.A., Jongen, W.M.F., 2006. New insights into consumer-led food product development. Trends in Food Science & Technology 17 (8), 457.

Das, T.K., Teng, B.S., 2000. A resource-based theory of strategic alliances. Journal of Management 26 (1), 31-61.

De Jong, J.P.J., Vermeulen, P.A.M., 2006. Determinants of product innovation in small firms - A comparison across industries. International Small Business Journal 24 (6), 587-609.

De Man, A.P., Duysters, G., 2005. Collaboration and innovation: a review of the effects of mergers, acquisitions and alliances on innovation. Technovation 25 (12), 1377-1387.

De Noble, A.F., Gustafson, L.T., Hergert, M., 1988. Planning for post-merger integration--eight lessons for merger success. Long Range Planning 21 (4), 82.

Dekker, H.C., 2004. Control of inter-organizational relationships: evidence on appropriation concerns and coordination requirements. Accounting Organizations And Society 29 (1), 27-49.

Dhanaraj, C., Parkhe, A., 2006. Orchestrating innovation networks. Academy of Management Review 31 (3), 659-669.

Dittrich, K., Duysters, G., 2007. Networking as a means to strategy change: The case of open innovation in mobile telephony. Journal of Product Innovation Management 24 (6), 510-521.

References

Dons, H.J.M., Bino, R.J., 2008. Innovation and knowledge transfer in the Dutch horticultural system. In: Hulsink, W., Dons, H.J.M. (Eds.), Pathways to High-tech Valleys and Research Triangles: Innovative Entrepreneurship, Knowledge Transfer and Cluster Formation in Europe and the United States. Springer Science+Business Media: Amsterdam.

Dosi, G., Freeman, C., Nelson, R., Silverberg, G., Soete, L., 1988. Technical Change and Economic Theory. Pinter Publishers Limited: London.

Doz, Y.L., Olk, P.M., Ring, P.S., 2000. Formation processes of R&D consortia: Which path to take? Where does it lead? Strategic Management Journal 21 (3), 239-266.

Du Chatenier, E., Verstegen, J.A.A.M., Biemans, H.J.A., Mulder, M., 2008, August 8-13. A competence profile for open innovation professionals. Paper presented at the Academy of Management Annual Meeting, Anaheim, California.

Dyer, J.H., Nobeoka, K., 2000. Creating and managing a high-performance knowledge-sharing network: The Toyota case. Strategic Management Journal 21 (3), 345-367.

Dyer, J.H., Singh, H., 1998. The relational view: Cooperative strategy and sources of interorganizational competitive advantage. Academy of Management Review 23 (4), 660-679.

Edwards, T., Delbridge, R., Munday, M., 2005. Understanding innovation in small and medium-sized enterprises: a process manifest. Technovation 25 (10), 1119-1127.

Eisenhardt, K.M., 1989. Building Theories from Case-Study Research. Academy of Management Review 14 (4), 532-550.

Emden, Z., Calantone, R.J., Droge, C., 2006. Collaborating for new product development: Selecting the partner with maximum potential to create value. Journal of Product Innovation Management 23 (4), 330-341.

Epstein, M.J., 2004. The drivers of success in post-merger integration. Organizational Dynamics 33 (2), 174-189.

Ernst, H., Vitt, J., 2000. The influence of corporate acquisitions on the behaviour of key inventors. R & D Management 30 (2), 105-119.

European Commission, 2000. The Lisbon European Council – An Agenda of Economic and Social Renewal for Europe. European Commission: Brussels.

European Commission, 2005. Working together for growth and jobs. A new start for the Lisbon Strategy. Brussels.

Faems, D., Van Looy, B., Debackere, K., 2005. Interorganizational collaboration and innovation: Toward a portfolio approach. Journal of Product Innovation Management 22 (3), 238-250.

Fagerberg, J., 2004. Innovation - A guide to the literature. In: Fagerberg, J., Mowery, D.C., Nelson, R.R. (Eds.), The Oxford Handbook of Innovation (pp. 1-26). Oxford University Press.

Fetterhoff, T.J., Voelkel, D., 2006. Managing open innovation in biotechnology. Research-Technology Management 49 (3), 14-18.

Fey, C.F., 2005. External sources of knowledge, governance mode, and R&D performance. Journal of Management 31 (4), 597-621.

Finkelstein, S., Haleblian, J.J., 2002. Understanding acquisition performance: The role of transfer effects. Organization Science 13 (1), 36-47.

Firth, R.W., Narayanan, V.K., 1996. New product strategies of large, dominant product manufacturing firms: An exploratory analysis. Journal of Product Innovation Management 13 (4), 334-347.

Fontana, R., Geuna, A., Matt, M., 2006. Factors affecting university-industry R&D projects: The importance of searching, screening and signalling. Research Policy 35 (2), 309-323.

Fortuin, F.T.J.M., 2006. Aligning Innovation to Business Strategy. Combining Cross-Industry and Longitudinal Perspectives on Strategic Alignment in Leading Technology-based Companies., Wageningen University.

Freel, M.S., 2003. Sectoral patterns of small firm innovation, networking and proximity. Research Policy 32 (5), 751-770.

Freeman, C., Soete, L., 1997. The economics of industrial innovation. MIT-Press: Cambridge.

Fritsch, M., Lukas, R., 2001. Who cooperates on R&D? Research Policy 30 (2), 297-312.

Galbraith, J.R., 1974. Organizational design. Addison-Wesley: Reading, MA.

Garcia Martinez, M., Briz, J., 2000. Innovation in the Spanish food & drink industry. The International Food and Agribusiness Management Review 3 (2), 155.

Gassmann, O., 2006. Opening up the innovation process: towards an agenda. R & D Management 36 (3), 223-228.

Gassmann, O., Sandmeier, P., Wecht, C.H., 2006. Extreme customer innovation in the front-end: learning from a new software paradigm. International Journal of Technology Management 33 (1), 46-66.

Gellynck, X., Vermeire, B., Viaene, J., 2007. Innovation in food firms: contribution of regional networks within the international business context. Entrepreneurship and regional development 19 (3), 209-226.

Gemunden, H.G., Ritter, T., Heydebreck, P., 1996. Network configuration and innovation success: an empirical analysis in German high-tech industries. International Journal of Research in Marketing 13, 449-462.

Gerpott, T.J., 1995. Successful Integration Of Research-And-Development Functions After Acquisitions - An Exploratory Empirical-Study. R & D Management 25 (2), 161-178.

Gilsing, V.A., 2003. Exploration, Exploitation and Co-evolution in Innovation Networks. Erasmus University Rotterdam, Rotterdam.

Gopalakrishnan, S., Damanpour, F., 1997. A review of innovation research in economics, sociology and technology management. Omega-International Journal of Management Science 25 (1), 15-28.

Graebner, M.E., 2004. Momentum and serendipity: How acquired leaders create value in the integration of technology firms. Strategic Management Journal 25 (8-9), 751-777.

Granovetter, M.S., 1973. Strength of Weak Ties. American Journal of Sociology 78 (6), 1360-1380.

Granovetter, M.S., 1985. Economic Action and Social Structure: The Problem of Embeddedness. American Journal of Sociology 91, 481-510.

Granstrand, O., Bohlin, E., Oskarsson, C., Sjoberg, N., 1992. External Technology Acquisition In Large Multitechnology Corporations. R & D Management 22 (2), 111-133.

Grant, R.M., 1996. Toward a knowledge-based theory of the firm. Strategic Management Journal 17, 109-122.

Green, W.H., 2003. Econometric Analysis (5th ed.). Prentice Hall: New Jersey.

Griffin, A., 1997. PDMA research on new product development practices: Updating trends and benchmarking best practices. Journal of Product Innovation Management 14 (6), 429-458.

References

Grimpe, C., 2007. Successful product development after firm acquisitions: The role of research and development. Journal of Product Innovation Management 24 (6), 614-628.

Gulati, R., Singh, H., 1998. The architecture of cooperation: Managing coordination costs and appropriation concerns in strategic alliances. Administrative Science Quarterly 43 (4), 781-814.

Hagedoorn, J., 1990. Organizational Modes Of Interfirm Cooperation And Technology-Transfer. Technovation 10 (1), 17-30.

Hagedoorn, J., 2002. Inter-firm R&D partnerships: an overview of major trends and patterns since 1960. Research Policy 31 (4), 477-492.

Hagedoorn, J., Cloodt, M., 2003. Measuring innovative performance: is there an advantage in using multiple indicators? Research Policy 32 (8), 1365-1379.

Hagedoorn, J., Duysters, G., 2002a. The effect of mergers and acquisitions on the technological performance of companies in a high-tech environment. Technology Analysis & Strategic Management 14 (1), 67-85.

Hagedoorn, J., Duysters, G., 2002b. External sources of innovative capabilities: The preference for strategic alliances or mergers and acquisitions. Journal of Management Studies 39 (2), 167-188.

Hagedoorn, J., Link, A.N., Vonortas, N.S., 2000. Research partnerships. Research Policy 29 (4-5), 567-586.

Hagedoorn, J., Sadowski, B., 1999. The transition from strategic technology alliances to mergers and acquisitions: An exploratory study. Journal of Management Studies 36 (1), 87-107.

Hair, J.F., Anderson, R.E., Tatham, R.L., Black, W.C., 1998. Multivariate data analysis (Fifth Edition). Prentice-Hall, Inc: New Jersey.

Haleblian, J.J., Finkelstein, S., 1999. The influence of organizational acquisition experience on acquisition performance: A behavioral learning perspective. Administrative Science Quarterly 44 (1), 29-56.

Haleblian, J.J., Kim, J.Y.J., Rajagopalan, N., 2006. The influence of acquisition experience and performance on acquisition behavior: Evidence from the US commercial banking industry. Academy of Management Journal 49 (2), 357-370.

Hall, B.H., 1989. The Impact of Corporate Restructuring on Industrial Research and Development (Working Paper No. 3216). National Bureau of Economic Research: Cambridge, Massachusetts.

Hamel, G., 1991. Competition For Competence And Inter-Partner Learning Within International Strategic Alliances. Strategic Management Journal 12, 83-103.

Hamel, G., Doz, Y.L., Prahalad, C.K., 1989. Collaborate with Your Competitors - and Win. Harvard Business Review 67 (1), 133-139.

Hanna, V., Walsh, K., 2002. Small firm networks: a successful approach to innovation? R and D Management 32 (3), 201-207.

Hanna, V., Walsh, K., 2008. Interfirm cooperation among small manufacturing firms. International Small Business Journal 26 (3), 299-321.

Harrison, J.S., Hitt, M.A., Hoskisson, R.E., Ireland, R.D., 1991. Synergies And Postacquisition Performance - Differences Versus Similarities In Resource Allocations. Journal of Management 17 (1), 173-190.

Hartwich, F., Gottret, V., Babu, S., Tola, J., 2007. Building public-private partnerships for agricultural innovation in Latin America. IFPRI Discussion Paper 00699. International Food Policy Research Institute: Washinton.

Haspeslagh, P.C., Jemison, D.B., 1991. Managing Acquisitions: Creating Value Through Corporate Renewal. Free Press: New York.

Hassink, R., 1996. Technology transfer agencies and regional economic development. European Planning Studies 4 (2), 167-184.

Henderson, R., Cockburn, I., 1996. Scale, scope, and spillovers: The determinants of research productivity in drug discovery. Rand Journal of Economics 27 (1), 32-59.

Henderson, R.M., Clark, K.B., 1990. Architectural Innovation - The Reconfiguration Of Existing Product Technologies And The Failure Of Established Firms. Administrative Science Quarterly 35 (1), 9-30.

Hitt, M.A., Harrison, J.S., Ireland, R.D., Best, A., 1998. Attributes of Successful and Unsuccessful Acquisitions of US Firms. British Journal of Management 9 (2), 91-114.

Hitt, M.A., Hoskisson, R.E., Ireland, R.D., Harrison, J.S., 1991. Effects Of Acquisitions On Research-And-Development Inputs And Outputs. Academy of Management Journal 34 (3), 693-706.

Hitt, M.A., Hoskisson, R.E., Johnson, R.A., Moesel, D.D., 1996. The market for corporate control and firm innovation. Academy of Management Journal 39 (5), 1084-1119.

Hoang, H., Antoncic, B., 2003. Network-based research in entrepreneurship - A critical review. Journal of Business Venturing 18 (2), 165-187.

Hoffmann, W.H., Schlosser, R., 2001. Success factors of strategic alliances in small and medium-sized enterprises - An empirical survey. Long Range Planning 34, 357-381.

Hollander, J., 2002. Improving performance in business development. Genesis, a tool for product development teams. PhD Dissertation, Groningen.

Homburg, C., Bucerius, M., 2006. Is speed of integration really a success factor of mergers and acquisitions? An analysis of the role of internal and external relatedness. Strategic Management Journal 27 (4), 347-367.

Howells, J., 2005. Innovation and regional economic development: A matter of perspective? Research Policy 34 (8), 1220-1234.

Howells, J., 2006. Intermediation and the role of intermediaries in innovation. Research Policy 35 (5), 715-728.

Huggins, R., 2000. The success and failure of policy-implantedinter-firm network initiatives: motivations, processes and structure. Entrepreneurship and regional development 12, 111-113.

Hult, G.T.M., Hurley, R.F., Knight, G.A., 2004. Innovativeness: Its antecedents and impact on business performance. Industrial Marketing Management 33 (5), 429-438.

Ikeda, K., Doi, N., 1983. The Performances Of Merging Firms In Japanese Manufacturing-Industry - 1964-75. Journal of Industrial Economics 31 (3), 257-266.

Innovatieplatform, 2008. www.innovatieplatform.nl.

Isaksen, A., Remøe, S.O., 2001. New Approaches to Innovation Policy: Some Norwegian Examples. European Planning Studies 9 (3), 285-302.

Izushi, H., 2003. Impact of the length of relationships upon the use of research institutes by SMEs. Research Policy 32 (5), 771-788.

Janszen, F.H.A., 2000. The Age of Innovation, Making Business Creativity a Competence, not a coincidence. Pearson Education Limited: London.

Jemison, D.B., Sitkin, S.B., 1986. Corporate Acquisitions - A Process Perspective. Academy of Management Review 11 (1), 145-163.

Johnson, W.H.A., 2008. Roles, resources and benefits of intermediate organizations supporting triple helix collaborative R&D: The case of Precarn. Technovation 28 (8), 495-505.

Kamath, R.R., Liker, J.K., 1990. Supplier dependence and innovation: a contingency model of supplier's innovative activities. Journal of Engineering and Technology Management 7, 111-127.

Katila, R., Ahuja, G., 2002. Something old, something new: A longitudinal study of search behavior and new product introduction. Academy of Management Journal 45 (6), 1183-1194.

Katz, R., Allen, T.J., 1982. Investigating the Not Invented Here (Nih) Syndrome - a Look at the Performance, Tenure, and Communication Patterns of 50 R-and-D Project Groups. R & D Management 12 (1), 7-19.

Kaufmann, A., Tödtling, F., 2001. Science-industry interaction in the process of innovation: the importance of boundary-crossing between systems. Research Policy 30 (5), 791-804.

Kaufmann, A., Tödtling, F., 2002. How effective is innovation support for SMEs? An analysis of the region of Upper Austria. Technovation 22 (3), 147-159.

Keil, T., Maula, M., Schildt, H., Zahra, S.A., 2008. The effect of governance modes and relatedness of external business development activities on innovative performance. Strategic Management Journal 29 (8), 895-907.

Kemp, R.G.M., Folkeringa, M., De Jong, J.P.J., Wubben, E.F.M., 2003. Innovation and firm performance (Research report). EIM: Zoetermeer.

King, D.R., Dalton, D.R., Daily, C.M., Covin, J.G., 2004. Meta-analyses of post-acquisition performance: Indications of unidentified moderators. Strategic Management Journal 25 (2), 187-200.

King, D.R., Slotegraaf, R.J., Kesner, I., 2008. Performance implications of firm resource interactions in the acquisition of R&D-intensive firms. Organization Science 19 (2), 327-340.

Klerkx, L., Leeuwis, C., 2008a. Balancing multiple interests: Embedding innovation intermediation in the agricultural knowledge infrastructure. Technovation 28 (6), 364-378.

Klerkx, L., Leeuwis, C., 2008b. Matching demand and supply in the agricultural knowledge infrastructure: Experiences with innovation intermediaries. Food Policy 33 (3), 260-276.

Klomp, L., Van Leeuwen, G., 1999. The importance of innovation for firm performance. Statistcs Netherlands.

Kogut, B., 1988. Joint Ventures - Theoretical and Empirical-Perspectives. Strategic Management Journal 9 (4), 319-332.

Kogut, B., Zander, U., 1992. Knowledge Of The Firm, Combinative Capabilities, And The Replication Of Technology. Organization Science 3 (3), 383-397.

Kok, W., 2004. Facing the Challenge. The Lisbon Strategy for growth and employment. High Level Group.

Kolodny, H., Stymne, B., Shani, R., Figuera, J.R., Lillrank, P., 2001. Design and policy choices for technology extension organizations. Research Policy 30 (2), 201-225.

Larsson, R., Bengtsson, L., Henriksson, K., Sparks, J., 1998. The interorganizational learning dilemma: Collective knowledge development in strategic alliances. Organization Science 9 (3), 285-305.

Larsson, R., Finkelstein, S., 1999. Integrating strategic, organizational, and human resource perspectives on mergers and acquisitions: A case survey of synergy realization. Organization Science 10 (1), 1-26.

Laschewski, L., Phillipson, J., Gorton, M., 2002. The facilitation and formalisation of small business networks: Evidence from the North East of England. Environment and Planning C: Government and Policy 20 (3), 375-391.

Laursen, K., Salter, A., 2004. Searching high and low: what types of firms use universities as a source of innovation? Research Policy 33 (8), 1201.

Laursen, K., Salter, A., 2006. Open for innovation: The role of openness in explaining innovation performance among UK manufacturing firms. Strategic Management Journal 27 (2), 131-150.

Leiblein, M.J., Reuer, J.J., Dalsace, F., 2002. Do make or buy decisions matter? The influence of organizational governance on technological performance. Strategic Management Journal 23 (9), 817-833.

Lowe, J., Taylor, P., 1998. R & D and technology purchase through licence agreements: complementary strategies and complementary assets. R & D Management 28 (4), 263-278.

Lubatkin, M., 1983. Mergers And The Performance Of The Acquiring Firm. Academy Of Management Review 8 (2), 218-225.

Lundvall, B.A., 1992. National Systems of Innovation. Towards a Theory of Innovation and Interactive Learning. Pinter: London.

Maidique, M.A., Zirger, B.J., 1985. The New Product Learning Cycle. Research Policy 14 (6), 299-313.

Major, E.J., Cordey-Hayes, M., 2000. Engaging the business support network to give SMEs the benefit of foresight. Technovation 20 (11), 589-602.

Malecki, E.J., Tootle, D.M., 1996. The role of networks in small firm competitiveness. International Journal of Technology Management 11 (1-2), 43-57.

Malerba, F., 2002. Sectoral systems of innovation and production. Research Policy 31 (2), 247-264.

March, J.G., 1991. Exploration and Exploitation in Organizational Learning. Organization Science 2 (1), 71-87.

Menrad, K., 2004. Innovations in the food industry in Germany. Research Policy 33 (6-7), 845-878.

Meyer, M.H., Tertzakian, P., Utterback, J.M., 1997. Metrics for managing research and development in the context of the product family. Management Science 43 (1), 88-111.

Miles, M.B., Huberman, A.M., 1994. Qualitative data analysis. An expanded sourcebook (2nd ed.). Sage: Beverly Hills, CA.

Miller, C.C., Cardinal, L.B., Glick, W.H., 1997. Retrospective reports in organizational research: A reexamination of recent evidence. Academy of Management Journal 40 (1), 189-204.

Miotti, L., Sachwald, F., 2003. Co-operative R&D: why and with whom? An integrated framework of analysis. Research Policy 32 (8), 1481-1499.

Mohnen, P., Dagenais, M., 2002. Towards an Innovation Intensity Index: The Case of CIS 1 in Denmark and Ireland. In: Kleinknecht, A., Mohnen, P. (Eds.), Innovation and Firm Performance. Econometric Explorations of Survey Data (pp. 3-30). Palgrave.

Mol, M.J., 2005. Does being R&D intensive still discourage outsourcing? Evidence from Dutch manufacturing. Research Policy 34 (4), 571-582.

References

Mora-Valentin, E.M., Montoro-Sanchez, A., Guerras-Martin, L.A., 2004. Determining factors in the success of R&D cooperative agreements between firms and research organizations. Research Policy 33 (1), 17-40.

Mueller, D.C., 1985. Mergers and Market Share. Review of Economics and Statistics 67 (2), 259-267.

Nadler, D.A., Tushman, M.L., 1997. Competing by design: The power of organizational architecture. Oxford University Press: Oxford, U.K.

Narin, F., Breitzman, A., 1995. Inventive Productivity. Research Policy 24 (4), 507-519.

Narula, R., 2004. R&D collaboration by SMEs: new opportunities and limitations in the face of globalisation. Technovation 24 (2), 153-161.

Negassi, S., 2004. R&D co-operation and innovation a microeconometric study on French firms. Research Policy 33 (3), 365-384.

Nelson, R.R. Ed. 1993. National Systems of Innovation. Oxford University Press: Oxford.

Nieto, M., 2003. From R&D management to knowledge management - An overview of studies of innovation management. Technological Forecasting and Social Change 70 (2), 135-161.

Nooteboom, B., 1994. Innovation And Diffusion In Small Firms - Theory And Evidence. Small Business Economics 6 (5), 327-347.

Nooteboom, B., 1999a. Innovation and inter-firm linkages: new implications for policy. Research Policy 28 (8), 793-805.

Nooteboom, B., 1999b. Inter-Firm Alliances - Analysis and Design. Routledge: London.

OECD, 1996. OECD Proposed Guidelines for Collecting and Interpreting Technological Innovation Data: Oslo Manual. Revised edition. OECD: Paris.

OECD, 2007. OECD Science, Technology and Industry Scoreboard 2007. OECD.

Omta, S.W.F., 1995. Critical Succes Factors In Biomedical Research And Pharmaceutical Innovation. Kluwer Academic Publishers: Dordrecht, London, Boston.

Omta, S.W.F., 2002. Innovation in chains and networks. Journal on Chain and Network Science 2 (2), 73-80.

Omta, S.W.F., Van Rossum, W., 1999. The Management of Social Capital in R&D Collaborations. In: Leenders, R.T.A.J., Gabbay, S.M. (Eds.), Corporate Social Capital and Liability (pp. 356-376). Kluwer Academic Publishers: Boston, Dordrecht, London.

Oughton, C., Landabaso, M., Morgan, K., 2002. The Regional Innovation Paradox: Innovation Policy and Industrial Policy. The Journal of Technology Transfer 27 (1), 97-110.

Pannekoek, L., Kooten, O.v., Kemp, R.G.M., Omta, S.W.F., 2005. Entrepreneurial innovation in chains and networks in Dutch greenhouse horticulture. Journal on Chain and Network Science 5 (1), 39-50.

Paruchuri, S., Nerkar, A., Hambrick, D.C., 2006. Acquisition integration and productivity losses in the technical core: Disruption of inventors in acquired companies. Organization Science 17 (5), 545-562.

Pavitt, K., 1984. Sectoral patterns of technical change: Towards a taxonomy and a theory. Research Policy 13 (6), 343-373.

Petersen, K.J., Handfield, R.B., Ragatz, G.L., 2003. A model of supplier integration into new product development. Journal of Product Innovation Management 20 (4), 284-299.

Pisano, G.P., 1990. The Research-and-Development Boundaries of the Firm - an Empirical-Analysis. Administrative Science Quarterly 35 (1), 153-176.

Pittaway, L., Robertson, M., Munir, K., Denyer, D., Neely, A., 2004. Networking and innovation: a systematic review of the evidence. International Journal of Management Reviews 5-6 (3-4), 137-168.

Pollard, D. (2006). Innovation and Technology Transfer Intermediaries: A Systemic International Study, Advances in Interdisciplinary Studies of Work Teams (Vol. 12, pp. 137-174).

Porter, M.E., 1985. Competitive Advantage, Creating and Sustaining Superior Performance. Free Press: New York.

Powell, W.W., 1990. Neither Market Nor Hierarchy: Network Forms of Organization. In: Staw, B.M., Cummings, L.L. (Eds.), Research in Organizational Behavior (pp. 295-336). Jai Press Inc.: London.

Powell, W.W., Koput, K.W., SmithDoerr, L., 1996. Interorganizational collaboration and the locus of innovation: Networks of learning in biotechnology. Administrative Science Quarterly 41 (1), 116-145.

Prabhu, J.C., Chandy, R.K., Ellis, M.E., 2005. The impact of acquisitions on innovation: Poison pill, placebo, or tonic? Journal of Marketing 69 (1), 114-130.

Prahalad, C.K., Hamel, G., 1990. The Core Competence of the Corporation. Harvard Business Review 68 (3), 79-91.

Puranam, P., Singh, H., Zollo, M., 2006. Organizing for innovation: Managing the coordination-autonomy dilemma in technology acquisitions. Academy of Management Journal 49 (2), 263-280.

Ragatz, G.L., Handfield, R.B., Scannell, T.V., 1997. Success factors for integrating suppliers into new product development. Journal of Product Innovation Management 14 (3), 190-202.

Ranft, A.L., Lord, M.D., 2002. Acquiring new technologies and capabilities: A grounded model of acquisition implementation. Organization Science 13 (4), 420-441.

Rasmussen, E., 2008. Government instruments to support the commercialization of university research: Lessons from Canada. Technovation 28 (8), 506-517.

Ravenscraft, D.J., Scherer, F.M., 1987. Mergers, Sell-Offs & Economic Efficiency. The Brookings Institution: Washington, D.C.

Raymond, W., Mohnen, P., Palm, F., Van der Loeff, S.S., 2006. A classification of Dutch manufacturing based on a model of innovation. Economist-Netherlands 154 (1), 85-105.

Rindfleisch, A., Moorman, C., 2001. The acquisition and utilization of information in new product alliances: A strength-of-ties perspective. Journal of Marketing 65 (2), 1-18.

Ring, P.S., Van de Ven, A.H., 1992. Structuring Cooperative Relationships Between Organizations. Strategic Management Journal 13 (7), 483-498.

Ring, P.S., Van de Ven, A.H., 1994. Developmental Processes Of Cooperative Interorganizational Relationships. Academy of Management Review 19 (1), 90-118.

Ritter, T., Gemunden, H.G., 2003. Interorganizational relationships and networks: An overview. Journal of Business Research 56 (9), 691-697.

Rogers, D.M.A., 1996. The challenge of fifth generation R&D. Research-Technology Management 39 (4), 33-41.

Rogers, M., 2004. Networks, firm size and innovation. Small Business Economics 22 (2), 141-153.

References

Röller, L.-H., Stennek, J., Verboven, F., 2006. Efficiency gains from mergers. In: Ilzkovitz, F., Meiklejohn, R. (Eds.), European Merger Control: Do we need an efficiency defence? (pp. 84-201). Edward Elgar: Cheltenham, UK.

Rothaermel, F.T., Hess, A.M., 2007. Building dynamic capabilities: Innovation driven by individual-, firm-, and network-level effects. Organization Science 18 (6), 898-921.

Rousseau, D.M., Sitkin, S.B., Burt, R.S., Camerer, C., 1998. Not so different after all: A cross-discipline view of trust. Academy of Management Review 23 (3), 393-404.

Roussel, P.A., Saad, K.A., Erickson, T.J., 1991. Third Generation R&D Harvard Business School Press: Boston, Mass.

Sampson, R.C., 2007. R&D alliances and firm performance: The impact of technological diversity and alliance organization on innovation. Academy of Management Journal 50 (2), 364-386.

Sapsed, J., Grantham, A., DeFillippi, R., 2007. A bridge over troubled waters: Bridging organisations and entrepreneurial opportunities in emerging sectors. Research Policy 36 (9), 1314-1334.

Schartinger, D., Rammer, C., Fischer, M.M., Frohlich, J., 2002. Knowledge interactions between universities and industry in Austria: sectoral patterns and determinants. Research Policy 31 (3), 303-328.

Schenk, H., 2006. Mergers and Concentrarion Policy. In: Bianchi, P., Labory, S. (Eds.), International Handbook of Industrial Policy. Cheltenham: Edward Elgar.

Schmidt, J.B., Calantone, R.J., 1998. Are really new product development projects harder to shut down? Journal of Product Innovation Management 15 (2), 111-123.

Schweiger, D.M., 2002. M&A integration: a framework for executives and managers. McGraw-Hill: New York.

Schweizer, L., 2005. Organizational integration of acquired biotechnology companies into pharmaceutical companies: The need for a hybrid approach. Academy of Management Journal 48 (6), 1051-1074.

Seth, A., 1990. Value Creation In Acquisitions - A Reexamination Of Performance Issues. Strategic Management Journal 11 (2), 99-115.

Singh, H., Montgomery, C.A., 1987. Corporate Acquisition Strategies and Economic Performance. Strategic Management Journal 8 (4), 377.

Sirmon, D.G., Hitt, M.A., Ireland, R.D., 2007. Managing firm resources in dynamic environments to create value: Looking inside the black box. Academy of Management Review 32 (1), 273-292.

Smits, R., Kuhlmann, S., 2004. The Rise of Systemic Instruments in Innovation Policy. International Journal of Foresight and Innovation Policy 1 (1/2), 4-32.

Snow, C.C., Miles, R.E., Coleman, H.J., 1992. Managing 21st-Century Network Organizations. Organizational Dynamics 20 (3), 5-19.

Snyder, D.R., Blevins, D.E., 1986. Business and University Technical Research Cooperation: Some Important Issues. Jounal of Product Innovation Management 3 (2), 136-144.

Sousa, M., 2008. Open innovation models and the role of knowledge brokers. Inside Knowledge Magazine 11 (6), 18-22.

Stuart, T.E., 2000. Interorganizational alliances and the performance of firms: A study of growth and innovation rates in a high-technology industry. Strategic Management Journal 21 (8), 791-811.

Teece, D.J., 1986. Profiting From Technological Innovation - Implications For Integration, Collaboration, Licensing And Public-Policy. Research Policy 15 (6), 285-305.

Teece, D.J., Pisano, G., Shuen, A., 1997. Dynamic capabilities and strategic management. Strategic Management Journal 18 (7), 509-533.

Tidd, J., Bessant, J., Pavitt, K., 2005. Managing Innovation. Integrating Technological, Market and Organizational Change. (3 ed.). John Wiley & Sons.

Tidd, J., Trewhella, M.J., 1997. Organizational and technological antecedents for knowledge acquisition and learning. R & D Management 27 (4), 359-375.

Todlting, F., Trippl, M., 2005. One size fits all? Towards a differentiated regional innovation policy approach. Research Policy 34 (8), 1203-1219.

Tsai, K.-H., Wang, J.-C., 2007. Inward technology licensing and firm performance: a longitudinal study. R&D Management 37 (2), 151-160.

Tushman, M.L., Anderson, P., 1986. Technological Discontinuities And Organizational Environments. Administrative Science Quarterly 31 (3), 439-465.

Utterback, J.M., 1974. Innovation In Industry And Diffusion Of Technology. Science 183 (4125), 620-626.

Utterback, J.M., Meyer, M., Roberts, E., Reitberger, G., 1988. Technology And Industrial-Innovation In Sweden - A Study Of Technology-Based Firms Formed Between 1965 And 1980. Research Policy 17 (1), 15-26.

Uzzi, B., 1997. Social structure and competition in interfirm networks: The paradox of embeddedness. Administrative Science Quarterly 42 (1), 35-67.

Van de Vrande, V., 2007. Not Invented Here: Managing Corporate Innovation in a New Area. Technische Universiteit Eindhoven, Eindhoven.

Van de Vrande, V., Lemmens, C., Vanhaverbeke, W., 2006. Choosing governance modes for external technology sourcing. R & D Management 36 (3), 347-363.

Van Gils, A., Zwart, P., 2004. Knowledge acquisition and learning in Dutch and Belgian SMEs: The role of strategic alliances. European Management Journal 22 (6), 685-692.

Van Lente, H., Hekkert, M., Smits, R., Van Waveren, B., 2003. Roles of systemic intermediaries in transition processes. International Journal of Innovation Management 7 (3), 1-33.

Van Looy, B., Debackere, K., Andries, P., 2003. Policies to stimulate regional innovation capabilities via university-industry collaboration: an analysis and an assessment. R & D Management 33 (2), 209-229.

Van Poppel, A., 1999. Nieuwe producten, Te Veel Missers. Trends May 13, 78-79, in Dutch.

Vanhaverbeke, W.P.M., De Rochemont, M.H., Meijer, E., Roijakkers, A.H.W.M., 2007. Open Innovation in the Agri-Food Sector. Research paper commissioned by TransForum.

Veugelers, R., 1997. Internal R&D expenditures and external technology sourcing. Research Policy 26 (3), 303-315.

Veugelers, R., Cassiman, B., 1999. Make and buy in innovation strategies: evidence from Belgian manufacturing firms. Research Policy 28 (1), 63-80.

Von Hippel, E., 1988. The Sources of Innovation. Oxford University Press: New York, Oxford.

Weber, R.A., Camerer, C.F., 2003. Cultural conflict and merger failure: An experimental approach. Management Science 49 (4), 400-415.

West, J., Gallagher, S., 2006. Challenges of open innovation: the paradox of firm investment in open-source software. R&D Management 36 (3), 319-331.

West, J., Vanhaverbeke, W., Chesbrough, H., 2006. Open Innovation: A Research Design. In: Chesbrough, H., Vanhaverbeke, W., West, J. (Eds.), Open innovation: Researching a New Paradigm. Oxford University Press: New York.

Wheelwright, C., Clark, K.B., 1992. Revolutionizing product development. Quantum leaps in speed, efficiency and quality. Free Press.

Williamson, O.E., 1985. The economic institutions of capitalism; firms, markets and relational contracting. Free Press: New York.

Winch, G.M., Courtney, R., 2007. The organization of innovation brokers: An international review. Technology Analysis & Strategic Management 19 (6), 747-763.

Wissema, J.G., Euser, L., 1991. Successful Innovation through Inter-Company Networks. Long Range Planning 24 (6), 33-39.

Wubben, E.F.M., Batterink, M.H., Simonse, L.W.L., Omta, S.W.F., 2007. Realizing innovation synergies through Post Merger Integration. Paper presented at the RADMA conference, Bremen.

Yin, R.K., 2003. Case Study Research - Design and Methods (3 ed.). Sage Publications.

Zaheer, A., McEvily, B., Perrone, V., 1998. Does trust matter? Exploring the effects of interorganizational and interpersonal trust on performance. Organization Science 9 (2), 141-159.

Zollo, M., Singh, H., 2004. Deliberate learning in corporate acquisitions: Post-acquisition strategies and integration capability in US bank mergers. Strategic Management Journal 25 (13), 1233-1256.

Appendices

Appendix 1

Table A1.1. Distribution of (innovating) firms across OECD technology sector classification.

Sectors	NACE/SBI[1]	CIS-2 (N)	[2] [3]	CIS-2.5 (N)	[2] [3]	CIS-3 (N)	[2] [3]	CIS-3.5 (N)	[2] [3]	CIS-4 (N)	[2]
High-tech		230	12%	231	12%	159	11%	132	11%	160	12%
Pharmaceuticals	24.4	20	9% *	25	11%	28	18%	19	14%	28	18%
Electronics	30;31;32;33	210	91% *	206	89%	131	82%	113	86% *	132	83%
Medium high-tech		604	32%	610	30%	470	32%	452	36% *	418	32%
Basic chemicals	24.1;24.7	61	10%	66	11%	60	13%	47	10%	45	11%
Chemical end-products	24.3;24.6	87	14%	90	15%	80	17%	73	16%	74	18%
Machinery	29	313	52%	317	52%	251	53%	254	56%	226	54%
Car and transport	34;35	143	24% *	137	22%	79	17%	78	17%	73	17%
Medium low-tech		431	23%	509	25%	386	26%	326	26%	322	25%
Petrol	23	12	3%	16	3%	6	2%	6	2%	9	3%
Plastics	25	135	31%	144	28%	97	25%	95	29%	92	29%
Basic metal	27	43	10%	43	8%	39	10%	33	10%	30	9%
Metal products	28	241	56%	306	60%	244	63%	192	59%	191	59%
Low-tech		637	33%	653	33%	451	31%	336	27% *	407	31%
Food	15	273	43% *	269	41% *	196	43%	157	47%	204	50%
Textile	17;18	122	19% *	99	15% *	55	12%	42	13%	42	10%
Paper	21	86	14%	91	14%	82	18%	60	18%	59	14%
Printing and publishing	22	156	24%	194	30%	118	26%	77	23%	102	25%
Total industry		1902		2003		1466		1246		1307	

[1] The EC statistical office (Eurostat) classification scheme of economic activities. SBI is the Dutch equivalent of NACE. We followed the 2-digit SBI codes, except for the chemicals sector (SBI = 24), where we followed the 3-digit SIC codes, so we were able to differentiate between basic chemicals, the pharmaceutical sector, and the chemical end products.

[2] Percentage of this sub-sector (e.g. food) relative to the relevant technology class (e.g. low-tech). In the rows of the technology classes (e.g. low-tech), the percentage refers to the overall number of firms in the total industry in that period.

[3] * indicates that the share of this sector relatively to the technology class, or technology class relatively to the total industry is significantly different (according to a 2-proportion z-test, at 5% level) from this share in the last period (CIS-4).

Table A1.2. Distribution of (innovating) firms across size classes among the different years.

Sectors	Size class (employees)	CIS-2 1994-1996 (N)	CIS-2.5 1996-1998 (N)	CIS-3 1998-2000 (N)	CIS-3.5 2000-2002 (N)	CIS-4 2002-2004 (N)
Industry	10-50	655	734	475	325	440
	50-250	970	979	760	722	653
	>250	277	290	231	199	214
	Total	*1902*	*2003*	*1466*	*1246*	*1307*
High-tech	10-50	109	110	57	38	65
	50-250	86	87	66	64	66
	>250	35	34	36	30	29
	Total	*230*	*231*	*159*	*132*	*160*
Medium high-tech	10-50	183	203	140	127	141
	50-250	336	322	254	264	217
	>250	85	85	76	61	60
	Total	*604*	*610*	*470*	*452*	*418*
Medium low-tech	10-50	148	180	129	91	112
	50-250	238	272	221	194	175
	>250	45	57	36	41	35
	Total	*431*	*509*	*386*	*326*	*322*
Low-tech	10-50	215	241	149	69	122
	50-250	310	298	219	200	195
	>250	112	114	83	67	90
	Total	*637*	*653*	*451*	*336*	*407*

Table A1.3. Distribution of (innovating) cooperating firms across size classes among the different years.

Sectors	Size class (employees)	CIS-2 1994-1996 (N)	CIS-2.5 1996-1998 (N)	CIS-3 1998-2000 (N)	CIS-3.5 2000-2002 (N)	CIS-4 2002-2004 (N)
Industry	10-49	122	135	85	86	171
	50-249	309	292	231	304	345
	>250	174	157	137	140	171
	Total	*605*	*584*	*453*	*530*	*687*
High-tech	10-49	24	27	13	19	30
	50-249	34	35	26	36	46
	>250	25	23	27	21	24
	Total	*83*	*85*	*66*	*76*	*100*
Medium high-tech	10-49	31	46	30	41	52
	50-249	102	111	77	119	113
	>250	53	47	48	42	52
	Total	*186*	*204*	*155*	*202*	*217*
Medium low-tech	10-49	39	29	19	17	44
	50-249	90	82	65	79	94
	>250	32	34	23	30	27
	Total	*161*	*145*	*107*	*126*	*165*
Low-tech	10-49	28	33	23	9	45
	50-249	83	64	63	70	92
	>250	64	53	39	47	68
	Total	*175*	*150*	*125*	*126*	*205*

Table A1.4. Share of innovation firms engaged in licensing-in.

	Size class (employees)	1994-1996 [a]		1996-1998 [a]		1998-2000 [a]		2000-2002 [a]		2002-2004 [b]	
Total industry	10-49	8%	**	13%		10%		12%	**	22%	**
	50-249	14%		17%	**	12%	**	17%	**	28%	**
	>250	28%		27%	*	19%		27%		35%	
	Total	14%	**	17%	**	12%	**	17%	**	27%	**
High-tech	10-49	10%		14%		14%		21%		22%	*
	50-249	23%		18%		15%		14%	*	29%	
	>250	49%		38%		31%		40%		48%	
	Total	21%		19%		18%		22%		29%	
Medium high-tech	10-49	10%		14%		11%		13%		17%	
	50-249	20%		19%		13%		16%	**	35%	**
	>250	24%		26%		21%		26%		35%	
	Total	17%		18%		14%		16%	**	29%	**
Medium low-tech	10-49	7%	**	17%		13%		9%	**	23%	**
	50-249	12%	**	21%	**	11%		18%		22%	**
	>250	29%		35%		28%		24%		29%	
	Total	12%	**	21%	**	13%		16%	*	23%	**
Low-tech	10-49	5%		10%		5%		10%	*	25%	**
	50-249	7%		11%		10%	*	19%		25%	**
	>250	24%		19%	*	8%	*	22%		33%	
	Total	9%		12%	*	8%	**	18%	**	27%	**

[a] Reports z-test whether the percentage changes significantly between the two periods.
[b] Reports z-test whether the percentage in 2004 changes significantly from 1996.
* P-value <0.05, ** P-value <0.01.

Table A1.5. Share of innovating firms engaged in outsourcing.

	Size class (employees)	1994-1996 [a]		1996-1998 [a]		1998-2000 [a]		2000-2002 [a]		2002-2004 [b]	
Total industry	10-49	24%	*	29%	*	24%		27%		31%	*
	50-249	40%		41%	**	34%	**	43%	**	51%	**
	>250	64%		62%		60%		64%		72%	*
	Total	38%		40%	**	35%	**	42%	**	48%	**
High-tech	10-49	25%		35%		30%		39%		40%	*
	50-249	43%		44%		42%		47%		59%	*
	>250	80%		74%		69%		53%		72%	
	Total	40%		44%		44%		46%		54%	**
Medium high-tech	10-49	26%		31%	*	21%	*	33%		30%	
	50-249	41%		44%		39%	*	48%	*	59%	**
	>250	62%		66%		59%		67%	*	87%	**
	Total	39%		43%	*	37%	**	47%	*	54%	**
Medium low-tech	10-49	26%		27%		30%		22%		32%	
	50-249	39%		40%	*	30%		38%	*	49%	
	>250	69%		61%		75%		76%		63%	
	Total	38%		38%		34%		38%		44%	
Low-tech	10-49	22%		26%		18%		14%	*	27%	
	50-249	36%		39%	*	29%	*	40%		39%	
	>250	61%		55%		49%		58%		67%	
	Total	36%		37%	**	29%	**	38%		42%	

[a] Reports z-test whether the percentage changes significantly between the two periods.
[b] Reports z-test whether the percentage in 2004 changes significantly from 1996.
* P-value <0.05, ** P-value <0.01.

Table A1.6. Share of innovating firms cooperating with customers for innovation.

	Size class (employees)	1994-1996 [a]	1996-1998 [a]	1998-2000 [a]		2000-2002 [a]		2002-2004 [b]	
Total industry	10-49	12%	10%	12%		15%	**	23%	**
	50-249	15%	18%	18%	**	27%	**	34%	**
	>250	36%	33%	32%	**	45%		52%	**
	Total	18%	17%	18%	**	27%	**	33%	**
High-tech	10-49	15%	15%	12%	*	32%		32%	**
	50-249	21%	25%	21%		34%		41%	**
	>250	49%	47%	42%		47%		48%	
	Total	22%	24%	23%	*	36%		39%	**
Medium high-tech	10-49	10%	11%	16%		16%		23%	**
	50-249	17%	20%	17%	**	29%		36%	**
	>250	38%	35%	33%		43%	*	65%	**
	Total	18%	19%	19%	**	27%	**	36%	**
Medium low-tech	10-49	18%	12%	11%		12%	*	23%	
	50-249	21%	19%	19%	*	29%		33%	**
	>250	36%	30%	44%		56%		49%	
	Total	22%	18%	19%	**	28%		31%	**
Low-tech	10-49	6%	4%	8%		9%		18%	**
	50-249	11%	12%	16%		22%	*	30%	**
	>250	36%	27%	23%	*	39%		47%	
	Total	14%	12%	15%	**	22%	*	30%	**

[a] Reports z-test whether the percentage changes significantly between the two periods.
[b] Reports z-test whether the percentage in 2004 changes significantly from 1996.
* P-value <0.05, ** P-value <0.01.

Table A1.7. Share of innovating firms cooperating with suppliers for innovation.

	Size class (employees)	1994- [a] 1996	1996- [a] 1998	1998- [a] 2000		2000- [a] 2002		2002- [b] 2004	
Total industry	10-49	8%	9%	10%	**	16%	**	29%	**
	50-249	16%	17%	16%	**	32%	**	43%	**
	>250	38%	35%	31%	**	52%	**	65%	**
	Total	17%	17%	17%	**	31%	**	42%	**
High-tech	10-49	9%	13%	16%	*	34%		34%	**
	50-249	19%	21%	14%	**	41%	*	61%	**
	>250	40%	41%	39%		50%		59%	
	Total	17%	20%	20%	**	41%		49%	**
Medium high-tech	10-49	7%	8%	9%	**	21%		28%	**
	50-249	14%	19%	16%	**	33%		41%	**
	>250	35%	32%	25%	**	48%	*	67%	**
	Total	15%	17%	16%	**	31%	**	40%	**
Medium low-tech	10-49	9%	11%	9%		7%	**	25%	**
	50-249	21%	18%	18%	**	33%	*	44%	**
	>250	36%	40%	44%		54%		60%	*
	Total	18%	18%	18%	**	28%	**	39%	**
Low-tech	10-49	7%	7%	9%		10%	**	33%	**
	50-249	15%	14%	15%	**	27%	**	41%	**
	>250	39%	32%	28%	**	55%		68%	**
	Total	16%	14%	15%	**	29%	**	44%	**

[a] Reports z-test whether the percentage changes significantly between the two periods.
[b] Reports z-test whether the percentage in 2004 changes significantly from 1996.
* P-value <0.05, ** P-value <0.01.

Table A1.8. *Share of innovating firms cooperating with competitors for innovation*

	Size class (employees)	1994-1996 [a]	1996-1998 [a]	1998-2000 [a]	2000-2002 [a]	2002-2004 [b]
Total industry	10-49	5%	6%	5% **	10%	10% **
	50-249	9%	8%	8% **	13%	12% *
	>250	20%	23%	19% *	30%	29% *
	Total	9%	9%	9% **	15%	14% **
High-tech	10-49	2% *	9% *	0% **	21%	15% **
	50-249	9%	8%	9%	17%	12%
	>250	17%	29%	25%	37%	38%
	Total	7%	12%	9% **	23%	18% **
Medium high-tech	10-49	4%	6%	8%	10%	10% *
	50-249	7%	9%	9%	14%	13% *
	>250	15%	19%	17%	25%	33% *
	Total	7%	9%	10% *	14%	15% **
Medium low-tech	10-49	5%	6%	3%	7%	9%
	50-249	10%	9%	8%	13%	10%
	>250	29%	23%	25%	34%	26%
	Total	10%	10%	8% **	14%	11%
Low-tech	10-49	5%	5%	5%	6%	10%
	50-249	9% *	5%	8%	11%	12%
	>250	20%	24%	17%	28%	24%
	Total	9%	8%	8% *	13%	14% *

[a] Reports z-test whether the percentage changes significantly between the two periods.
[b] Reports z-test whether the percentage in 2004 changes significantly from 1996.
* P-value <0.05, ** P-value <0.01.

Table A1.9. Share of innovating firms cooperating with knowledge institutions for innovation.

	Size class (employees)	1994- 1996 [a]	1996- 1998 [a]	1998- 2000 [a]	2000- 2002 [a]	2002- 2004 [b]
Total industry	10-49	8%	8%	8%	11% *	17% **
	50-249	14% *	18% **	13% **	25% *	31% **
	>250	28%	35%	35% *	46% **	60% **
	Total	*16%*	*17%*	*15%* **	*24%* **	*31%* **
High-tech	10-49	7%	13%	12%	26%	28% **
	50-249	17%	22%	21% *	39%	41% **
	>250	54%	47%	56%	57%	66%
	Total	*18%*	*21%*	*26%* *	*39%*	*40%* **
Medium high-tech	10-49	8%	10%	11%	15%	16% *
	50-249	14% **	23% **	11% **	28%	36% **
	>250	36%	39%	36%	48% *	70% **
	Total	*15%* *	*21%* *	*15%* **	*27%* *	*34%* **
Medium low-tech	10-49	9%	8%	6%	7% *	16%
	50-249	18%	17%	13% *	22%	26%
	>250	42%	32%	39%	49%	51%
	Total	*18%*	*15%*	*13%* **	*21%*	*25%* *
Low-tech	10-49	6%	4%	5%	1% **	12% *
	50-249	12%	13%	13%	18%	26% **
	>250	38%	31%	24%	37% *	54% *
	Total	*14%*	*13%*	*12%* *	*18%* **	*28%* **

[a] Reports z-test whether the percentage changes significantly between the two periods.
[b] Reports z-test whether the percentage in 2004 changes significantly from 1996.
* P-value <0.05, ** P-value <0.01.

Appendix 2

Table A2.1. Comparing the longitudinal sample with the original CIS-3 sample of innovating firms.

	Longitudinal sample (N=686) Mean	CIS-3 sample (N=1654) Mean
Dependent variables		
Innovative sales incremental innovation 2001	21%	20%
Innovative sales radical innovation 2001	5.6%	6.5%
Independent variables		
Licensing-in	13%	13%
Outsourcing	40%	36%
Cooperation	33%	31%
Acquisition	5.2%	6.3%
In-house innovation	42%	45%
Control variables (firm characteristics)		
Firm size (employees)	323	221
Innovation intensity	0.027	0.023
Firm part of group	80%	75%
Search breadth	2.08	2.04
Control variables (sectors)		
Food and drink	13%	11%
Textiles	3%	3%
Paper	6%	5%
Printing and publishing	5%	7%
Petrol	1%	0%
Chemical basic products	4%	4%
Pharmaceutics	3%	2%
Chemical end products	5%	5%
Plastics	6%	6%
Basic metals	3%	2%
Fabric. metal products	13%	14%
Machinery	13%	15%
Electrical	7%	8%
Automobile and transport	4%	5%
Furniture	14%	14%

Appendix 3

A3.1. Description of the four innovation brokers in the study

KnowHouse

KnowHouse, which began operations in 2003, presents itself as a facilitator of innovation, specifically aimed at stimulating innovation in the agri-food sector in the south-eastern part of the Netherlands (North Limburg). It can be characterized as a 'pure' innovation broker (Klerkx and Leeuwis, 2008b). *KnowHouse* started operations in 2003. As of June 2007, *KnowHouse* employed 9 FTEs, 5 as 'co-innovators' involved as brokers in innovation projects, and 4 as support staff. *KnowHouse* is currently involved in about 30 projects, and has been involved in more than 100 projects since its beginning. *KnowHouse* has public shareholders (e.g. local governments, universities) and private shareholders (e.g. privatized research institutes, banks, agricultural supplies firms). Although *KnowHouse* obtained starting capital from its shareholders to bridge over the first three years, these days the organization's turnover comes directly from the innovation intermediation activities it conducts for its clients.

my eyes

Officially founded in September 2005, *my eyes* started operations in April 2006. The company is not a 'pure' innovation broker, although it carries out specific intermediation functions; *my eyes* also offers specific knowledge intensive services, such as ICT support. As of June 2007, *my eyes* employed 5 FTEs and was involved in about 30 projects (including unpaid projects). It is the mission of *my eyes* to bring producers and consumers closer together by making and facilitating the necessary connections. The company is directed by 3 individuals who hold some, but not the majority, of the shares. *My eyes* also has a certificate structure with B-shares, which are held primarily by *my eyes* partners (in projects and networks). Of the 5 FTEs currently employed at *my eyes*, only 2 are on the payroll. The other employees can be seen as entrepreneurs who should be able to earn directly from the company's activities and projects. Although the head office is located in the Dutch province of Gelderland, the company does not have a specific regional focus.

GIQS

GIQS (Grenzüberschreitende Integrierte Qualitätssicherung e.V.) focuses on facilitating cross-border public-private partnerships between Germany and the Netherlands. Its two parent organizations are the University of Bonn and Wageningen University. *GIQS* has 5 employees, 3 appointed by *GIQS* and 2 who are 'virtually appointed' through the University of Bonn. *GIQS* has about 30 official members, of which most participate or have participated in projects. The core funding for *GIQS* is only €15,000. In terms of funding and cooperation, *GIQS* is active in complex projects such as large EU INTERREG frameworks of cooperation. *GIQS* 'translates' complex projects into smaller projects or work packages that are accessible to SMEs. *GIQS* is involved in the entire life cycle of the projects.

PEACRITT

The mission of *PEACRITT* (Le Pôle Européen Agroalimentaire pour la Communication la Recherche, l'Innovation et le Transfert de Technologies) is to improve economic development of the agri-food sector in Rhône-Alpes (France) through various activities aimed at SMEs and other stakeholders. *PEACRITT* functions primarily as a broker between SMEs and knowledge institutes, and in addition, is involved in training SMEs in the fields of innovation and cooperation. *PEACRITT* employs 7 FTEs and is involved in a substantial number of regional projects. An important feature of *PEACRITT* is a programme called 'OPTIréseaux' (Opti-network), which focuses on themes related to innovation and technical or organizational development. An OPTIréseaux programme comprises a minimum of 6 and a maximum of 12 SMEs. The firms forming an OPTIréseaux programme are supported by at least two experts from technical centres or other research institutes. *PEACRITT* safeguards the OPTIréseaux concept, and takes on the role of coordinator and facilitator between the experts and the enterprises. The activities of *PEACRITT* in an OPTIréseaux programme involve individual elements (diagnostics of the project for each involved enterprise, technical assistance, training in the enterprise, engineering) and collective elements (connecting the enterprises in the OPTIréseaux network). *PEACRITT* is a non-profit organization which relies completely on public funding, mainly from the regional and national governments. Members pay a small contribution. *PEACRITT* is also involved in European projects, making them accessible to regional SMEs.

A3.2. General interview questions

- What are the main objectives of the organization?
- Can you explain the kind of projects you are involved in?
- How is the organization linked to SMEs?
- How is the organization linked to research organizations?
- What are the main activities your organization carries out related to the innovation projects?
- What are the main activities your organization carries out un-related to the innovation projects?
- How do innovation projects get started?
- How are the innovation networks developed?
- How are the 'rules, coordination mechanisms, administrative procedures' within the network set up?
- What kind of conflicts occur in the networks you are involved in? How are such conflicts tackled?
- What enhances trust and what erodes trust? / How important is trust and how is it facilitated?
- How do network members interact?
- What is the main contribution / added value of your organization to SMEs?
- What are the most important lessons learned during your time so far in this organization?
- Can you distinguish important events / factors that influenced performance of innovation networks (positively or negatively)?

Appendix 4

List of interview questions

The semi-structured interviews included the following major questions:
- M&A motives
  - What was/were the main motive(s) for the M&A?
- Technological relatedness
  - Can you describe the main technological areas of the firms involved in the M&A?
- Post M&A integration
  - What post M&A integration approach has been chosen? Can you describe it?
  - How was the post M&A integration organized?
  - (How) was the R&D function integrated?
  - Which mechanisms have been put in place for linking or integrating the original different R&D functions? Please illustrate and indicate why?
  - What were the main changes in the R&D functions after the M&A?
  - Has there been a transfer of certain R&D/innovation management practices? Can you mention specific practices and how they were exchanged?
  - What were the main challenges during the Post M&A integration process?
  - Would you judge the acquisition and subsequent integration as having been successful?
- Innovation synergy realization
  - Was the firm able to reduce the cost of R&D / innovation as a result of the acquisition? If yes, can you explain how many costs were reduced and how?
  - Was the firm able to improve the innovation process in terms of efficiency and effectiveness as a result of the acquisition? If yes, can you explain what has improved and how?
  - Was the firm able to gain access to new technological or knowledge resources as a result of the acquisition? If yes, can mention them and describe how?
  - Was the firm able to set up new innovation or R&D trajectories as a result of the acquisition? If yes, can you explain how many and describe them?
  - Was the firm able to increase the scale and/or scope of research and development? If yes, can you explain how much and how?
  - Are there new products/processes or services that are the result of combining the two organizations? If yes, can you explain how these innovations were the result of the combination of the organizations?

Summary

In recent years, innovation has become essential for the competitive advantage of firms in a growing number of industries. Due to the fast development of technologies, changing customer demands, shortening of product life cycles, increased global competition and changing regulations, modern firms constantly have to look for new ways to prosper in this very dynamic business environment. To survive in this dynamic environment, firms increasingly look for ways to profit from knowledge in other organizations, like supply chain partners, universities and research institutes, and even competitors. Firms may choose from several strategies for external knowledge acquisition, such as inter-organizational cooperation, venture capital investments, outsourcing of Research and Development (R&D), licensing-in, but also Mergers and Acquisitions (M&As).

When firms try to acquire external knowledge they will face major management challenges. Several empirical studies have indicated that acquiring external knowledge can be time consuming, expensive and laborious. Moreover, establishing relationships with external organizations raises several complex issues, such as appropriation concerns, motivational problems, leakage of sensitive information, and partner dependency. In this respect, the management of innovating firms should not only strategically consider which knowledge acquisition strategy is to be preferred when they want to profit from knowledge developed elsewhere, but they should also consider carefully how to manage their external knowledge acquisition processes. The main objective of this book is therefore as follows:

To analyze how firms can profit from external knowledge using different knowledge acquisition strategies.

In order to realize this objective, four empirical studies are carried out. The first two studies are primarily concerned with the relevance of different strategies for acquiring external knowledge (such as licensing-in, outsourcing and cooperation), using a quantitative approach. Both studies use data of industrial firms from Dutch Community Innovation Surveys (CIS, 1994-2004), which explore the innovation process inside firms. The first study (Chapter 2) concentrates on the occurrence of different external knowledge acquisition strategies over time. The second study (Chapter 3) complements the first study by analyzing whether the different knowledge acquisition strategies have an impact on innovation performance.

Next, the other two studies apply a qualitative approach and concentrate on specific management challenges of two different knowledge acquisition strategies, namely inter-organizational cooperation and M&As. The first qualitative study (Chapter 4) provides in-depth information on innovation brokers orchestrating innovation networks of Small and Medium sized Enterprises (SMEs) in the agri-food sector, in different European countries. The second qualitative study (Chapter 5) provides in-depth information on the integration processes of the R&D function, following large, (medium) high-tech M&As in life science industries. In this study we link technological relatedness to specific R&D integration mechanisms, and subsequently to innovation synergy realization.

In the innovation management literature there is a growing attention for the open innovation model, introduced by Henry Chesbrough in 2003. This model emphasizes that the innovation process should be flexible and may cross organizational boundaries, so that it enables the transfer of knowledge and capabilities from and to other independent organizations. According to the open innovation model, firms should not only consider internal, but also external knowledge, capabilities and paths to markets. Yet, despite the recent emphasis on open innovation by innovation management scholars, the empirical evidence of its relevance to innovating firms has so far surprisingly been limited, mainly to high-tech industries. Nevertheless, anecdotal evidence suggests that open innovation can be beneficial for low-tech industries as well. An important question is therefore whether the concepts of open innovation also apply to lower-tech industries. In addition, whereas the relevance of open innovation is shown for a number of large firms, it remains unclear to what extent open innovation is also relevant for SMEs. The research question in Chapter 2 is therefore:

To what extent do different types (size and technology classes) of innovating firms pursue an open innovation strategy?

The results show that especially since the turn of the century, an increasing share of innovating firms pursue an open innovation strategy, i.e. using external knowledge acquisition strategies, such as cooperation, outsourcing, and licensing-in. In addition, we found an increase in cooperation for different types of cooperation partners, such as suppliers, customers and research institutes. The most prevalent cooperation partners are actors from within the supply chain, i.e. suppliers and customers. Interestingly, the results showed that small firms and low- and medium-tech firms in particular are catching up large and high-tech firms in pursuing open innovation strategies since 2000. Yet, in general, large firms and firms from high-tech industries are still the most inclined to adopt open innovation strategies.

We conclude in Chapter 2 that open innovation has become more common, but is it also a successful strategy? Chapter 3 concentrates on the performance consequences of different knowledge acquisition strategies. In Chapter 3 we addressed the following research question:

What is the impact of different external knowledge acquisition strategies on the short-term and long-term innovation performance of innovative firms?

Drawing from a sample of 686 industrial firms from the Dutch CIS database we analyzed what the impact is of different knowledge acquisition strategies; both open innovation strategies such as licensing-in, outsourcing, cooperation, as closed innovation strategies such as M&As and the contrasting case of in-house innovation, on the short-term and long-term performance of incremental and radical innovation. We found that open innovation is often a successful strategy. More specifically, cooperation was found to have a positive impact on incremental and radical innovation, both in the short and long term. Thus, cooperation is not only increasingly practiced (see Chapter 2), it also turns out to be a successful strategy to profit from external knowledge. Furthermore, we found that outsourcing has a positive impact on a firm's short-term and long-term performance of innovations, whereas licensing-in only contributes to short-term innovation performance. That licensing-in only contributes to the short-term innovation performance suggests that licensing-in is especially useful for acquiring knowledge and technologies that are relatively rapidly applicable for creating innovations. This knowledge is often also available to other organizations, so that licensing-in does not lead to long-term competitive advantage. The results suggest as well that there may be several sub-modes of outsourcing and inter-organizational cooperation that facilitate innovation in different ways.

Contrary to our expectations, we found that the acquisition of a relatively large firm boosts the innovation performance significantly, although only after a substantial number of years. Apparently, it takes considerable time and effort to integrate the acquired firm in such a way that it improves the innovation performance. Finally, exclusive in-house innovation turned out to be a sub-optimal strategy, as we found that exclusive in-house innovation had a consistently significant negative impact on the performance of both short and long-term performance of incremental and radical innovation.

Chapter 4 presents a study on the innovation networks in which SMEs cooperate. Although cooperation can have a positive impact on innovation performance (see Chapter 3), for SMEs it can be a major challenge to cope with all the issues stemming from inter-organizational cooperation, such as cultural differences (e.g. between academics/researchers and entrepreneurs), appropriation concerns, motivational problems, and leakage of sensitive knowledge. In the innovation management literature there is a growing attention to intermediary organizations, such as innovation brokers, which assist SMEs with the challenges that come with innovating in a network. In Chapter 3, we therefore asked the following research question:

How do innovation brokers orchestrate SME innovation networks in the agri-food sector?

Drawing from the rich experience of four innovation brokers in the agri-food sector in The Netherlands, Germany and France, we substantiated the network orchestration processes that are important for innovation processes of SMEs. First, innovation brokers assist SMEs in the early stage of the innovation project, to develop ideas independently of large institutional actors, and to find complementary partners such as other SMEs, or research institutes. In contrast to an individual SME, an innovation broker can typically draw from a large and diverse network, in order to compose a network of complementary actors. Second, innovation brokers take the lead in setting up appropriate coordination mechanisms to facilitate the inter-organizational cooperation within the new innovation network. Third, innovation brokers often are involved in the network during the whole innovation trajectory, in order to manage the inter-organizational cooperation between the different parties. Especially in the case of conflict between the parties, innovation brokers are of added value in SME innovation networks. Being in a neutral position in an innovation network in which all other parties have a commercial stake, and having ample experience with inter-organizational innovation processes, enables innovation brokers to do so.

As stated in Chapter 3, we found that major acquisitions have a positive impact on the long-term performance of innovations. In Chapter 5 we analyze how major M&As can contribute to innovation performance. The research question in Chapter 5 is:

What is the role of technological relatedness in realizing innovation synergies in M&As?

Our study of 10 large, medium- and high-tech M&As in life-science industries showed that there are three categories of innovation synergies: innovation cost synergy, innovation process synergy, and new growth platforms. Furthermore, we concluded that depending on the level of technological relatedness between the involved firms, different integration mechanisms are applied. The results suggest that there are three levels of R&D integration, starting with a minimal form integration, which is the standardization of system, such as the harmonization of information, reporting, and control systems. Systems standardizing is applied in the case of lowly technological related M&As and does not or hardly lead to innovation synergies. The second level of R&D integration focuses, in addition to system standardization, on structural linking, e.g. in terms of integrated R&D management, R&D teams, or even R&D departments. This level of integration is primarily applied in moderately technological related M&As and may lead to innovation process synergy and new growth platforms. The third and most far-reaching level of R&D integration focuses, in addition to system standardization and structural linking on process re-design, i.e. rationalization processes (eliminating duplicate R&D), specialization, and re-prioritizing of innovation projects. Process re-design is mainly applied in highly technologically related M&As, and is associated with each of the three types of innovation synergy.

On the issue of organizing the Post M&A Integration process, we conclude that there are several factors that enhance innovation synergy realization, such experience, integration planning, and open communication. For instance, we found that firms with a track record of similar acquisitions, draw explicitly from their experience by using dedicated PMAI tools and guidelines. These firms are likely to integrate the R&D functions more quickly than firms without relevant experience.

To conclude, we found that external knowledge becomes increasingly important for the innovation activities of firms. Although it can be difficult to profit from the knowledge and capabilities from other organizations, more and more firms manage to do so. This research has shown that companies use different knowledge acquisition strategies and this research has arrived at concrete possibilities and guidelines to improve this process.

Finally, this research has made a number of main contributions to literature.

- First, we advanced the external validity of the open innovation model. Several studies have pointed at the importance of the open innovation model, but previous studies mainly concentrated on a small amount of case studies, or on one sector only. Our longitudinal research shows that firms from different industries and size classes increasingly pursue an open innovation strategy. In addition, our research shows that open innovation strategies contribute to innovation performance. The impact of licensing-in and outsourcing on innovation performance in particular has so far hardly been investigated. The extension on knowledge acquisition strategies and industries brings research on open innovation to a higher level.
- Second, we presented new empirical evidence on the socially relevant academic discussion on whether M&As have a positive impact on the innovation performance of firms. With our large scale quantitative study we showed that major acquisitions have a positive impact on the long-term performance of incremental and radical innovations. Contrary to previous studies, which focused on the number of patents as indicator for innovation performance, we used an indicator for innovation performance that also captures the commercial impact of innovations. In addition, we not only included high-tech, but also lower-tech firms.
- Third, we developed a conceptual model for innovation synergy realization in M&As. Although several studies investigated the R&D integration process in M&As, so far it has remained unclear if, and if so how, innovation synergies are realized in large M&As. In our research we combined insights from the strategic management and the post M&A integration literature to gain a better understanding of the process of innovation synergy realization. The model shows that depending on the technological relatedness between the involved firms, specific R&D integration mechanisms should be applied and that depending on these R&D integration mechanisms, different innovation synergies can be realized.
- Fourth, we substantiated the network orchestration processes of innovation brokers active in SME innovation networks. Previous studies in the innovation management literature focused primarily on identifying and describing the functions and roles of innovation brokers in the (regional) innovation system. Our research shows specifically which contributions innovation brokers make at the innovation network level, and how they make these contributions.

About the author

Maarten Harmen Batterink was born in 1979 in De Noordoostpolder, the Netherlands. In 2003 he received his MSc degree in *Agrosysteemkunde* at the Wageningen University with a specialization in Operations Research & Logistics. During his study, he carried out research in the company Friesland Foods and in AFSG (Agrotechnology and Food Sciences Group) on the topics of location-allocation problems and agro-logistic simulation. In 2002 he spent a five-month internship at the Lincoln Ventures Supply Chain Systems Group (a spin-off from Lincoln University, New Zealand) and carried out a research project in the kiwi-fruit sector. In 2003 he started his PhD research at the Business Administration group of Wageningen University. Related to his PhD research, he was involved in a number of research projects, such as the NWO project *The impact of M&A-driven market dominance on innovation dynamics* (within the Dynamics of Innovation Program) and the Interreg project PromSTAP (Promoting the Stable-to-Table APproach). He presented his work at various international conferences and has published in a number of scientific journals, such as the *International Food and Agribusiness Management Review* and the *Journal on Chain and Network Science*. Furthermore, he was co-editor of the book *Tools for cooperating in chains and networks* (in Dutch) and has co-organized the first Mansholt PhD-day in 2004 and the PREBEM (PhD Researchers in Business, Economic & Management) conference in 2005. Since September 2008 Maarten Batterink works as assistant professor in entrepreneurship and innovation management at the Business Administration group of Wageningen University.

Innovation and sustainability series

The fields of innovation and sustainability are more and more recognized as the major drivers of business success in the 21st century. Today's companies are facing ever-faster changes in their business environment, to which they must respond through continuous innovation. The growing concern regarding the quality and environmental friendliness of products and processes call for fundamentally new ways of developing, producing and marketing of products. New ways of organizing supply chains, with new network ties between firms are needed to cope with these new demands. This series aims to assist industry to conduct the (interorganizational) innovations needed to meet the challenges that are fundamental for the transition from a production orientation to a 'cradle-to-cradle' demand-orientation. However, innovation can be disruptive, not only concerning the organization of the processes, but also regarding the allocation of resources and power bases. Existing companies are increasingly challenged by newcomers, e.g. start-up firms and spin-off ventures. In the transition process, supplier bases might be reorganized, activities reallocated, and relations and role allocations changed as new entities occur. We want to study these new organizational forms and their consequences – as we view them as core for these business networks in transition.

About the editor

Onno Omta is chaired professor in Business Administration at Wageningen University and Research Centre, the Netherlands. He received an MSc in Biochemistry and a PhD in innovation management, both from the University of Groningen. He is the Editor-in-Chief of The Journal on Chain and Network Science, and he has published numerous articles in leading scientific journals in the field of chains and networks and innovation. He has worked as a consultant and researcher for a large variety of (multinational) technology-based prospector companies within the agri-food industry (e.g. Unilever, VION, Bonduelle, Campina, Friesland Foods, FloraHolland) and in other industries (e.g. SKF, Airbus, Erickson, Exxon, Hilti and Philips).

Guest editor

Dr Emiel F.M. Wubben is Associate Professor in Strategic Management at the Management Studies Group of Wageningen University (2000-). He has an MSc in Theoretical Economics (Erasmus University), and an internationally awarded PhD-thesis on The introduction of uncertainty into economics (Tinbergen Institute). Wubben was Assistant Professor Strategic Management and Business Environment and ERIM research fellow at the Rotterdam School of Management. Currently he is research fellow of Mansholt Graduate School, member of its

PhD assessment committee, and in the board of the Association for Institutional and Political Economy VIPE. In recent years Wubben run the NWO-funded research project 'Synergies and dynamic efficiencies in dominant mergers and acquisitions', together with projects on Food Safety Authorities, innovation intermediaries, (horticultural) chains and networks, and biorefinery. Wubben participates in and organizes international conferences and publishes in academic journals, books, reports and popular journals. From a strategic management, innovation management and/or industrial organization-perspective he supervises MSc- and PhD-projects, and has an teaching history in economics and management, e.g. 'Industrial Organization' and 'Advanced Management Marketing'.

Printed in the United States
by Baker & Taylor Publisher Services